ISLAMIC

ISLAMIC LAW AND ETHICS

Edited by

David R. Vishanoff

IIIT

LONDON · WASHINGTON

IIIT, P.O. Box 669, Herndon, VA 20172, USA • www.iiit.org
P.O. Box 126, Richmond, Surrey TW9 2UD, UK • www.iiit.org.uk

ISBN 978-1-56564-950-7 limp
ISBN 978-1-56564-951-4 cased
E-BOOK ISBN 978-1-64205-346-3

Layout and Design by Shiraz Khan
Printed in the USA

Contents

FOREWORD

To what extent is ethics theology and to what extent is it philosophy? The dynamic of interpretation, of trying to extrapolate to modernity and its challenges, is the nature of the conversation emerging in this set of essays, in which we see scholars engage with Islamic traditions and provide rationales for their views.

Society is incapable of evolution without formulation of legislation rooted in an understanding of law undergirded by a respect for and practical application of ethics, which gives it direction. Under Islamic Law this ethics becomes a more powerful driving force, determined by a Divine moral code whose authority lies in the Qur'an and Sunnah (actions) of the Prophet Muhammad (*ṢAAS*)*, rather than pure intuition and moral consequentialism (secular reasoning) as arbiters of the rightness or wrongness of an action.

Fundamental to the expression of Islamic Law therefore is scriptural and hadith authority, which position continues to be the basis of personal conduct as well as actions and decisions taken in relation to the social/political/economic and other functioning of society and life. Fuelling debate down the centuries has been how best to derive and realise the Divine intent. Thus, while the Shariʿah sits uncomfortably in the Western imagination, considered provocative even, it forms a strictly integral and unapologetic part of the ethical, moral society envisaged by Islam (provided it is applied *genuinely* and under *genuine* governance). There are important parallels both in the Western and Islamic traditions that can be explored, once the dust of controversy settles.

The papers in this anthology explore Islamic Law in relation to ethics in general as well as certain ethical and moral issues of the day. They were first presented at the 2014 IIIT Summer Institute for

***ṢAAS* (*Ṣallā Allāhu ʿalayhi wa sallam*: May the peace and blessings of God be upon him said whenever the name of the Prophet Muhammad is mentioned).

Scholars, an annual event dedicated to studying contemporary approaches in Islamic thought, and meant to bring together scholarly contributions that update our understanding of various sub-fields, methodologies, and topics.

Where dates are cited according to the Islamic calendar (hijrah) they are labelled AH. Otherwise they follow the Gregorian calendar and are labelled CE where necessary. Arabic words are italicized except for those which have entered common usage. Diacritical marks have been added only to those Arabic names not considered contemporary. English translations taken from Arabic references are those of the author.

Since its establishment in 1981, the IIIT has served as a major center to facilitate serious scholarly efforts. Towards this end it has, over the decades, conducted numerous programs of research, seminars and conferences, as well as publishing scholarly works specialising in the social sciences and areas of theology, which to date number more than seven hundred titles in English and Arabic, many of which have been translated into other major languages.

We are grateful to Professor David Vishanoff for the expertise he brought to bear as Editor. We also thank the contributors, as well as all those directly or indirectly involved in the completion of this book.

IIIT
May 2020

Editor's Introduction
Islamic Law and Ethics: From Integration to Pluralism

David R. Vishanoff

Does Islamic law define Islamic ethics? Or is the law one branch of a broader ethical system? Or is it one of several independent ethical discourses, Islamic and otherwise, competing for Muslims' allegiance? This is no idle academic question. It has far-reaching implications for epistemology, for the authority of jurists and lay Muslims, for the practical moral challenges of daily life, and for relationships with non-Muslims. This question evoked varied and passionate answers over the course of a week-long summer institute on "Islamic Law and Ethics" hosted by the International Institute of Islamic Thought at its headquarters in Herndon, Virginia in June of 2014.

A range of possible answers were laid out by the distinguished guest speakers who opened the conference. Jasser Auda made the case that if Islamic law is reformed from within, with a focus on its moral objectives, it can incorporate other dimensions of ethics, such as virtue, and systematically ground them all in revelation. Abdulaziz Sachedina likewise called for a systematic and integrated methodology for Islamic ethics, but one that looks beyond the interpretive tools of traditional legal theory to incorporate universal ethical intuitions. Ebrahim Moosa argued that Islamic law should not be the sole marker of Muslims' identity that governs all aspects of their lives, but that Islamic ethics should be constituted by a plurality of normative discourses. Carl Ernst agreed with Moosa that ethics cannot be reduced to a single moral calculus such as fiqh, and argued that even the "foreign" cultural norms and ethical philosophies that have entered into

Islamic life and thought should be regarded as integral components of Islamic ethics.

The group of young scholars who stayed and engaged one another in a rich conversation over the course of the following week offered historical examples and constructive proposals spanning this whole range of answers. None of them specialized in Islamic ethics, and not many were trained in Islamic law, but all of them brought to bear on the subject the rich particulars of their own research and their personal engagement with the dilemmas of contemporary Islamic thought. Their contributions were exploratory rather than definitive, but together they constituted a profound interrogation of the relationship between fiqh and ethics. Most of their papers are assembled in this volume, arranged in the following order: first those in which Islamic law is the starting point and the defining framework for ethics, then those that insert Islamic law into a broader ethical framework, then those that present law as just one among several parallel Islamic ethical discourses, and finally those that suggest how Islamic ethics should relate to non-Muslim normative systems.

My own paper comes first because it is the simplest: it assumes that one's ethical system is defined by one's legal theory, and then asks what kind of ethical theory is embedded in one particular eleventh–century work on Islamic legal theory. Imām al-Ḥaramayn al-Juwaynī's ethics is found to be a kind of moral realism and divine command theory that can be characterized as deontic, deontological, agent-centered, individualistic, and particularistic. The paper does not look beyond legal theory, but attempts to imagine what that discipline might look like if it were structured around different ethical categories like the cultivation of virtues, the establishment of interpersonal relationships, or the articulation of general moral principles, rather than around the eternal consequences of particular actions for the individuals who perform them. Samy Ayoub's paper likewise shows how broad ethical considerations may be integrated into legal theory: it demonstrates that although Hanafite legal theory appears deontological, because it assigns to each action a definite legal value based on God's commands, the maxims governing its application are consequentialist because they consider the consequences of actions in particular circumstances. This makes law subject to the overarching moral priorities of the jurists, but it integrates those ethical values into the disciplinary framework of legal theory.

The next two papers suggest that law is not a fully adequate framework for ethics. Hamid Mavani's paper argues that traditional Islamic legal theory has been unable to adapt the law to changing contexts, and must be reimagined and placed within a broader ethical framework grounded in theological, scientific, and societal considerations. This makes the law subject to rationally discerned and widely accepted ethical norms (*siyar al-ʿuqalāʾ*), just as the Qur'an articulated its laws within the framework of a socially defined ethic (*al-maʿrūf*). Kamal Abu-Shamsieh's paper then illustrates why such a reframing of law within broader ethical concerns proves necessary in practice: for a Muslim hospital chaplain, the emotional and cultural forces at play in the face of sickness and death make the rote application of legal rules contextually inadequate, so an applied ethic must address moral and spiritual flourishing more holistically, taking into account character, custom, benefit, and harm. Both Hamid Mavani and Kamal Abu-Shamsieh retain the discourse of Islamic legal theory, but they place it under the tutelage of higher and more universal ethical values.

The next paper presents Islamic law as but one ethical discourse alongside others. Christopher Taylor argues that Islamic ethics is constituted as much by what ordinary people do as by what scholars say, and shows how the legal doctrine and the social practice of zakah in Lucknow have diverged: the agent–centered ethic of classical fiqh, which focuses on the duty and intention of the donor, is being displaced in practice by a patient–centered ethic focused on the development of the recipient's work ethic and economic status. Christopher Taylor notes that this shift is tolerated by many legal scholars, who acknowledge its divergence from their prescriptions but regard its aims as compatible with their own.

In a just world, Christopher Taylor's paper would have been followed by another innovative essay challenging the traditional framing of Islamic law in terms of obligation and prohibition, and retrieving some early Muslim precedent for a rights–based ethic. Sadly, there are political gains to be had by denying the internal diversity and sophistication of Islamic thought that are illustrated so well by that essay and by this whole volume, and it was just such a politically-motivated denial of the obvious that compelled the omission of that essay, robbing this volume of its elegantly symmetrical four-part structure and, more importantly, of an original and eye-opening contribution.

That lost paper also would have illustrated the challenge posed to Islamic law today by ethico-religious pluralism. Few Muslims today are in a position to view the world through a singular moral lens. Ethical categories like human rights, developed outside the framework of any Islamic discourse, nevertheless resonate deeply with some strands of Islamic moral thought. Muslims' encounters with ethico-religious others have evoked some strident calls for ideological purity and opposition, as documented in Asaad Alsaleh's paper; but he argues that this rhetoric of opposition rests on a misreading of the Qur'an's statement that "never will the Jews or the Christians approve of you until you follow their religion" (2:120), and that a properly contextualized reading of the verse requires not hostility but rather coexistence with different ethico-religious systems. Katrin Jomaa's paper goes further by showing how ethico-religious pluralism might be positively accommodated within an Islamic political theory. She takes her cue from a close rereading of the Madinah Constitution, which she argues makes space not only for multiple tribes and religious communities but also for multiple moral and legal systems, within the context of a shared polity that is pluralistic without being secular.

Of course, these seven papers represent far more than just a progression through four possible views of the relationship between Islamic law and ethics. Each presents a fascinating body of material from a specific historical or contemporary context. And each wrestles independently with the relationship between Islamic law and ethics, resisting the simplified classification into which I have forced it in this introductory outline. But together these papers, tentative and exploratory as they are, vividly illustrate the significance of the question addressed by the IIIT's 2014 Summer Institute for Scholars: should Muslims pursue a common, universal, overarching methodology and framework for judging all ethical questions, or should they relish the rhetorical and political competition of alternative but not necessarily incompatible moral discourses?

The papers also demonstrate the generous hospitality with which the International Institute of Islamic Thought welcomed such a wide range of approaches, perspectives, and answers from such a young group of emerging scholars.

1
The Ethical Structure of Imām al-Ḥaramayn al-Juwaynī's Legal Theory

David R. Vishanoff

ABSTRACT: Imām al-Ḥaramayn al-Juwaynī's definition of law (fiqh) as knowledge of legal values (*aḥkām*), his definitions of those legal values, several of his interpretive principles, and other features of his legal theory (*uṣūl al-fiqh*) give Islamic law the structure of an ethical system that can be characterized in limited respects as a form of moral realism, as a divine command theory, and as deontic, deontological, agent-centered, individualistic, and particularistic. Comparing his vision of the law with other types of ethical systems suggests alternative ways in which Islamic law might be envisioned and defined, and reveals some profound implications of seemingly minor points of legal theory like the definitions of technical terms. In this paper, the ethical structure of al-Juwaynī's widely taught legal theory is contrasted with virtue ethics, constructivism, consequentialism, utilitarianism, existentialism, natural law and social contract theories, as well as patient-centered, rights-centered, and relational ethical systems. Several alternative possibilities for structuring legal theory and defining its key terms are suggested by these comparisons. The goal is to imagine what legal theory might look like if it were structured around the cultivation of virtues, the establishment of certain kinds of interpersonal relationships, or the articulation of general moral principles, rather than around the eternal consequences of particular actions for the individuals who perform them. These possibilities would require not only different definitions of key terms, but also different approaches to the interpretation of revealed texts and the construction of ethical norms. Resources for reshaping legal theory around such alternative ethical structures are identified within the discipline of *uṣūl al-fiqh* itself and in other Islamic disciplines. No particular reformulation of legal theory is advocated, but it is argued that imagining alternatives helps us to understand al-Juwaynī's own legal theory. We do not fully understand the significance of the theoretical choices made by scholars of *uṣūl al-fiqh* until we imagine what Islamic law would look like if they had chosen differently.

Introduction: Comparative Imagination

When in the fall of 1999, after a semester studying Islamic legal theory in Fez, Morocco, I decided to make that discipline the focus of my research, I sat down with two scholars at Emory University to perform a comparative reading of Imām al-Ḥaramayn al-Juwaynī's *Kitāb al-Waraqāt fī Uṣūl al-Fiqh* and a modern textbook on Western hermeneutical thought, *New Horizons in Hermeneutics*, by Anthony Thiselton.[1] This turned out to be the most difficult intellectual enterprise I had ever undertaken, but it proved very worthwhile, and laid the conceptual groundwork for my dissertation and, eventually, my book on *The Formation of Islamic Hermeneutics*.[2]

This essay attempts a similar comparison, reading al-Juwaynī's *Kitāb al-Waraqāt* in light of some basic categories of Western ethical discourse. Such comparative reading has the potential to illuminate features of texts that would otherwise remain implicit and unnoticed. By exposing the ethical structure implied by al-Juwaynī's technical definitions and theoretical choices, and by imagining what other kinds of ethical systems he could have envisioned if he had made different choices, we may hope to discern what kinds of ethical system his legal theory presupposes, and what ethical structures it leaves unthought or even unthinkable.

This will not enable us to generalize about the structure of all Islamic ethics. The *Kitāb al-Waraqāt* is just one work by one scholar of one school in one of the many Islamic disciplines that bear on ethics. As other papers in this volume demonstrate, other scholars in other disciplines thought about ethics in very different ways. For one thing, Islamic legal theory does not necessarily determine the ethical structure of Islamic law itself: Ḥanafī legal scholars have shared a mainstream Sunni legal theory very similar to al-Juwaynī's, yet Samy Ayoub's paper shows that some of their actual legal views have been much more concerned with the consequences of actions and the rights of individuals than their legal theory would suggest. Furthermore, Islamic law itself does not determine the structure of all Islamic ethics. Other moral discourses such as *adab* (comportment), *akhlāq* (character), and *taṣawwuf* (spirituality) are far more concerned with the cultivation of the moral self than with the evaluation of actions as right or wrong, which is the main focus of Islamic law. Discerning the ethical structure implicit in the *Waraqāt*, therefore, will not reveal the overall shape of Islamic ethics as a whole, or even of al-Juwaynī's own ethical thought, which encompassed much more than law.

Nevertheless, this analysis will shed some important light on the challenge of formulating a comprehensive Islamic ethic. If, as some of the contributors to this volume suggest, all Islamic moral discourses are to be seen as complementary parts of a coherent ethical vision, then the implicit ethical structures of those discourses will have to be understood and reconciled. Law may not be the queen of the Islamic sciences, as is often too easily assumed, but few Muslims would want to exclude law altogether from their ethical discourse, and many would give it a central place. Legal theory may not fully determine the law, but legal scholars at least aspire to render decisions compatible with their legal theory. Not all legal theorists would follow the *Kitāb al-Waraqāt*, but it remains one of the most influential legal theory texts ever written. The ethical structure that it presupposes and embodies, therefore, will have to be integrated somehow into almost any comprehensive Islamic ethic.

The *Kitāb al-Waraqāt*

The *Kitāb al-Waraqāt fī Uṣūl al-Fiqh* is attributed to the eleventh-century Shafiʿite Ashʿarite scholar Imām al-Ḥaramayn al-Juwaynī (1028–1085). It is not his magnum opus; quite the contrary, it is a text for schoolboys, a leaflet easy to memorize but useless without the guidance of a teacher or a commentary. In his monumental, eloquent, and brilliant *Kitāb al-Burhān* al-Juwaynī argued his way through every little point of legal theory, and articulated some innovative ideas. In this diminutive 'Leaflet on the Sources of Law', however, he provides only what every beginning student is expected to learn: basic definitions and uncontroversial principles of interpretation and reasoning that were taken more or less for granted by the end of the eleventh century. He omits debatable sources of law, such as the Practice of the People of Madinah or Public Interest (*maṣlaḥah*), and he withholds judgment on several disputed questions. This little booklet is therefore an ideal object of comparative analysis, because it represents not al-Juwaynī's own idiosyncratic conception of ethics, but the concepts which he felt were so widely taken for granted that every student needed to know them. It therefore reveals the underlying conceptual structure of the discipline: how ethics was and still is imagined by many if not most legal theorists, and, indeed, the boundaries of how ethics can be imagined from within that classical discipline.

This little text has been copied and reprinted countless times, often with one or another of the many commentaries and super-commentaries that have been written upon it. I have identified about sixty such commentaries, and I have written one myself, which incorporates many of the ideas presented in this paper and is freely available at http://waraqat.vishanoff.com, where readers may post their own comments on my translation and commentary. But there are surely many more that I have not counted, including oral commentaries in several languages at www.YouTube.com. There are also many variant texts of the *matn* or base text, the *Kitāb al-Waraqāt* itself. The translation used here is based on my reconstruction of a very early critical edition produced by one of the work's earliest commentators, Tāj al-Dīn Abū Muḥammad ʿAbd al-Raḥīm ibn Ibrāhīm al-Fazārī, better known as Ibn al-Firkāḥ, who died in 1291, two centuries after al-Juwaynī. (That edition, with critical apparatus, as well as a complete annotated translation, are available at http://waraqat.vishanoff.com.) Ibn al-Firkāḥ worked from at least three copies of the *Waraqāt*, and he carefully preserved many textual differences while indicating what he felt was the original *matn* even when he disagreed with it. My own reconstruction of his reconstructed *matn* is based on three early manuscripts, Landberg 256 and Sprenger 601 from the Staatsbibliothek in Berlin and British Museum Oriental 3093 at the British Library, as well as a laudable edition of Ibn al-Firkāḥ's commentary produced by Sarah Shafi al-Hajiri using four later manuscripts.[3]

Ibn al-Firkāḥ already expressed some doubt as to whether the text really was authored by al-Juwaynī. He had good reason to be skeptical: the opinions given in the *Waraqāt* do not always align with the views upheld by al-Juwaynī in his *Burhān*. It seems to me, however, that the differences are readily explained by the different goals of the two works: the *Kitāb al-Waraqāt* was not intended to advance al-Juwaynī's own idiosyncratic views but to introduce students to a widely accepted way of thinking about the law. For the purposes of this paper, therefore, it matters little whether al-Juwaynī himself actually wrote this little book, or whether it was ascribed to him by an admiring student or a pretentious teacher. Either way, it articulates a set of assumptions about law and ethics that have been shared, studied, and commented upon by countless teachers and students up to the present day, even outside the Shafiʿite school to which al-Juwaynī belonged.

I will proceed by commenting briefly on several sections of the text in sequence, providing a translation of each one, while the import of other sections for this analysis will only be noted in passing.

Section 1 – Legal Science and its Roots

> Here are some pages encompassing information on various subdivisions of 'the roots of legal science'. That is a phrase composed of two distinct parts, 'roots' and 'legal science'. A root is that on which something else is built, whereas a branch is that which is built on something else. Legal science is awareness of those revealed legal values that are arrived at by diligent inquiry.

Al-Juwaynī begins his 'Leaflet on the Sources of Law' by saying, according to Ibn al-Firkāḥ's reconstruction of the text, that *uṣūl al-fiqh* "is a phrase composed of two distinct parts, 'roots' (*uṣūl*) and 'legal science' (fiqh)." This seems obvious, but deserves scrutiny. The other principal textual tradition, which is embedded in the more famous commentary of Jalāl al-Dīn al-Maḥallī (d. 1460), is more ambiguous here and hence, I think, more likely to be authentic. It reads simply "that is composed of two distinct parts," leaving the referent of the demonstrative pronoun "that" deliberately unspecified, so that one remains unsure whether it is the phrase *uṣūl al-fiqh* that is divided into two parts, the discipline of *uṣūl al-fiqh* itself, or the *Kitāb al-Waraqāt fī Uṣūl al-Fiqh*. This ambiguity may be deliberate, because all three are composed of two parts in some sense: the first word in the phrase, the first part of the discipline, and the first half of the book all have to do with the roots or sources of the law – the stuff or material of revelation – while the second part of each deals with the construction of law by reasoning based on those sources.

This distinction suggests that al-Juwaynī's ethics may combine features of two different types of ethical theory: divine command theory and constructivism. First, its reliance on revealed sources makes it a kind of divine command theory in which ethical norms are established by and known through God's speech rather than being naturally and universally binding and knowable, as in most natural law theories. Second, the acknowledgement that in addition to revelation the formulation of Islamic law requires human agreement (consensus) and reasoning (analogy and diligent inquiry), which are discussed in the second half of the *Waraqāt*, suggests that al-Juwaynī's ethic may also have a constructivist dimension: he may hold that ethical norms are not eternally fixed prior to their application in particular situations, but are arrived at through a process of human deliberation and agreement in view of particular conditions. It may turn out that the construction of law, for al-Juwaynī, consists entirely of deliberation and agreement about the proper interpretation of God's speech, so that rather than construction of new laws he is envisioning the discovery of eternally fixed ethical norms. That would make him more of a divine command theorist than a constructivist. It will be instructive, however, to consider further whether he might believe that ethical norms themselves are actually constructed (and not merely discovered) through human deliberation.

The next phrase provides one clue as to which aspect of Islamic ethics – its being commanded in revelation or its being constructed through deliberation – al-Juwaynī wishes to emphasize. He proceeds to define the words *uṣūl* and *fiqh*, starting with the singular of the first word, *aṣl*: "A root is that on which something else is built, whereas a branch is that which is built on something else." *Aṣl* could be translated source, root, or foundation, and I have chosen root because it contrasts nicely with branch (*far*ᶜ), but al-Juwaynī is not thinking of a tree; his definition shows that he is thinking of a building. The metaphor of a tree, which is pervasive in Islamic legal thought, suggests organic growth, as though every rule of law was predetermined by the genetic material of revelation. The building metaphor however suggests human constructive labor: Islamic law is like a house built upon revelation, constrained by the footprint of that foundation but shaped as well by human creativity. This shows that while al-Juwaynī regards the source of law (its *uṣūl*) as revelation rather than human deliberation, consensus, or reasoning, he regards the content or "branches" (*furū*ᶜ) of law (fiqh) as literally a human construct – "that which is built on" revelation.

This is a point on which not all conceptions of Islamic legal ethics agree. Some legal theorists emphasize instead the metaphor of the tree, describing the process of interpreting revelation as *istithmār*, a word that suggests the idea of making something yield fruit. Some define *aṣl* as "whatever something [else] derives its substance from" (or "comes from" or "is part of" – *mā minhu al-shay'*)[4] or as "whatever something else branches off from."[5] If al-Juwaynī had chosen one of these definitions, this would have reinforced the idea, conveyed by the tree metaphor, that the content of law stems entirely from revelation. Such horticultural language suggests that every little detail of the law is fully determined by revelation, just as the shape of every leaf on a tree is already encoded in the roots from which it grows. Diligent inquiry, in this picture, is like the work of a gardener, who merely provides the environment that is needed for the unfolding of a plant's DNA. Human thought and culture provide the environment to which the law adapts itself, but they can no more determine its content than a gardener can choose to grow oranges on a persimmon tree.

Al-Juwaynī, however, chooses to evoke the image of a foundation (revelation) upon which a building (fiqh, legal science) is erected. He even goes so far as to define *farʿ* as "that which is built on (*buniya ʿalā*) something else," even though *farʿ* normally means branch, not building. This definition suggests that diligent inquiry involves much more than just teasing out the implicit meaning of revelation. It conveys the idea that while revelation may dictate the building's footprint, human thought and culture may make a material contribution to the edifice of legal science through methods of diligent inquiry (ijtihad) such as consensus and analogy. Of course, al-Juwaynī means building in an abstract rather than a concrete sense, so perhaps he does not mean to imply all that the image of a builder suggests; but if our word choices convey something about how we think, and even shape how we think, then it is significant that although al-Juwaynī echoes the tree metaphor, and thus implies that law stems entirely from revelation, he explicitly and quite literally defines law as a human construct.

This is reaffirmed by his definition of the second word, fiqh: "Legal science is awareness of those revealed legal values (*aḥkām*) that are arrived at by diligent inquiry (ijtihad)." By way of contrast, Abū al-Ḥasan al-Ashʿarī (d. 935) defined fiqh as understanding the meaning of speech, or, more technically, as understanding the meaning of revelation as it relates to law.[6] The difference is subtle but important: legal science is not knowing the legal values of actions, it is understanding God's speech. Had al-Juwaynī adopted al-Ashʿarī's definition, he would have been emphasizing the divine command theory that law is spoken by God, and that humans know the law only insofar as they grasp the intent of God's speech. Al-Juwaynī's chosen definition has the opposite effect of emphasizing the constructive role of human reasoning: legal science is the product of ijtihad.

Section 2 – Legal Values

There are seven legal values: obligatory, recommended, permitted, forbidden, disapproved, valid, and invalid. Obligatory means what one is rewarded for doing and punished for omitting. Recommended means what one is rewarded for doing but not punished for omitting. Permitted means what one is neither rewarded for doing nor punished for omitting. Forbidden means what one is rewarded for omitting and punished for doing. Disapproved means what one is rewarded for omitting but not punished for doing. Valid means effective and relied upon. Invalid means neither effective nor relied upon.

The object of legal science, according to al-Juwaynī's definition, is legal values (*aḥkām*). To know the law is to know the legal values of actions. In section two al-Juwaynī enumerates seven possible legal values that a human action can have: obligatory, recommended, permitted, forbidden, disapproved, valid, and invalid. He could have listed more. An act can have the legal value of being a cause (*sabab*) that gives rise to another legal value of another act. The act of murder, for example, has the legal value of 'forbidden', but it also has the legal value of being the cause that renders an act of retaliation permissible. An act can also be a necessary condition (*sharṭ*) for the existence of another legal value, or an obstacle (*māni*ʿ) to it. These too are legally important features of actions, and they are considered 'legal values' of a particular kind. As al-Juwaynī and most legal theorists would agree, however, the first five legal values are the basic ones: obligatory, recommended, permitted, forbidden, and disapproved. Valid, invalid, cause, condition, and obstacle are legal values only in the secondary sense that they are features of actions that have implications for the basic legal values of other actions. To say that a sale is valid means that it effectively transfers ownership, which changes what the former and new owners are permitted or forbidden to do with the exchanged property. Similarly, to call something an occasion, condition, or obstacle is just to specify which situations make actions obligatory, recommended, permitted, forbidden, or disapproved. In the end all legal knowledge serves to establish which of the main five legal values some action has in a certain situation.

As has often been pointed out, the inclusion among these five fundamental legal values of two intermediate values, recommended and disapproved (or disliked, *makrūh*), makes this normative system more ethical than strictly legal: Islamic law is not just about what one is required to do but about what is best, not just about what one must do but about what one should do.

Just as important is the way al-Juwaynī defines those legal values entirely in terms of reward and punishment. This too makes Islamic law more ethical than legal, because the reward and punishment he has in mind are not those meted out by human authorities and institutions, but those administered by God in the life to come. This is not explicit in al-Juwaynī's definitions of the five main legal values; he merely says that "obligatory means what one is rewarded for doing and punished for omitting," and so on, without specifying whether that reward or punishment will occur on earth or in the hereafter. But he is clearly not imagining rewards or punishments meted out by a human judge. He is not talking about *aḥkām* in the sense of court judgments (*aqḍiyah*). Instead he uses the Qur'an's vocabulary for describing God's reward (*thawāb*) and punishment (*ʿiqāb*) in the hereafter. He would not deny that certain acts should be punished by human rulers in this life, but he is not talking here about *ḥudūd*. The penalty of flogging is not God's punishment (*ʿiqāb*) for making unfounded accusations of adultery; it is just another human action, which would ordinarily be forbidden but which, because an accusation of adultery has been made without proper justification, becomes permissible or even obligatory for the ruler to carry out. Technically, according to al-Juwaynī's definitions, legal science is not the knowledge that one who makes an unfounded accusation of adultery should be flogged; it is the knowledge that God will punish such accusers in the afterlife, and that He will also reward rulers who apply the penalty of flogging to such accusers. This amounts to the same thing in practice, but technically the legal value of any action is defined not by its consequences in this life but by its consequences in the hereafter, and this tells us that al-Juwaynī understood law as primarily about eternal rather than earthly consequences. Earthly consequences are secondary effects of the pursuit of heavenly consequences.

This makes Islamic legal ethics, at least in theory, a private affair between the individual and God. Of course one's actions will have effects on others, but one's fundamental responsibility and accountability, as al-Juwaynī defines it here, is to God, not to other individuals or to society. Ethical norms are not grounded in or dependent upon a social contract. One can certainly imagine an Islamic social contract theory: philosophers like Ibn Sīnā regarded prophetic revelation and law as necessary means of promoting social cohesion,[7] so that the law's *raison d'être* is not individual reward in the afterlife but social wellbeing on earth. But for al-Juwaynī the fundamental basis and ultimate goal of revealed law are not found in society but in God's commands to the individual and God's future judgment upon the individual. Society, one infers, is at best a vehicle that helps the individual toward eternal happiness.

Already we can see that al-Juwaynī's simple enumeration of legal values bears within it a great deal of information about the structure of his ethical thought. His definitions appear innocuous and uncontroversial, and so obvious that they hardly need to be stated, but because he has defined legal science as awareness of the legal values of particular actions, how he defines those legal values determines the nature of his legal ethics.

From al-Juwaynī's definitions of legal science and legal values we learn that his ethic is deontic, deontological, and agent-centered. First, it is deontic because it is concerned with knowledge of what one ought to do. (*Deon* is the Greek word for duty.) For every conceivable human action there is a legal value, and the task of legal science, as al-Juwaynī defines it, is to discover what mathematicians call a function: a relation f (for fiqh) that assigns a legal value v to every action a, which we could denote $f(a)=v$. This function maps the immense set A of all conceivable human actions onto a tiny set V containing just the five legal values that al-Juwaynī has just defined. For every act a, performed by a given person at a given time and place under a given set of circumstances, f(a) is one of those five legal values. Al-Juwaynī's definition of legal science makes ethics a matter of mapping or plotting on a graph as much of that legal function as one can, or at least as much as one actually needs for gaining God's reward and avoiding His punishment. When one has done that, one knows what any given agent may, should, or must do in any given circumstance.

This all seems obvious enough: ethics is knowing what one ought to do. Not all ethical systems are deontic in nature, however. Virtue ethics, for example, is not directly concerned with what one should do but with what kind of person one should be. We can imagine what an Islamic virtue ethic might look like. If al-Juwaynī had wanted to construct a legal virtue ethic, then instead of defining fiqh as awareness of certain legal values and then proceeding to define those values, he would have defined fiqh as the attainment of certain virtues and would have proceeded to define a whole list of virtues like wisdom, prudence, patience, and forbearance. Rather than defining five degrees of reward or punishment, he would have listed degrees of progress along the path to virtue. And rather than portraying his ethic as growing from or built upon the content of divine revelation, he would have mentioned divine grace and aid, or perhaps a set of character-building practices, as the foundations or roots or sources of virtue.

Muslims have developed systems of virtue ethics in disciplines other than legal theory. The literature on *akhlāq* (character or morals) spans materials as diverse as sayings of the Prophet and other pious figures, philosophical classifications of virtue, and Sufi descriptions of the stages and methods of personal spiritual development. The history of Islamic thought offers vast resources for constructing non-deontic ethical systems centered on the cultivation of virtue. That is not al-Juwaynī's concern, however – at least, not in his *Kitāb al-Waraqāt*. Here, in his terse summary of what every student of Islamic legal theory should know, he takes for granted that ethics means deontic ethics and, more specifically, deontological ethics.

His ethical system is deontological because it is concerned with deciding which actions an agent is obligated, permitted, or forbidden to perform. This may seem obvious, but not all deontic ethical systems are deontological. A consequentialist ethic, for instance, is deontic because it tries to assess what one ought to do, but instead of positing obligations and prohibitions that govern the moral agent who performs the actions (as in al-Juwaynī's definition of the law), it focuses on the consequences or outcomes of the agent's actions: what one ought to do is not that which one is somehow obligated to do, but that which results in the most good. Classic utilitarian ethics, for instance, says that one ought to do that which produces the most pleasure and the least pain for the greatest number of people.

Al-Juwaynī certainly talks about the consequences of one's actions: eternal reward and punishment are forms of pleasure and pain. Consequentialist ethics, however, generally has in view the consequences of one's actions for others as well as for oneself. (Ethical egoism, which aims solely at the agent's own benefit, is unusual in that regard). Such concern for others is notably absent from al-Juwaynī's definition of the law. This is not to say that he does not care about others. The content of Islamic law is in many respects more oriented toward the benefit of society than that of the individual. The basic duty of commanding what is good and forbidding what is evil, for example, is oriented toward the welfare of others. Nevertheless, al-Juwaynī's technical definition of legal science as knowledge of what actions will result in reward or punishment for the agent makes his ethics a matter of individual responsibility and personal consequences – just as the Qur'an declares that each individual will ultimately be judged alone, on the basis of his or her own deeds. The rules of Islamic law are often altruistic, but their goal, according to al-Juwaynī, is individualistic. One does not do things because one believes they will lead to the welfare of others; one does them because God has promised to reward them. The fact that they benefit others may be the reason why God has decided to command and reward them, but al-Juwaynī does not appear to be concerned with discerning the reasons for God's law; he is concerned with gaining reward and avoiding punishment.

The deontological and individualistic nature of al-Juwaynī's ethical vision has great significance for debates going on in Islamic law today. Nowhere in this treatise does al-Juwaynī mention *maṣlaḥah* (public welfare or the common good) or *sadd al-dharā'iʿ*

(blocking the means to harmful consequences). He was a Shafiʿite, and the Shafiʿites did not look kindly on sources of law beyond the traditional list of four sources: Qur'an, Sunnah, consensus, and analogy. Others, particularly among the Hanbalites and the Malikites, made more room for consequentialist reasoning. Thinkers such as the Hanbalite Najm al-Dīn al-Ṭūfī (d. 1316) provided conceptual resources for a consequentialist Islamic ethic, which have been exploited to great effect in the modern period, as evidenced by the burgeoning discourse about *maṣlaḥah* across the Muslim intellectual landscape. Such consequentialist thinking remained marginal in classical legal theory, however, and even in the modern period it is viewed with suspicion from some quarters. Al-Juwaynī's definition of law in terms of the five *aḥkām* reveals one reason for this suspicion: consequentialism is at odds with the fundamentally deontological and individualistic ethical structure of al-Juwaynī's legal theory, and his theory is so well entrenched in classical conceptions of law that few Muslims have ever thought to challenge his statement that fiqh means knowing the legal values of actions, or his definition of those legal values in terms of the act's consequences for the agent. Those seemingly innocuous definitions give Islamic legal ethics a deontological structure, and it would be difficult to transform it into a consequentialist system without revisiting al-Juwaynī's fundamental assumptions about the nature of legal knowledge.

Finally, al-Juwaynī's ethical vision is not only deontic and deontological but also agent-centered. That is, his ethic describes what is obligatory, permissible, or forbidden for particular agents given their particular situations. There are also patient-centered deontological ethical theories, which define the agent's obligations in terms of the rights of others: I am forbidden to kill because others have a right to live (or at least not to be killed); I am forbidden to use others for my own ends without their consent because others have a right to be treated as people rather than as tools; etc. The rights of the patient or victim of one's actions imply duties for the agent, but in patient-centered theories the patient's rights are more fundamental than the agent's duties.

If al-Juwaynī had conceived of Islamic law as rights- or patient-centered, he would have defined legal science (fiqh) as knowledge of whether the violation of a given right will or will not be compensated or punished in the afterlife, rather than as knowledge of which acts will or will not be rewarded or punished in the afterlife. There are resources within Islamic legal discourse itself for such a patient-centered and rights-based ethic: some legal obligations and prohibitions are said to be based on the rights of human beings (*ḥuqūq al-ʿibād*) as opposed to the rights of God. As we have seen, however, al-Juwaynī defines ethical norms in terms of divine reward and punishment for the agent. This puts the focus squarely on the agent's duty toward God, not the rights of the patient. It grounds the law in God's right to be obeyed, not in the rights of human individuals. If the modern discourse of human rights has been viewed with suspicion by some Muslims, this is not because Islamic law lacks the conceptual resources for a rights-based or patient-centered ethic, but because for centuries students of Islamic legal theory have started from al-Juwaynī's premise that legal science is a matter of knowing the duties of the agent, not the rights of the patient.

Section 3 – Knowledge and its Opposites

Legal science is a subcategory of knowledge.
Knowledge is awareness of the thing known as it actually is.
Ignorance is to imagine something as other than what it actually is.
Immediate knowledge is that which does not arise through rational or evidentiary inquiry, such as knowledge arising from one of the five senses (hearing, sight, smell, taste, and touch) or from collective transmission.
Acquired knowledge depends on rational and evidentiary inquiry.
Rational inquiry is reflection on what is true of the object of inquiry.
Evidentiary inquiry is the search for evidence. Evidence is that which leads to what is sought.
Belief is acknowledging two possibilities, one of which is more likely than the other.
Doubt is acknowledging two possibilities, neither of which is superior to the other.

Section Three offers still more of those preliminary definitions that appear purely technical but which are crucial for understanding the basic structure of al-Juwaynī's ethical thought. Here al-Juwaynī clarifies that legal science (fiqh) is a subcategory or particular type of knowledge. This reaffirms what we noted earlier: Islamic ethics is about gaining knowledge of moral truths, not about gaining virtues or upholding a social contract. He then defines knowledge as "awareness of the thing known as it actually is." This implies that legal values, which are the things known in legal science, are properties that actions actually have independent of human knowledge or deliberation. We have already noted a tension in al-Juwaynī's definition of the roots of law: law is given through revelation, as in divine command theories of ethics, yet also constructed through a human deliberative process. Al-Juwaynī's definition of knowledge implies the former rather than the latter: legal values already exist; human ethical deliberation does not create them, but merely discovers them "as they actually are."

This makes al-Juwaynī a moral realist: he regards the law as a true description of real properties of human actions. It must be remembered, however, that the moral properties he has in mind are the properties of being rewarded or punished by God. These are extrinsic, not intrinsic properties; they are grounded in God's future action, not in the nature of human action. In this al-Juwaynī differs from those Muʿtazilites who said that actions are good or bad by nature, and that God wills, commands, and rewards certain actions (and, indeed, must do so) because they are good, and prohibits other actions because they are bad. In al-Juwaynī's Ashʿarite theological framework human actions have no intrinsic properties that would necessitate divine reward. He is a moral realist of the divine command type, not of the natural law type. He regards obligations as imposed by divine revelation, not as grounded in the natural properties of actions. The legal values that one seeks to know "as they actually are" are the properties of being rewarded or punished by God, not the properties of being intrinsically good or evil.

Section 4 – Subdivisions of the Discipline of Legal Theory

The roots of legal science are the paths to it, considered generally, and the manner of using them in evidentiary inquiry, as well as what follows from that. By 'the manner of using them in evidentiary inquiry' we mean the prioritizing of some pieces of evidence before others. By 'what follows from that' we mean the status of those who engage in diligent inquiry.

The roots of legal science fall under the following headings:

[5] – Types of speech
[6] – Commands and prohibitions
[7] – General and particular expressions
[8] – Summarized, clarified, apparent, and reinterpreted speech
[9] – Actions
[10] – Abrogating and abrogated speech
[12][8] – Consensus
[13] – Reports
[14] – Analogy
[15] – Forbiddance and permission
[16] – The prioritizing of evidence
[17] – The characteristics of the issuer of legal opinions and the seeker of legal opinions
[18] – The status of those who engage in diligent inquiry

Section Four is a table of contents. Having finished with his all-important preliminary definitions, al-Juwaynī now moves on to the standard topics of legal theory proper. Once again he divides the discipline into two parts: the roots or sources or evidences of the law, which here he calls the paths to legal science, and "the manner of using those sources in evidentiary inquiry." This clarifies that when al-Juwaynī spoke of the human construction of law in Section One, he did not mean that human reasoning creates legal values out of nothing, but rather that humans construct their knowledge of legal values through a process of interpretive reasoning. Legal science – knowledge of the law – is a human construct; the law itself – the 'mathematical function' that assigns a legal value to every act – is not a human construct at all. Al-Juwaynī is not proposing a constructivist ethic, in which moral norms do not exist independently but are constructed through human deliberation.

This also demonstrates that al-Juwaynī's ethic is not an example of classic natural law theory, in which human reason is sufficient to discover legal norms on its own.[9] There were Muslims who advocated such theories, including important Muʿtazilī thinkers who held that some moral principles are intrinsic properties of actions and are knowable by and binding upon all rational creatures. Those Muʿtazilites also upheld revelation as a complementary source of knowledge that fills in the very extensive gaps in our natural moral knowledge, so they too developed legal theories embodying principles of interpretive reasoning that were, in their broad outlines, quite similar to al-Juwaynī's. Al-Juwaynī's starting point is different, however. The legal science that he says is built by human reasoning upon the foundation of revelation is a purely interpretive construct; it employs rational methods but not rational or natural sources of moral information.

Sections 5 and 6 – Types of Speech and Commands and Prohibitions

(5) At the very least, speech must consist of two nouns, a noun and a verb, a verb and a particle, or a noun and a particle.
It is divided into command, prohibition, statement, and question.
In another respect, it is divided into literal and figurative speech. Literal usage is that which retains the sense for which words were coined, or alternatively, usage according to the conventions of speech. Figurative usage is that which goes beyond the sense for which words were coined. Literal usage can be linguistic, revealed, or customary. Figurative usage can be based on surplus, deficiency, transference, or borrowing [of meaning]. Figurative usage by surplus [of meaning] is like God's saying "There is nothing like His likeness." Figurative usage by deficiency [of meaning] is like God's saying "Ask the town." Figurative usage by transference [of meaning] is like 'hollow' being used for what comes out of a person. Figurative usage by borrowing [of meaning] is like God's saying "a wall that wants to collapse."
(6) A command is a verbal request obliging an inferior to perform an act. Its verbal form, when unqualified and in the absence of contextual indications [to the contrary], is *ifʿal*, so [that verbal form] is interpreted [as a command], except when some evidence indicates that what is intended is a recommendation or a granting of permission, in which case it is interpreted accordingly.

> The correct view is that a command does not require the repetition of the act, unless some evidence indicates that repetition is intended; nor does it require immediate action, because its aim is to bring the action into being without specifying one time rather than another. The command to bring about an action is a command to perform both the act and whatever is required for the completion of the act, just as the command to perform the prayers is a command enjoining the purity that paves the way for them. If the act is performed, then the person to whom the command is addressed is released from the charge laid upon him.
>
> Who is included in command and prohibition, and who is not: The believers are included in God's command, but the inattentive, young people, and the possessed are not addressed by it. Unbelievers are addressed concerning the branches of the revealed laws, and concerning that without which their performance is invalid, namely *islām*, because God has said "[What has landed you in hell?] They said, we did not pray."
>
> The command to do something is the prohibition of its opposite, and the prohibition of something is the command to do its opposite.
>
> [A prohibition] is a verbal request obliging an inferior to omit an act, and it indicates that the prohibited act is invalid.
>
> The verbal form of command [also] occurs with the meaning of permitting, threatening, giving alternatives, or creating.

In Sections Five and Six al-Juwaynī establishes another extremely important feature of classical Islamic legal theory: its goal is to reduce all of God's speech, in all of its great variety, to a single form and mode of speech: indicative statements about the legal values of human actions.

Al-Juwaynī begins by defining and dissecting speech. His list of four kinds of speech act – command, prohibition, statement, and question – is hardly exhaustive: he could have included any number of other performative effects that an utterance can have, such as the expression of a wish, offer, oath, promise, or threat. His goal here, however, is simply to point out that all utterances do not accomplish the same kinds of things. In Section Six he reveals why this is important: commands and prohibitions are central to God's imposition of the law, but they have to be translated into statements of legal values.

Al-Juwaynī has already established that legal science means knowing that certain acts have certain legal values. Such knowledge is expressed in statements of the form "act a by person p under circumstance c has the legal value v." Commands and prohibitions, however, are not statements, so in Section Six al-Juwaynī describes exactly how to translate commands and prohibitions into indicative statements of the proper form. An imperative verb, which in Arabic has the form *ifʿal*, constitutes a command, and therefore should be translated as a statement of an obligation, unless there is some contextual indication to show that it is intended merely as a recommendation or a granting of permission, in which case it should be translated as a statement that the act is merely recommended or permitted. An imperative verb should also be translated into several correlative statements about other obligations, such as the obligation to perform any other act necessary for the completion of the commanded act. It should not, however, be translated into a statement about the legal value of performing the commanded act immediately or repeatedly. A prohibition should, in the absence of evidence to the contrary, be translated into a statement that an act is forbidden, and also into a separate statement that the act is legally invalid (which is another of al-Juwaynī's seven legal values).

This translation exercise may seem straightforward and inevitable, given the way al-Juwaynī has defined legal science, but it has monumental implications. Defining law as statements of legal values means that whatever form the language of the Qur'an may have – and it takes many forms, from tragic stories and dire warnings to vivid natural images and tender words of comfort – the jurist's job will be to extract from each sentence whatever propositional content it may yield regarding the consequences of human actions. Because law has been such a pervasive aspect of Muslim intellectual life, the Qur'an has often been treated as a book of legal information. Indeed, one legal theorist, the Muʿtazilī Qāḍī ʿAbd al-Jabbār (d. 1025), concluded that the Qur'an is only about law: it may appear to tell stories and preach sermons of warning, but the only beneficial information God can possibly intend to convey to us through those stories and sermons is which actions He will reward and which He will punish. The Qur'an is, or must be reduced to, a statement of the law.[10]

This is not the only way one can imagine the Qur'an revealing law. For instance, it is often pointed out that God's speech does not just convey information, it also frequently serves to create or bring things into being. "When He decrees something, He merely says to it 'be!' and it is" (Qur'an 2:117, 19:35, 40:68). If law or ethics were imagined as a set of relationships between people, instead of a set of properties of actions, then the Qur'an could be viewed as the speech by which God brings certain relationships into existence, performatively binding people to each other in covenants of mutual responsibility and submission, just as the words used to perform a marriage bring about a new bond of authority and mutual obligation between husband and wife. Many Islamic societies have relied heavily on networks of carefully defined relationships of responsibility, loyalty, and authority between people, and it would not seem unreasonable to conceive of God's lawgiving as an act of creating such networks of relationships. If revelation were understood in this way, law would not consist of statements of the form "this act by this person at this time under these circumstances has this legal value," but instead would take the form "this person now stands in this relationship to this other person." Those relationships would be discovered not by translating commands into statements of obligation, but by tracing the history of human and divine interactions (both verbal and nonverbal) through which those relationships were performatively brought into being.

Alternatively, we could imagine that the function of God's speech is not to convey information but to transform people's character. That would certainly fit the tone of the Qur'an, and it would result in a very different kind of ethical or legal system, in which Muslims evaluate the development of their personal virtues, rather than the eternal consequences of their actions. Legal science would then take the form "this person has achieved this degree of patience or that degree of generosity." As we noted earlier, resources for such a virtue-oriented ethic are already present in the fields of *akhlāq* and *taṣawwuf.*

Alternatively, we could think like modern existentialists, and focus on the way God's speech challenges people, confronts them, and demands choice and response. This too fits well the tone of the

Qur'an. It would result in an ethic that focuses not on consequences but on the authenticity of each individual's response to revelation. In such an ethic, the same action could be evaluated quite differently depending on one's reason for doing it: "this person's choice to drink beer last night constituted a spineless sellout to peer pressure, whereas that person's choice to drink was a courageous act of solidarity with downtrodden laborers." Approaching God's speech as a direct personal challenge rather than a timeless statement about future reward and punishment would yield a radically different kind of Islamic ethic. Al-Juwaynī appears to be interested in legal information rather than existential challenge, but even he, at the end of the book, will hint that it is the integrity of one's choices, rather than their correctness, that determines their value in God's sight.

All three of these alternative ways of imagining Islamic ethics regard God's speech as performative rather than merely informative. They require us to look at revelation not just as a text but as an interpersonal event – just like the nonverbal revelatory actions of the Prophet that al-Juwaynī will discuss below in Section Nine. He will say in Section Seven that such nonverbal actions are not statements expressing general legal rules; they are just individual events, from which any general law must be inferred by means of an argument about the relevance of that event to other situations. If even verbal revelation was viewed as such a historical event, it would not be viewed as a set of general propositions, but as a record of God's interactions with particular people in particular times and places. The task of diligent inquiry (ijtihad) would then be to investigate what we can learn about the present from God's past interactions with people, rather than just applying the words God used in those past interactions directly to present situations.

This is, in fact, how some modern Muslims have tried to reform Islamic law. Fazlur Rahman (d. 1988), for example, is famous for his "double movement" theory of interpretation: first one investigates what God was trying to accomplish through His interaction with people at the time of the Prophet's revelations, then one investigates how that same moral purpose can best be accomplished in the here and now – even if the answer is quite unlike the specific commands

God gave in the seventh century. Fazlur Rahman did not say he was looking for the 'performative effect' of God's speech, but he treated God's speech as a historical event rather than as a timeless statement, which is a step away from an indicative interpretation and toward a performative interpretation of God's commands.

These alternative ways of understanding the language of revelation, and of imagining Islamic law or ethics, would have seemed ludicrous to al-Juwaynī – but only because he, and with him the whole classical legal tradition, had already made the pivotal decision to regard God's speech as a set of indicative statements about which actions God will reward or punish. This was not an unreasonable decision, but by al-Juwaynī's time it had come to be taken so much for granted that other possibilities, like the ones suggested above, were no longer even thinkable for legal theorists. It is worthwhile trying to imagine other possibilities, however, because we do not fully understand the significance of al-Juwaynī's choices – of his definitions of speech and knowledge and legal science – until we imagine what it would have meant if he had chosen to define them differently.

Sections 7 – General and Particular

A general expression includes (*ʿamma*) two or more things. ([This is the sense that *ʿamma* has] when one says "I included both Zayd and ʿAmr in my gift," or "I included everyone in my gift.") It [can be expressed using] four verbal forms: a singular noun made definite by a *lām*; a plural noun made definite by a *lām*; pronouns such as 'who' for rational beings, 'what' for non-rational things, 'any' for both of these, 'where' for place, 'when' for time, 'what' for inquiry and partition and other things, and 'no' applied to indefinite nouns, as when one says "there is no man in the house." Generality is an attribute of utterances, and it is not permissible to claim generality for other things such as actions or the like.

Particular expressions are all those that are not general.

Particularization is to distinguish part of a whole. It is divided into connected and disconnected particularization. Connected particularization comprises exception, condition, and qualification by an attribute.

Exception is the exclusion of that which an expression would otherwise include. Exception is only valid on condition that there remains something

> of that from which the exception was made. Another condition is that the exception be connected to the expression [from which exception is being made]. That which is excepted can be mentioned before that from which it is excepted. A thing can be excepted from the class to which it belongs or from another class.
>
> A condition can precede that which is made conditional [upon it].
>
> Unqualified expressions are interpreted in accordance with those that are qualified by some attribute. For example, the word 'slave' is qualified by the attribute of faith in some passages but is unqualified in others, so the unqualified passages are interpreted in accordance with the qualified ones.
>
> The Book can be particularized by the Book, the Book by the Sunnah, the Sunnah by the Book, the Sunnah by the Sunnah, and utterance by analogy, where by utterance we mean the speech of God (He is Exalted) and the speech of the Prophet (God's blessing and peace be upon him).

In Section Seven al-Juwaynī broaches another major aspect of the legal theorists' analysis of language: *ʿāmm* and *khāṣṣ*, general and particular expressions (or unrestricted and restricted expressions, as Joseph Lowry has recently proposed to translate these terms[11]). Here and in Section Eleven al-Juwaynī articulates the classic Shāfiʿī position, which, in spite of some resistance from the Muʿtazilites and the Hanafites, came to dominate classical legal theory across school lines. It is this, and it bears reflection: the particular always trumps the general.

This principle is not just a guideline for interpreting texts when they appear to contradict each other; it is fundamental to al-Juwaynī's conception of the law. Recall that he defined legal science as knowledge of the legal values of human actions – not general classes of actions in the abstract, but particular actions performed by particular individuals under particular circumstances. The goal of ethical inquiry is not to establish general rules about the kinds of actions that are generally preferred, or general guidelines about the kinds of moral goods one should pursue; it is to establish whether this particular person will be rewarded or punished if he or she performs this act at this particular time and place. As has often been pointed out, Islamic law is casuistic in the technical, non-pejorative sense of the word: it proceeds by analysis of specific cases rather than by the formulation of universal rules.

This concern with evaluating particular actions, rather than identifying and applying general moral values or aims or principles, cannot be overemphasized, because failure to understand this feature of Islamic law can lead to considerable bewilderment among modern Westerners, particularly when they come to discuss thorny issues like human rights. The Western intellectual tradition, stemming from the Platonic and Aristotelian concern with universal truths, tends to operate on the assumption that general principles govern particular cases. If all bachelors are male, and Socrates is a bachelor, then Socrates must be male. More pertinently, if Islamic law guarantees religious freedom, and conversion is a religious act, then Islamic law must guarantee the freedom to convert. Some Muslims involved in human rights debates, however, insist that while Islamic law does guarantee religious freedom, because the Qur'an says that there is no compulsion in religion, it also forbids conversion from Islam to another religion. This cannot be considered a violation of religious freedom, however, because the Qur'an clearly says there is no compulsion in religion.

Such logic seems ludicrous until one understands that the logic of Islamic legal theory does not make the legal values of particular actions subject to general moral principles like 'freedom of religion'. To those steeped in Western intellectual traditions, 'being consistent' means applying one's general principles to all particular cases, whereas to al-Juwaynī 'being consistent' means reconciling conflicting texts to avoid inconsistencies within the corpus of revelation, and this requires modifying general rules to accommodate more particular ones. That is precisely what the discourse about general and particular expressions is designed to do: it provides a simple way to reconcile conflicting texts. If one text forbids eating the meat of animals that have not been ritually slaughtered, while another allows eating fish (which is not, and indeed cannot be, ritually slaughtered), this apparent contradiction is easily resolved by saying that the narrow, more particular ruling about fish 'particularizes', or is an exception to, the broader, more general ruling about the meat of unslaughtered animals, which must not ever have been meant to be as general as it sounds.

Apart from a few scholars like al-Shāṭibī, who sought to subject detailed rules to general Qur'anic principles, Muslim legal theorists have almost unanimously sided with al-Juwaynī in declaring that narrower and more particular rules always trump more general principles. Muslim thinkers like al-Juwaynī have long been aware of Aristotelian logic – indeed it was thanks to them that Europeans first rediscovered it during the Renaissance – but that logic was not the basis of their legal theory, despite attempts by some legal theorists to reconcile the two disciplines. This classical tendency to prioritize the particular over the general has been challenged by many modern and even some premodern Muslims. Al-Shāṭibī (d. 1388) argued that five overarching goals of Islamic law – the preservation of religion, life, reason, wealth, and lineage – could be extracted from revelation by inductive reasoning, and could in turn be used to interpret and even override more particular rules. Najm al-Dīn al-Ṭūfī (d. 1316) argued that the famous hadith "there is to be no harming and no reciprocating harm" (number 32 in al-Nawawī's *Forty Hadith*), though extremely general, modifies numerous more specific rules, rather than being particularized by them. Many modern Muslims such as Fazlur Rahman have tried to filter out the situation-specific rules that the Prophet implemented and modified as his community grew and his circumstances changed, and to isolate the general moral principles behind those rules, so as to re-implement those general principles in the form of new rules for contemporary societies. Classical Islamic thought offers ample resources for the development of an ethic that prioritizes general principles over particular cases, and those resources have received a great deal of attention in modern times, partly because they fit better with the Western preoccupation with general principles. It must be recognized, however, that such an ethical structure runs against the grain of classical legal theory's fundamental orientation toward evaluating particular actions, and is contrary to its basic interpretive rule of giving priority to particular expressions over general ones.

Sections 8 – 17

Similar observations could be made about each of the remaining sections, but the most significant chapter, for the purpose of characterizing the structure of al-Juwaynī's ethics, is the last. I will therefore give only a brief overview of sections 8–17, of which the full text may be found at http://waraqat.vishanoff.com.

Section Eight deals with clarity and ambiguity in the language of revelation, so it is important mainly for understanding al-Juwaynī's hermeneutic. Section Nine deals with the non-verbal parts of the Prophet's Sunnah: his actions and omissions. As he did with verbal revelation, al-Juwaynī explains how to translate non-verbal revelation into statements about the legal values of human acts. This shows that al-Juwaynī regards even non-verbal actions as informative rather than performative: the Prophet's revelatory actions do not accomplish things or bring about new states of affairs, but instead convey information about the legal values of acts. Section Ten deals with another interpretive device for resolving conflicts between revealed texts: abrogation. This highlights once again that al-Juwaynī conceives of moral norms not as timeless natural properties of actions but as arising from divine commands and thus subject to change whenever God chooses to issue a new command.

In Section Eleven al-Juwaynī shifts from discussing the stuff of revelation – the properties of various types of revealed evidence – to the methods for interpreting that evidence when it appears contradictory, unclear, or insufficient. He begins with an explanation of how to apply concepts like particularization and abrogation, which he has described in the first half of the book, to resolve conflicts or apparent contradictions between revealed texts. Section Twelve describes consensus, which al-Juwaynī treats not as an independent source that determines and fixes the law, but as a method of interpretive argument that, arguably, permits gradual development of the law. Section Thirteen, on reports (*akhbār*), highlights the fact that texts are not interpreted in a vacuum but in the context of a tradition of scholarship within which they are handed down, interpreted, and evaluated.

Section Fourteen, on reasoning by analogy, suggests the important idea that the law is internally coherent – that good acts are good because of some characteristic they have, and that other acts with similar characteristics are therefore also good. This appears to qualify our earlier characterization of al-Juwaynī as a divine command theorist. He appears to be saying that legal values are not simply imputed to actions by God's decree, but are grounded in an action's natural properties, which 'entail' or 'bring about' their legal values. Given his Ashʿarite outlook, which denies that God does anything out of necessity or 'for a reason', I think it better to understand al-Juwaynī as saying that God uses the common characteristics of actions as pieces of evidence that 'indicate' their legal values, and thus help to communicate God's law. God gives similar legal values to similar actions so that humans can more easily discover their legal values, not because the natural properties of actions dictate those legal values. This understanding, however, cannot be defended on the basis of the *Kitāb al-Waraqāt* alone. Al-Juwaynī's language here suggests that even an Ashʿarite thinker's legal theory provides some foundation for a natural law theory of ethics.[12]

In Section Fifteen al-Juwaynī avoids taking a position on the question of whether an action has any legal value at all in the absence of revelation that assigns it a legal value, and if so what that default legal value is. Presumably, being a divine command theorist, he believes that moral norms simply do not exist in the absence of a divine command. Nevertheless, by leaving this question unresolved, he leaves open the possibility of adopting a kind of natural law theory in which actions have legal values in and of themselves, independently of divine commands. In Section Sixteen he returns to the question of how to resolve contradictions between conflicting pieces of evidence or interpretive rules. In Section Seventeen he reiterates that ethical knowledge is the product of human interpretive reasoning: legal rules cannot simply be handed down from one generation of scholars to the next, but must be reconstructed through diligent inquiry by each interpreter. He adds the crucial qualification, however, that this ethical reasoning is not something that everyone can do; it can only be performed by qualified interpreters working within a certain horizon of interpretation. That horizon, shaped by formal training in several Islamic and linguistic disciplines, is handed down from one generation of scholars to the next, and thus ensures continuity in the law. Yet by insisting that each generation of scholars must reach its own conclusions about the legal implications of God's speech, al-Juwaynī makes the law something that can evolve, albeit slowly, rather than remaining fixed from one generation to the next. Law may be revealed, but it is also constructed by human interpretive labor, from within the horizon of each generation of interpreters. Although al-Juwaynī seeks to ensure continuity in that horizon of interpretation, he does not seek to freeze the results of interpretation for all time.

Section 18 – The Status of Those Who Engage in Diligent Inquiry

> Diligent inquiry is to go to the limits of one's ability to achieve one's objective. If a fully competent practitioner of diligent inquiry inquires diligently into the branches of law and judges correctly, he is rewarded twice. If he inquires diligently and errs, he is rewarded once. Some say that all who inquire diligently into the branches of law judge correctly, but it cannot be said that all who inquire diligently into fundamental issues judge correctly, because that would require us to declare correct those who are in error – Christians, Magians, infidels and atheists. The proof of those who say that not all who exercise diligent inquiry concerning the branches of law judge correctly is that the Prophet (peace be upon him) said "whoever inquires diligently and judges correctly is rewarded twice, and whoever inquires diligently and errs is rewarded once." This is a proof because the Prophet (God's prayers and peace be upon him) declared the practitioner of diligent inquiry to be in error in one instance and declared him to be correct in another.

Section Eighteen returns to our opening question about whether ethical and legal norms are to be discovered through analysis of divine commands or constructed through human deliberation. Some theologians and legal theorists, known as the *muṣawwiba*, held that whatever conclusion is reached by a proper attempt at diligent inquiry (ijtihad) is by definition correct, because God makes the law for that person correspond to the result of his ijtihad. This reflects a kind of ethical constructivism: legal norms are not merely discovered but actually brought into being through human deliberation and reasoning. Khaled Abou El Fadl has interpreted al-Juwaynī as belonging to this constructivist camp. The truth, says Abou El Fadl, is in the search, not in the conclusions one reaches; truth is a property of the interpretive process, not of statements about the legal values of acts. We might call Abou El Fadl both a constructivist and an existentialist with respect to interpretation: what matters is not what legal value one assigns to an act, but the authenticity of one's attempt to understand revelation.[13]

In the *Kitāb al-Waraqāt*, however, Imām al-Ḥaramayn al-Juwaynī does not in fact adopt this constructivist and existentialist position. In Section Three he unequivocally made ethics a matter of knowing the legal values of acts "as they actually are," and here in Section Eighteen he unmistakably sides not with the *muṣawwiba* but with the *mukhaṭṭi'a*, those who affirm that there is a single correct answer to every legal or ethical question, so that it is possible for a qualified interpreter to perform ijtihad diligently and yet reach the wrong conclusion. We noted in Section One that al-Juwaynī's definition of the roots of law as a foundation upon which law is built served to highlight the role of human reasoning in the construction of law. In concluding his handbook on legal theory, however, al-Juwaynī notes that the Prophet's statement that practitioners of diligent inquiry will be rewarded even if they err implies that not all interpretations are correct, no matter how diligent and authentic the interpreter's effort. The law is already out there, in God's mind, waiting to be discovered through analysis of God's speech; it is not indeterminate, waiting to be constructed by human deliberation.

Nevertheless, by citing sympathetically both sides of this debate, al-Juwaynī demonstrates that there are within the heritage of Islamic legal thought ample resources for a constructivist or even an existentialist Islamic ethic. Khaled Abou El Fadl is only one of several modern Muslim scholars who have called for Muslims to take greater responsibility for their interpretive choices, and have focused on how diligently and sincerely ethical choices are made and owned, rather than on the content of those choices. This is yet another of those approaches to ethics that al-Juwaynī could not quite bring himself to embrace, given his commitment to a divine command theory of ethics. Yet his own writing demonstrates that such alternative forms of ethics are live possibilities for Muslims willing to interrogate the definitions and principles of classical *uṣūl al-fiqh*.

Conclusion

That last statement encapsulates the principal point of this paper: the rules and definitions that constitute classical legal theory shape and circumscribe Islamic legal ethics, but identifying and articulating those limits through comparison with modern ethical categories makes it possible to imagine alternative ethical structures that could be grounded in other rules and definitions, or in other Islamic disciplines altogether. First and foremost, I hope that my use of modern ethical terminology has helped to bring out the hidden structure of al-Juwaynī's thought, and has thus helped provide a fuller historical appreciation for the specific contours of al-Juwaynī's ethical vision. Given the great and enduring influence of al-Juwaynī's little 'Leaflet on the Sources of Law', that historical understanding should contribute something to our understanding of the whole classical tradition of Islamic legal theory, which remains very influential today. But I also hope that this comparative exercise has provoked some insights into the kinds of possibilities that Muslim scholars have open to them today as they continue to reconstruct their conceptions of Islamic ethics. The discipline of *uṣūl al-fiqh* is being reassessed continuously on many levels, and I expect it will prove fruitful for those engaged in this effort to consider the particular structure of the ethical system that is presupposed in classical *uṣūl al-fiqh*, and to mine very deliberately the resources that may be found in other varieties of Islamic legal theory, in other Islamic disciplines, and even in non-Islamic disciplines, for the task of imagining and elaborating new structures for Islamic ethics.

REFERENCES

Abou El Fadl, Khaled, *Speaking in God's Name: Islamic Law, Authority, and Women* (Oxford: Oneworld, 2001).

Emon, Anver, *Islamic Natural Law Theories* (Oxford: Oxford University Press, 2010).

Ibn al-Firkāḥ, Tāj al-Dīn ʿAbd al-Raḥmān ibn Ibrāhīm al-Fazārī, *Sharḥ al-Waraqāt li-Imām al-Ḥaramayn al-Juwaynī*, (Ed.), Sarah Shafi al-Hajiri (Beirut: Dār al-Bashā'ir al-Islāmiyyah, 1422 AH /2001).

Ibn Fūrak, Abū Bakr, *Muǧarrad Maqālāt al-Ašʿarī (Exposé de la doctrine d'al-Ašʿarī).* (Ed.), Daniel Gimaret (Beirut: Dar al-Machreq, 1987).

Lowry, Joseph E. (Ed. and trans.), *The Epistle on Legal Theory, by Muḥammad ibn Idrīs al-Shāfiʿī* (New York: New York University Press, 2013).

Rahman, Fazlur, *Prophecy in Islam: Philosophy and Orthodoxy* (London: George Allen & Unwin, 1958).

Thiselton, Anthony C., *New Horizons in Hermeneutics: The Theory and Practice of Transforming Biblical Reading* (Grand Rapids: Zondervan, 1992).

Vishanoff, David R., *The Formation of Islamic Hermeneutics: How Sunni Legal Theorists Imagined a Revealed Law* (New Haven: American Oriental Society, 2011).

al-Zarkashī, Badr al-Dīn, *al-Baḥr al-Muḥīṭ fī Uṣūl al-Fiqh.* (Ed.), Abd al-Qadir Abd Allah al-Ani, Umar Sulayman al-Ashqar, and Abd al-Sattar Abu Ghuddah (Kuwait: Wizārat al-Awqāf wa al-Shu'ūn al-Islāmiyyah, 1409 AH / 1988).

NOTES

1. Anthony C. Thiselton, *New Horizons in Hermeneutics: The Theory and Practice of Transforming Biblical Reading* (Grand Rapids: Zondervan, 1992).
2. David R. Vishanoff, *The Formation of Islamic Hermeneutics: How Sunni Legal Theorists Imagined a Revealed Law* (New Haven: American Oriental Society, 2011).
3. This was her Master's thesis at the University of Kuwait, later published as Tāj al-Dīn ʿAbd al-Raḥmān ibn Ibrāhīm al-Fazārī Ibn al-Firkāḥ, *Sharḥ al-Waraqāt li-Imām al-Ḥaramayn al-Juwaynī.* (Ed.), Sarah Shafi al-Hajiri (Beirut: Dār al-Bashā'ir al-Islāmiyyah, 1422 AH / 2001).
4. Badr al-Dīn al-Zarkashī, *al-Baḥr al-Muḥīṭ fī Uṣūl al-Fiqh.* (Ed.), Abd al-Qadir Abd Allah al-Ani, Umar Sulayman al-Ashqar, and Abd al-Sattar Abu Ghudda (Kuwait: Wizārat al-Awqāf wa al-Shu'ūn al-Islāmiyyah, 1409 AH / 1988), vol.1, p.15. This definition is also mentioned by Ibn al-Firkāḥ, *Sharḥ al-Waraqāt* (fol.3a in MS Staatsbibliothek zu Berlin—Landberg 256, fol.3a in MS British Library—Oriental 3093, p.80 in the edition of al-Hājirī).

5. al-Zarkashī, *al-Baḥr al-Muḥīṭ*, vol.1, p.16.
6. Abū Bakr Ibn Fūrak, *Muǧarrad Maqālāt al-Aš'arī (Exposé de la doctrine d'al-Aš'arī)*. (Ed.), Daniel Gimaret (Beirut: Dar el-Machreq, 1987), p.190.
7. Fazlur Rahman, *Prophecy in Islam: Philosophy and Orthodoxy* (London: George Allen & Unwin, 1958), pp.52–53.
8. Al-Juwaynī does not mention here the section that I have numbered 11, which explains what to do "if two utterances contradict one another."
9. See, however, note 12 below.
10. See Vishanoff, *The Formation of Islamic Hermeneutics*, pp.135–45, and the sources cited there.
11. Joseph E. Lowry (Ed. and trans.), *The Epistle on Legal Theory, by Muḥammad ibn Idrīs al-Shāfiʿī* (New York: New York University Press, 2013).
12. Anver Emon presents al-Juwaynī as a 'soft natural law theorist' in *Islamic Natural Law Theories* (Oxford: Oxford University Press, 2010), pp.28, 103–6, 126–29.
13. Khaled Abou El Fadl, *Speaking in God's Name: Islamic Law, Authority, and Women* (Oxford: Oneworld, 2001), pp.145–50, 159, and *passim*.

2

"Neither Desiring It, nor Transgressing Its Limits:" Ethical Hierarchy in Islamic Law

Samy Ayoub

ABSTRACT: The inquiry into normative ethics within Islamic jurisprudence (fiqh) seeks to establish general principles for deriving specific rules and guidelines for human conduct. This article investigates the intersections of hardship (*mashaqqah*), relaxation of a requirement (*taysīr*), and necessity (*ḍarūrah*) in late Ḥanafite jurisprudence. I argue that Ḥanafite legal formulations in circumstances of hardship and necessity are rooted in moral choices inspired by the doctrine of the choice of the lesser evil. In circumstances of necessity and hardship, Ḥanafite jurists affirm a hierarchy of ethical values, for which they provide a consequentialist ethical justification, to guide believers to overcome emerging moral dilemmas.

Introduction

The title of this article, "Neither Desiring It, nor Transgressing Its Limits" is a partial rendering of the Qur'anic verse "*fa man iḍturra ghayr bāghin wa lā ʿādin fa lā ithm ʿalayhi*" (2:173). Yusuf Ali translates this "But if one is forced by necessity, without wilful disobedience, nor transgressing due limits, then is he guiltless;" but as a legal principle it amounts to "There is no sin/harm for those who need [to violate a legal norm as long as they do not transgress the boundaries of the proper conditions of such necessity]." Late Ḥanafites employ a number of legal categories (necessity, hardship, easing of requirements, excuse, and communal necessity) to justify modifying legal requirements or rights under certain circumstances. In this paper, an analysis of how Ḥanafites employ these categories will show that their use presupposes a consequentialist ethic and a certain hierarchy of values.

This article is concerned with the role and influence of hardship and necessity in late Ḥanafism.[1] I pursue two issues in this regard: (1) the boundaries of hardship and necessity, and (2) the place of individual and collective rights in these circumstances. Late Ḥanafites consistently held that an individual may violate a legal obligation when there is a fear of probable death or serious bodily injury, or in case of compelling need. This position is reflected in two central legal maxims: "hardship brings about relaxation of a requirement," and "necessitous circumstances permit the unlawful."[2] Zayn Ibn Nujaym (d. 970/1562), a key Ḥanafite authority, points out that legal maxims function as the frame of reference for substantive legal cases (*turadd ilayha masāʾil al-fiqh*).[3] Late Ḥanafite jurists – the focus of this article – based their judgments on a hierarchy of values whose order is governed by balancing harms in pursuit of lesser evils. The top value in this hierarchy is preserving human life and attaining public interest. Ḥanafite jurists asserted that individuals may violate a legal obligation in order to avoid a greater evil. For example, they emphasized the individual's moral responsibility to eat carrion or to drink wine to avoid death.[4]

Furthermore, under the doctrines of necessity and hardship, Ḥanafites justify infringement upon certain rights of others, such as taking others' money to buy food to avoid starvation.[5] The nature of rights affected in these circumstances, whether individual or collective, or rights of God, are essential components of Ḥanafite legal preferences. The legal choices made by late Ḥanafite jurists in such circumstances presuppose a consequentialist ethical framework, which requires jurists to attend to the consequences of legal actions in order to weigh their ethical value. This approach may be contrasted with a deontological framework, which would assert, for example, that telling a lie is bad universally regardless of the consequences in specific situations. In a consequentialist framework, telling a lie may be necessary to preserve one's life and, therefore, permissible.

Ḥanafite ethics, and the moral hierarchy it produces, provide a unique window into Islamic moral concerns and priorities.

I should stress that a consequentialist view of morality – as Ḥanafites deploy it – does not render the act good or rightful but merely excusable. For example, Ḥanafites will affirm that a person should lie to preserve his/her life, but this permission to commit a sin does not change the ontological moral nature of the act of lying itself. As Khaled Abou El Fadel put it, "I am not sure that a teleological view of morality is possible without a prior deontological commitment."[6] In other words, the point of departure for a jurist who would grant permission for theft or lying in compelling necessity is that these acts are sinful and morally wrong.

In late Ḥanafite jurisprudence, *ḍarūrah* (necessity) and *mashaqqah* (hardship) are discussed as both individual and collective experiences. For instance, Muḥammad Amīn ᶜĀbidīn (d. 1836), known as Ibn ᶜĀbidīn, dedicates a section in his magnum opus *Radd al-Muḥtār* to the legal issues of *al-maᶜdhūr* (the excused one).[7] *Al-maᶜdhūr* is a person who, for example, has a medical condition that does not allow him/her to maintain his/her *wuḍū'* (ritual ablution). The *maᶜdhūr*, on this individual level, is excused from repeating the *wuḍū'*, even after it has been violated by his/her medical condition. On a communal level, Ibn ᶜĀbidīn, following earlier Ḥanafite authorities, uses the term *ᶜumūm al-balwā* (communal necessity) to describe a general status of a group or a community in order to address a widespread necessity or social practice.[8]

Necessitous Circumstances Permit the Unlawful

Although the term *ḍarūrah* does not appear in the Qur'an, the passive verb *uḍṭrra* (was compelled to) appears five times in the Qur'an in connection with alleviating the rules and restrictions of prohibited food items in the event of force majeure (*iḍṭirār* in Arabic). *Iḍṭirār* means compulsion or coercion, as opposed to *ikhtiyār* or freedom of choice. There are three jurisprudential principles that represent the lynchpin of the *ḍarūrah* maxim in Ḥanafite legal thought: civil liability (*ḍamān*), concession (*rukhṣah*), and the choice of the lesser evil (*akhaff al-mafsadatayn*). The interrelations of these principles may be illustrated, for instance, by a case in which a person is compelled, due to an extreme hardship, to usurp another's food to avoid starvation. While this person might have a license (*rukhṣah*) to violate another's rights to save his/her life, s/he is liable for the value of the usurped property.

The doctrine of *ḍarūrah* was applied more widely by Ḥanafite jurists to address practical necessity and wider communal needs. They appealed to *ḍarūrah* in reconsidering the limitations of juristic analogy (*qiyās*) in legal reasoning. Ibn ᶜĀbidīn held that necessity is an acceptable justification for preferring a weak opinion to the preponderant opinion (*al-ra'y al-rājiḥ*) in the school.[9]

Secondary Scholarship

In his *Authority, Continuity, and Change in Islamic Law*, Wael Hallaq rightly argues that necessity (*ḍarūrah*) drives doctrinal change.[10] He contends that jurists have justified their adoption of new practices on the basis of necessity. Hallaq asserts that the principle of *ḍarūrah* finds justification in Qur'an 2:185: "God wants things to be easy for you and does not want any hardship for you." He says that Ibn ᶜĀbidīn bypasses authoritative doctrines held by the most influential figures of the school in favor of a weak opinion.[11] Hallaq also argues that Ibn ᶜĀbidīn solves new emergent problems in two ways: (1) by upholding custom as a sufficient justification; and (2) by resorting to the notion of necessity (*ḍarūrah*).[12] Hallaq explains that although the notion of necessity has been used to justify "a number of departures from the stringent demands of the law, it is, like custom, restricted to those areas upon which the explicit texts of revelation are silent."[13] He affirms that necessity was a legal device used to justify "departure from the authoritative doctrine of the school, that which represents the dominant mainstream of legal doctrine and practice."[14] "*Ḍarūra*," he says, "was a device that must have seemed handy when all other hermeneutical ventures appeared to have no prospect of success."[15]

However, in his *Sharīʿa: Theory, Practice, and Transformation*, Hallaq views the concept of *ḍarūrah* as a legal tool misused by contemporary jurists to justify predetermined legal outcomes. He maintains that the concept of *ḍarūrah* is among the methods that the emerging nation-states in the 19th century used to "restrict the scope and influence of Islamic law while strengthening their bureaucratic and legal powers."[16] He argues that the narrowing down of Shariʿah must be seen more as "an inherent part of the power dynamics of the evolving modern state rather than as teleological efforts to progress toward a more sophisticated legal culture."[17] Hallaq emphasizes that modern legists transformed this concept in two ways: (1) it was transposed from the realm of substantive law to the realm of legal theory, and (2) the scope of *ḍarūrah* was widened beyond recognition.[18]

Hallaq's sentiment about the exploitation of *ḍarūrah* in contemporary legal discourse is valid. However, frustration with contemporary legal discourses should not overshadow the fact that *ḍarūrah* is a legitimate tool of legal theory.[19] It has been applied to a variety of topics in the legal literature, and has been an essential legal device in Ḥanafite legal thought.[20] Ibn ʿĀbidīn justifies the shift in some of his legal doctrines by change of time (*ikhtilāf al-zamān*), corruption of the people of the time (*fasād ahl al-zamān*), and general necessity (*ḍarūrah*).[21] He argues that although these doctrinal shifts may be perceived to be outside the realm of the authoritative doctrinal commitments espoused by the school, these new positions would have been endorsed by the early authorities of the school if they had been exposed to the new customs and compelling social needs of his day.[22] The concept of *ḍarūrah* is an indispensable tool of legal reasoning used by Ḥanafite jurists to admit or reject new emergent forms of social customs and dealings.

Hardship Brings About Relaxation of a Requirement *(Al-Mashaqqah Tajlib al-Taysīr)*[23]

The legal maxim "hardship brings about relaxation of a requirement" is one of the six universal maxims included in Ibn Nujaym's *al-Ashbāh wa al-Naẓā'ir*.[24] Ibn Nujaym starts the discussion on this maxim by emphasizing that the source of this legal maxim is the

Qur'an and Sunnah.[25] He supports this claim by invoking two verses from the Qur'an and a Prophetic tradition (Hadith).[26] Ibn Nujyam's objective here is to drench this maxim in the two authoritative texts of Islamic law in order to emphasize its authenticity. The verses he quotes are "God intends for you ease (*al-yusr*) and does not intend for you hardship (*al-ʿusr*)" (2:185), and "He has not placed upon you in the religion any hardship (*ḥaraj*)" (22:78). The word *mashaqqah* does not appear in these verses, but rather the word *ḥaraj* (hardship), as well as the word *yusr* (ease) and its antonym *ʿusr* (difficulty), which are key words in any legal discussion of hardship and necessity. Ibn Nujaym also cites a Prophetic tradition to support the authority of this maxim. The hadith states that the Prophet said: "The best religion in the sight of God is the easy *Ḥanīfiyya* (referring to the religion of Abraham)." Then he emphasizes that this maxim is the fulcrum of all concessions and relaxations of requirements (*rukhaṣ al-sharʿ wa takhfīfātih*) in the legal literature.[27] In this legal maxim, Ibn Nujaym finds the flexibility to accommodate new emerging cases and address urgent social issues within the Muslim community. He employs this maxim to justify the legality of some transactions and to alleviate hardship in ritual acts.[28] For example, late Ḥanafites use this maxim to sanction many contracts such as *salam* sale,[29] conditioned sale, and commercial partnership, which are considered essential for people's everyday business.[30]

Hierarchy of Hardship

In his *al-Ashbāh wa al-Naẓā'ir*, Ibn Nujaym includes a set of legal norms or restatements (*fawā'id*) that determine the contours of hardship in Ḥanafite jurisprudence. The first restatement defines the degrees of hardship and divides them into two types, the first of which is intrinsic hardships that are inseparable from the act.[31] Examples of this type are the hardship of performing minor ablution during cold weather, fasting during hot weather on long days, and traveling for Hajj. Ibn Nujaym emphasizes that these intrinsic hardships intertwined with acts of worship do not reduce, alleviate, or remove the duty to perform these acts. According to Ibn Nujaym, fasting inherently involves *mashaqqah*; such difficulty in abstaining from food and drinks is not a legally compelling reason to remove the duty of fasting during the month of Ramadan, since the *mashaqqah* is intrinsic to the ritual act itself.[32]

The second type of *mashaqqah* is extrinsic to ritual acts. For instance, Ibn Nujaym permits dry ablution (*tayammum*) if individuals have serious fears about the severity of cold weather for performing major ritual ablution (*ghusl*). Ibn Nujaym restricts this ruling to cases in which one fears for one's life or limb if one performs a complete ablution (*ghusl*) to remove *janābah* (major ritual impurity). Ibn Nujaym invokes the doctrine of *taysīr* to circumvent this hardship. He divides this extrinsic hardship into three levels, the first of which is grave hardship (*mashaqqah ʿaẓīmah*), which primarily involves endangering one's life, limb, or the functionality of a body organ. Ibn Nujaym asserts that relaxation of requirements here is obligatory, and he provides some examples in this regard. For instance, Ḥanafites consider dry ablution sufficient to remove major ritual impurity (*janābah*) if the individual fears death or material harm to his/her body. Also, Ḥanafites remove the duty of performing Hajj if the only way to visit Makkah is traveling by sea and it is established that it is unsafe to make such a journey. The second level is light hardship (*mashaqqa khafīfa*), which is defined as equivalent to the least possible pain that a person suffers in his finger, the least headache he may incur, or having a bad temper.[33] Ibn Nujaym affirms that these symptoms have no legal consequence because, according to him, bringing about benefits takes priority over fending off these minor personal difficulties. The third level is intermediate hardship (*mashaqqah mutawassiṭah*), which Ibn Nujaym does not define but which he considers adequate grounds for relaxing a legal requirement. He cites as an example of intermediate hardship the case of a sick person during Ramadan. Ḥanafites allow this person to break his/her fast if s/he is concerned that fasting will worsen his/her health condition or slow his/her recovery.[34] The problem that Ibn Nujaym might have grappled with in his hierarchical framework is that these levels of hardship are intimately intertwined with individual situations, and it would be impossible for jurists to define these instances precisely. However, he lays down the overall criterion that guides jurists in this regard: fear for one's life or limb necessitates (*yūjib*) lightening of a requirement (*al-takhfīf*).[35]

Hardship Brings about Relaxation of a Requirement

Ibn Nujaym establishes seven grounds for lightening a requirement (*takhfīf*) in ritual and non-ritual acts.[36] These seven grounds fall under the rubric of extrinsic hardship. The first ground is travel (*safar*) and it has two types, the first of which is travel that involves a long journey and is composed of three days and nights. In this travel situation, *takhfīf* entails a license (*rukhṣah*) for shortening prayer (*qaṣr*), breaking the fast (*ifṭār*), and wiping over the leather socks (*al-masḥ ʿalā al-khuffayn*) instead of removing them to perform ablution for a period of a day and a night. The second type of travel is travel that is not specified by a time frame, meaning indefinite travel from one's home.[37] Here, a legal license (*rukhṣah*) is granted to skip Friday prayers, the two feasts (*al-ʿīdayn*), and the five daily prayers in congregation. Furthermore, the act of traveling makes performing supererogatory prayers valid while riding one's means of travel (e.g. a camel). For Ḥanafites, shortening prayer during travel is a required license in the sense of resolve (*ʿazīmah*). In other words, shortening prayer during travel is the default Ḥanafite position. Ibn Nujaym declares that Ḥanafites consider the prayers of a person who does not shorten his/her prayers during travel to be invalid, and the individual is considered sinful. The exception to this rule is that this person intends to stay (*iqāmah*) in a certain place before the third unit of prayer (*rakʿah*).

The second ground for relaxation of a requirement is sickness (*maraḍ*). For example, a person can perform dry ablution (*tayammum*) if s/he has concerns for his/her life or limb. Also, a *rukhṣah* is given to perform dry ablution if water will result in worsening a patient's medical condition or decelerating the process of his/her recovery and healing. In this case, Ibn Nujaym allows using substances that are legally determined to be impure, as well as wine, for medical reasons, though he also mentions two opposing opinions within the school. In addition, Ibn Nujaym states that permission is given to the medical doctor to see and examine one's private parts.

Ibn Nujaym considers illness to be a valid ground for *takhfīf.* However, he does not admit mild illness to be sufficient to trigger any type of dispensation; the individual must become concerned about his/her life and well-being. Ibn Nujaym raises the question of why jurists do not permit relaxation of a requirement due to an ailment in general terms, i.e. without conditioning a specific degree of hardship.[38] This inquiry on the part of Ibn Nujaym addresses one of the legal principles (*uṣūl*) of the Ḥanafite legal school. Ḥanafites differentiate between the operative cause (*ʿilla*) and the legal wisdom (*ḥikma*) behind a requirement, which do not have the same effect in legal reasoning. This is explained by ʿUbayd Allāh al-Karkhī (d. 340/951), who points to the Ḥanafite school's principle that it is solely the existence of an *ʿilla* that renders legal determinations, regardless of the existence of a clear wisdom.[39] Hence, travel (*safar*) is grounds for a license (*rukhṣah*) to shorten prayers (*qaṣr*) and for other types of *takhfīfāt*, regardless of the degree of hardship associated with the act of travel.

The third, fourth, and fifth grounds for relaxation of a requirement are duress (*ikrāh*), forgetfulness (*nisyān*), and ignorance (*jahl*), respectively. Ibn Nujaym does not elaborate on these circumstances, but we can see their legal consequences in his work. The sixth ground for relaxation of a requirement is comprised of extreme hardship (*ʿusr*) and predominant communal need (*ʿumūm al-balwā*). A practical manifestation of the concept of *ʿumūm al-balwā* is that Ḥanafites hold that fire purifies animals' droppings for the sake of lightening a requirement (*li al-taysīr*), i.e., that these droppings are pure when they are used as fuel. (Farmers used these droppings in mud ovens to bake their bread and prepare their food.) Ibn Nujaym justifies this position by arguing that if animal droppings were considered impure this would result in declaring the impurity of bread in most major cities.[40]

Ibn Nujaym deploys the principle of *takhfīf* in the realm of commercial transactions, utilizing the flexibility of the *taysīr* maxim to address people's recurring needs and spare them hardship. He uses this maxim to justify the legality of contracts of hire and lease (*ijārah*), mercantile partnerships (*sharikah*), loans of money (*qarḍ*), the agricultural contract of *muzāraʿah*, and several other kinds of sale contracts.[41] Ibn Nujaym refers to the fact that engaging in a commercial transaction is necessary to assist with people's practical needs, and in cases of bankruptcy.[42] He invokes the same argument to justify specifying certain conditions in sale contracts to avoid injustice in transactions.[43]

The seventh ground for relaxation of a requirement is deficiency (*naqṣ*). Ibn Nujaym views deficiency in legal capacity (*ahliyyah*) as a situation that warrants relaxation of a requirement (*takhfīf*). For instance, the legal capacity (*ahliyyah*) of both the child and the mad person is deficient (*naqīṣah*); therefore, their legal matters are delegated to their guardian (*walī*). In addition, under this justificatory ground, Ibn Nujaym explains that women are not legally responsible for many of the duties that men are asked to fulfill, such as attending prayers in congregation and Friday prayers, participating in jihad, or, for non-Muslim women, paying taxes (*jizyah*).[44] Also, unlike men, women are permitted to wear silk and gold.[45]

The Second Restatement: Seven Types of Takhfīfāt

Ibn Nujaym delves into seven types of lightening a requirement (*takhfīfāt*). The first type is the cessation (*takhfīf isqāṭ*) of ritual acts (*ʿibādāt*) in the presence of their legal excuses (*aʿdhār*). Although Ibn Nujaym does not provide examples, a perfect case would be skipping ritual prayers during a woman's menstrual period. The second type is reducing ritual acts (*takhfīf tanqīṣ*); such as shortening prayer during travel. The third type is performing an alternate ritual act (*takhfīf ibdāl*) such as replacing ablution (*wuḍū'*) with a dry ablution (*tayammum*), or replacing fasting with feeding the needy. The fourth type is performing the ritual act before its due time (*takhfīf taqdīm*), such as paying out the annual obligatory charity (zakah) before its due time.[46] The fifth type is delaying the ritual act (*takhfīf ta'khīr*), such as delaying fasting Ramadan for the sick person and the traveler.[47] The sixth type grants concessions for individuals to violate a legal norm to achieve a higher legal value (*takhfīf tarkhīṣ*), such as permitting drinking wine due to a medical need or necessity.[48] The seventh type is changing the ritual act entirely (*takhfīf taghyīr*); such as changing the order of ritual prayer in the state of fear.[49]

Mashaqqah Is Considered in the Absence of Textual Evidence

The third restatement states that *mashaqqah* and *ḥaraj* are legally considered in the absence of a *naṣṣ* (textual evidence). This means that the maxim does not seek to unnecessarily alleviate a textually established ritual act such as fasting or pilgrimage. If there is a *naṣṣ*, these legal rules may not run against it. Ibn Nujaym cites the example that Abū Ḥanīfah and Muḥammad al-Shaybānī prohibited cutting the grass in the Makkan Ḥaram (sanctuary) or tending a flock of animals on it because it is a violation of the conditions of pilgrimage (*iḥrām*); however, Abu Yūsuf allowed tending animals there, justifying his position by invoking the need to alleviate the *ḥaraj* incurred.[50] This example shows that the application of this maxim to textually stated prohibitions can be contentious, and that the concept of *ʿumūm al-balwā* can be used to construe texts malleably, albeit within the school's legal norms.[51]

Ibn ʿĀbidīn reiterates the established maxims in the Ḥanafite school, "hardship brings about ease" and "when a matter becomes difficult it is eased," throughout his legal work. Ibn ʿĀbidīn explains: "From among the maxims of our authoritative scholars is to adopt ease in cases of necessity and all-encompassing public need (*balwā ʿāmmah*)."[52] For example, in his discussion of the purity of well water, Ibn ʿĀbidīn explains that the urine and feces of both mice and cats is ritually impure in most of the authentic narrations of the *madhhab*, which renders the water impure if they are found in a well. However, Ḥanafi jurists did not consider the well to be impure and thus they did not require draining it, justifying their position by appeal to necessity (*ḍarūrah*).[53] The same ruling applies to the droppings of pigeons because it is not possible to prevent them from approaching the wells. Ibn ʿĀbidīn explains that it is an impurity that was forgiven due to necessity. Although there is a difference of opinion on pigeons' droppings among scholars of the *madhhab*, what has been established in the *Hidāyah* and many other authoritative works is that pigeons' droppings are not considered an impurity. This is due to the consensus, in practice (*ijmāᶜ ᶜamalī*), of domesticating pigeons in the Sacred Mosque without any dispute about what comes out of them.[54]

Moral Dilemmas

Late Ḥanafites debated the use of ritually impure materials for medical recovery and in circumstances of necessity. Ibn ᶜĀbidīn argued, relying upon Ibn Nujaym, that if ritually impure materials such as wine and carrion have been determined to preserve life, it is permissible to resort to such materials for medication. Abū Ḥanīfah had prohibited drinking the urine of animals that are ritually permissible to consume, but late Ḥanafites allowed it if it was believed to assist in medical recovery. Ibn ᶜĀbidīn and late Ḥanafites in general affirmed the permissibility of consuming ritually impure substances for medication due to compelling necessity. They argued that these situations provide a license, in which the stated prohibitions cease to exist.[55]

Ḥanafites only apply the prohibition of food items when one has freedom of choice (*ikhtiyār*) regarding one's food. Therefore, in circumstances of compelling necessity, there is a wide window for the applications of *ḍarūrah*, in which one can identify the interrelations between necessity and harm (*ḍarar*). For example, in necessitous circumstances such as fear of death or sickness, Ḥanafites enjoin the individual to eat prohibited food to save his life. It is a moral obligation for the person to preserve his life. Furthermore, the consumption of these prohibited foods and drinks is not conditioned upon the extreme situation when a person is on the verge of death. Ḥanafites permit violating these rules if the person fears such an extreme status. Ḥanafites stipulate some guidelines for *ḍarūrah*. For instance, they stress that the individual should not exceed the amount of food or drink that would be enough for him not to suffer starving or harm.[56] They frame *ḍarūrah* within the contours of avoiding serious consequences. Nevertheless, this guideline is flexible and accommodates numerous situations. For instance, a person is permitted to eat or drink his fill if he/she is going to walk a distance, or is running away.

Ḥanafites define the realm of the doctrine of *ḍarūrah* through a hierarchy of ethical choices. Ḥanafites such as Abū Jaᶜfar al-Ṭaḥāwī and Ibn Ṣamāᶜa argue that a person who is destitute should prioritize taking others' money to buy food over eating carrion. Yet Ibn Nujaym points out that other Ḥanafites assert that this person should prioritize eating carrion over usurping others' money.[57] By the same token, they state that a person should eat the meat of the animals that were slaughtered improperly by a non-believer rather than eating carrion. Moreover, a person should prioritize eating the meat of a prohibited animal over carrion. Here, Ḥanafites consistently follow a legal reasoning that assigns ethical values to legal determinations.

This legal and ethical dimension is manifest, for example, when Ḥanafites discuss the legal choices of a person who suffers an injury that would cause blood leaks if this person prostrates in prayer, but would not if the person did not engage in prostration. Ḥanafites give license to this person to pray sitting, and only ask him to signal his prostration with his hands. Ḥanafites contend that omitting prostration in prayer is less severe than praying while ritually impure (as in the case of blood leaks from an injury). Similarly, according to *al-Fatāwā al-Bazzāziyya*, if a pilgrim finds him/herself in a situation of necessity and has the option to either consume carrion or engage in hunting (which is ritually prohibited during the pilgrimage), Ḥanafites argue that this pilgrim should consume carrion and avoid hunting. This is the authoritative opinion in the school. However, if this pilgrim were compelled to choose between hunting or usurping others' money, Ḥanafites agree that this person should engage in hunting and avoid wrongful appropriation of people's money.[58] Similarly, although telling a lie is morally prohibited, Ḥanafites contend that if such a lie will bring about a benefit that will supersede the evil of telling a lie, such as reconciling two enemies, the act is permissible.[59]

To summarize, *ḍarūrah* centers on the doctrine of the choice of the lesser evil (*akhaff al-mafsadatayn*). This maxim weighs benefits in relation to damages or harm. Ibn ᶜĀbidīn uses this doctrine to describe the choices made in circumstances of necessity. He asserts, for example, that collective rights take precedence over individual rights. Based on the doctrine of *ḍarūrah*, if someone's wall blocks a public road, this wall will be demolished and this person will be compensated. This does not suggest that individual rights will always be trumped. Muslim jurists affirm that individual rights are protected, but they frame these rights within their social context, so these rights are not absolute in themselves. Legal discretion in the case of necessity is tied to the doctrine of balancing benefits and harms. Therefore, it is considered a remedy to the overly strict application of legal rules in consideration of special circumstances.

The doctrine of necessity is not accepted as a valid justification in cases of homicide. In this area of law, the focus is not on consequences but on the deontological status of actions, even under circumstances of necessity. Ibn ʿĀbidīn, for example, rejects necessity as an excuse in murder.[60] He states that if a Muslim is forced to kill another Muslim, on pain of being killed himself, this is not a legal license for him to kill this person. He emphasizes that the person under duress should avoid killing this individual Muslim (*yaṣbir ʿalā al-qatl*) because being killed is a lesser evil than killing a Muslim. Also, he invokes the consensus (*ijmāʿ*) prohibiting killing without a legal reason. In other words, for Ḥanafites, the doctrine of necessity does not mitigate homicide charges.

Conclusion

Since applying the principles of necessity and hardship is not always a simple matter, but often involves moral dilemmas, the choices Ḥanafite jurists make between alternative relaxations of the law reveal a hierarchy of values that generally favors public interest over private interest and the performance of ritual over the technical correctness of ritual. Their reasoning reveals that in most areas of law (with the exception of homicide crimes) their concern for consequences – achieving the benefit of the law while minimizing harm – trumps their concern for following legal prescriptions, so the ethic underlying their legal reasoning may be called consequentialist even though the basic structure of the law appears deontological.

This exposition of Ḥanafite consequentialist ethics shows how the legal discipline is guided by practical and ethical rather than purely theoretical or theological concerns.[61] The doctrine of necessity is not a monolithic legal framework. It has different manifestations in different areas of the law. For Ḥanafites, necessity does not alter the essential nature of actions. Rather, it provides a legal framework for assessing the intricate factors involved in a situation of necessity so as to allow, and sometimes obligate, the individual to violate a legal norm. For Ibn ʿĀbidīn, the doctrine of necessity cannot be used to justify material harm to others' life or limb. In homicide cases, Ibn ʿĀbidīn and late Ḥanafites in general reject the defense of necessity as an acceptable excuse for this criminal activity.

Ibn ʿĀbidīn utilized the doctrine of necessity to justify infringement upon certain rights such as taking others' food to avoid starvation.[62] The challenge of this doctrine lies in conflicting interests that are close in value. In such situations, the legal choices made are based on a hierarchy of values whose order is governed by balancing the harms in pursuit of the lesser evil.

Ibn Nujaym utilized the maxim of *taysīr* to justify certain legal choices such as permitting drinking alcohol to avoid starvation or death.[63] He identifies the realm of the maxim of *taysīr* through a hierarchy of ethical choices. The person who is caught in a situation of necessity should prioritize doing the lesser evil.[64] The applications of such a framework appear in a case where Ibn Nujaym discusses the legal choices of doing a ritual act while suffering some sort of impurity.[65] He stresses that priority will be given to performing the ritual act if the impurity is insignificant or if removing it will lead to a major harm. The justification he gives is that the person should weigh the harms and benefits and make a decision.[66]

NOTES

1. Late Ḥanafism as a category emerged ca. 11th century. It manifested in a fully-fledged tradition in the Mamluk period and early modern Ottoman Empire.

These late Ḥanafites developed their own distinct identities, opinions, and consensus in relation to earlier Ḥanafite opinions. See ʿAbd al-Ḥayy al-Laknawī, *ʿUmdat al-Riʿāya ʿalā Sharḥ al-Wiqāya* (Beirut: Dār al-Kutub al-ʿIlmiyyah, 2009), pp.15–16.

2. Legal maxims (*al-qawāʿid al-fiqhiyya*) are pithily expressed principles that function as jurisprudential frameworks in order to identify legal schools' doctrinal commitments and facilitate the process of legal discretion.
3. Ibn Nujaym, *al-Ashbāh wa al-Naẓā'ir*, (Ed.), Muhammad al-Hafiz (Cairo: Dār al-Fikr, 2005), p.3.
4. Ibn Nujaym, *al-Baḥr al-Rā'iq Sharḥ Kanz al-Daqā'iq* (Cairo: Dār al-Kitāb al-Islāmī, n.d), vol.1, p.122.
5. Ibn Nujaym, *al-Ashbāh wa al-Naẓā'ir* (Beirut: Dār al-Kutub al-ʿIlmiyyah, 1999), p.98.
6. Khaled Abou El Fadl, "Between Functionalism and Morality", in *Islamic Ethics of Life: Abortion, War, and Euthanasia.* (Ed.), Jonathan E. Brockopp (Columbia: University of South Carolina Press, 2003), p.106.
7. Muḥammad Amīn ʿĀbidīn, *Radd al-Muḥtār ʿalā al-Durr al-Mukhtār* (Beirut: Dār al-Fikr, 1992), vol.1, p.305.
8. Ibn ʿĀbidīn, *Radd al-Muḥtār*, vol.1, p.191.
9. Ibn ʿĀbidīn, *Radd al-Muḥtār*, vol.1, p.74.
10. Wael Hallaq, *Authority, Continuity, and Change in Islamic Law* (Cambridge: Cambridge University Press, 2004), pp.211–13.
11. Ibid.
12. Ibid., p.227.
13. Ibid.
14. Ibid., p.231.
15. Ibid., p.232.
16. Wael Hallaq, *Shari'a: Theory, Practice, Transformations* (Cambridge: Cambridge University Press, 2009), pp.447–48.
17. Ibid.
18. Ibid.
19. The discussion on *ḍarūrah* appears in Ḥanafite *uṣūl* works such as ʿUbayd Allāh al-Dabūsī, *Taqwīm al-Adilla fi Uṣūl al-Fiqh* (Beirut: Dār al-Kutub al-ʿIlmiyyah, 2001), p.81; Alī b. Muḥammad al-Bazdawī, *Kanz al-Wuṣūl ilā Maʿrifat al-Uṣūl* (Istanbul: Şirket-i Sahafiye-'i Osmaniye, 1890), p.213; Aḥmad al-Shāshī, *Uṣūl al-Shashī* (Beirut: Dār al-Kutub al-ʿIlmiyyah, 2002), p.164. There are also extended discussions on *ḍarūrah* in *qawāʿid* works such as Ibn Nujaym, *al-Ashbāh wa al-Naẓā'ir*. (Ed.), Muhammad al-Hafiz, pp.84–92.
20. Ibn Nujaym, *al-Ashbāh wa al-Naẓā'ir*, p.84.
21. Ibn ʿĀbidīn, *Majmūʿat Rasā'il Ibn ʿĀbidīn* (Istanbul: Dār-i Saʿādat, 1907), p.44.
22. Ibid.
23. Ibn ʿĀbidīn, *Radd al-Muḥtār*, vol.1, p.190.

24. Ibn Nujaym, *al-Ashbāh wa al-Naẓā'ir*, p.84.
25. Ibid.
26. Ibid.
27. Ibid., p.90.
28. Ibid., p.92.
29. *Salam* is a sale whereby the seller undertakes to supply some specific goods to the buyer at a future date in exchange for an advanced price paid fully on the spot. The contract of salam creates a legal obligation for the seller to deliver the goods.
30. Ibn Nujaym, *al-Ashbāh wa al-Naẓā'ir*, p.92.
31. Ibid., p.90.
32. Ibid.
33. Ibid.
34. Ibid.
35. Ibid., p.91.
36. Ibid.
37. Ibid., p.84.
38. Ibid., p.92.
39. ʿUbayd Allāh b. al-Ḥusayn al-Karkhī, "Risāla fī al-Uṣūl", in *Ta'sīs al-Naẓar.* (Ed.), Muhammad Mustafa al-Qabbani al-Dimashqi (Cairo: Maktabat al-Kulliyāt al-Azhariyya, n.d.), p.172.
40. Ibn Nujaym, *al-Ashbāh wa al-Naẓā'ir*, p.92.
41. Ibid.
42. Ibid.
43. Ibid.
44. Ibid., p.90.
45. Ibid., p.92.
46. Ibid.
47. Ibid.
48. Ibid.
49. Ibid.
50. Ibid.
51. Ibid.
52. Ibn ʿĀbidīn, *Radd al-Muḥtār*, vol.1, p.189.
53. Ibid., vol.1, p.220.
54. Ibid., vol.1, p.221.
55. Ibid., vol.1, p.210
56. Ibn Nujaym, *al-Ashbāh wa al-Naẓā'ir*, p.95.
57. Ibid., p.98.
58. Ibid., p.99.
59. Ibid.

60. Ibn ʿĀbidīn, *Nuzhat al-Nawāẓir ʿalā al-Ashbāh wa al-Naẓā'ir*. (Ed.), Muhammad al-Hafiz (Cairo: Dār al-Fikr, 2005), p.128.
61. Ayman Shihadeh, "Theories of Ethical Value in Kalām: A New Interpretation", Oxford Handbooks Online, http://www.oxfordhandbooks.com/view/10.1093/oxfordhb/9780199696703.001.0001/oxfordhb-9780199696703-e-007. Accessed April 6, 2016.
62. Ibn ʿĀbidīn, *Radd al-Muḥtār*, pp.124–25.
63. Ibn Nujaym, *al-Baḥr al-Rā'iq*, p.82.
64. Ibid., p.231.
65. Ibid.
66. Ibid.

3

Structural Ijtihad: A Radical Paradigm Shift in Twelver Shiʿi Legal Theory

Hamid Mavani

ABSTRACT: Ijtihad is generally touted as the panacea that can successfully respond to the challenges of modernity. However, this optimism and confidence is only partially valid because the "traditional ijtihad" paradigm that is in current usage to deal with present-day challenges has reached its limits and is unable to deal methodically with contemporary contingencies. In the face of new challenges, the traditional ijtihad model is forced to invoke secondary juridical devices such as public welfare (*maṣlaḥah*), imperative necessity (*ḍarūrah*), distress (*ḥaraj*), and averting difficulty (*ʿusr*). I will argue that these devices are highly subjective, lack rigor, and sometimes produce rulings that would be viewed as unethical by an ordinary person. Moreover, these secondary principles could undermine the integrity of juristic theory altogether if they were invoked to justify a disregard for the law or to legitimize a stratagem (*ḥīlah*). I will argue that such juridical devices provide only partial, patchy, and petty formal modifications to existing legal rulings at the level of *furūʿ*, for they are motivated primarily by pragmatic considerations. Advocates of "structural ijtihad," however, are seeking fundamental changes in the *uṣūl* of Islamic legal theory through their holistic approach, incorporating other disciplines like ethics, theology, cosmology, anthropology, linguistics, soft and hard sciences, and critical thinking in their formulations of legal theory and their derivation of legal rulings, in an attempt to reconstruct Islamic thought in keeping with universal moral and ethical values that accord with the present time and are in harmony with the Qur'anic ethos and worldview.

Contemporary Muslim interpreters face a number of instances in which employing the traditional model of ijtihad produces outcomes that are legal from the perspective of the Islamic divine law, but are arguably unethical, immoral, and unjust in the eyes of reasonable people (*sīrat al-ʿuqalāʾ*). This raises several interesting questions: Are ethical considerations secondary to legal rulings? Are ethics and law mutually exclusive domains? If Islamic law were made compatible with ethics or became subservient to it, would it not be secularized and, as a consequence, lose its divine quality? Does classifying acts into the five normative categories (i.e., prohibited, discouraged, permissible, recommended, and mandatory) constitute an ethical or a legal judgment? If the latter, does this classification of divine law have any relationship with ethics? Does Islam have an ethical theory and, if so, is it compatible with natural law theory, divine command theory (deontological ethics), utilitarianism, virtue ethics, or some other ethical theory? My submission is that there is an organic relationship between fiqh and ethics but that in the final analysis fiqh remains subservient to ethics. In other words, a *fiqhī* legal ruling cannot transgress the boundaries of *al-maʿrūf* (what is universally acknowledged to be good, moral, and ethical at the time, or *ʿurf al-zamān*).

The answers to these pivotal and complex questions depend a great deal upon one's underlying theology and the nature and scope of ethics in that theological paradigm. In the past, scholars were fixated upon resolving issues that affected the laity on the personal level and did not provide an ethical framework for the process of ijtihad. Moreover, the source of ethics is generally considered to be the practical intellect (*ʿaql amalī*), whereas for jurisprudence it is revelation (*waḥy*). In other words, obligation in the context of morality is distinctly different from obligation in the context of divine law, because due to the principle of leniency (*qā'idat al-tasāmuḥ*) in deducing proofs the former has a far lower threshold for acceptance than does the latter, which deals with mandatory (*wājib*) and prohibited (*ḥarām*) actions.

In the past, ethics, theology, intellect, anthropology, cosmology, linguistics, modern science, and the foundational principles in

Islamic legal theory were either minimal or absent from Islamic law. Traditional ijtihad was therefore anchored in proof texts, which provided a very limited role for reason and other sciences, and thus jurists even today still engage in derivative ijtihad (*al-ijtihād fi al-furūʿ*) to resolve new issues. But this approach allows little room for innovative and creative thinking because it sanctifies precedence and addresses modern contingencies only through minor adaptations, based on the prophetic statement: "Acts assessed to be lawful (*ḥalāl*) by Muhammad will remain so forever until Judgment Day, and his prohibitions will remain so forever until Judgment Day."[1] As a result, traditional ijtihad gradually became a rigid, standardized, fixed, and sacrosanct methodology (*al-ijtihād al-jāmid*).[2] On the other hand, structural or foundational ijtihad (*al-ijtihād fi al-uṣūl wa al-mabānī*),[3] a term invoked by Muhammad Iqbal (d. 1938) in its generalities but provided specificity by Mohsen Kadivar,[4] focuses on the fundamentals and principles of Islamic legal theory and attempts to reconstruct the Islamic tradition's indigenous type of thought and cosmology, a system that encompassed philosophy, ontology, theology, linguistics, anthropology, sociology, morality, and fiqh. It is also characterized by an organic relationship among reason, theology, law and ethics, history, soft and hard sciences, the fundamental principles of Islamic legal theory, and fiqh.

Shiʿi reformists have invoked ijtihad's legal-ethical dynamism by advancing hermeneutical, exegetical, and juridical devices within the existing framework of their school of thought's legal theory. However, they have done this without underlining the vital role of foundational principles (*uṣūl*), theological ethics, cosmology, anthropology, linguistics, soft and hard sciences, and critical thinking when formulating legal theory and deriving legal rulings at the center. They limit themselves to expanding the scope of reason (*ʿaql*) and the lacunae or discretionary areas (*mantaqat al-farāgh*) in fiqh, and thus find themselves forced to introduce such juridical devices as time (*zamān*), place (*makān*), customary practice (*ʿurf*), public welfare (*maṣlaḥah*), and objectives of the law (*maqāṣid al-sharīʿah*). In addition, they have to invoke such secondary principles as harm (*ḍarar*), necessity (*ḍarūrah*), emergency (*iḍṭirār*), need (*ḥājah*), averting difficulty (*ʿusr*) and distress (*ḥaraj*), and hardship (*mashaqqah*) as exceptions that justify the minor legal adjustments needed to allow dispensations or exemptions (*rukhṣah*).

But such devices do not resolve the problems associated with traditional ijtihad when it seeks to tackle modern challenges.[5] Moreover, these secondary principles could undermine the integrity of juristic theory altogether if they were invoked to justify a disregard for the law or to legitimize a stratagem (*ḥīlah*). Such juridical devices provide only partial, patchy, and petty formal modifications to existing legal rulings, for they are motivated primarily by pragmatic considerations. Advocates of structural ijtihad, however, are seeking fundamental changes in Islamic legal theory by incorporating other disciplines – ethics, theology, linguistics, and the sciences being central to them – in an attempt to reconstruct Islamic thought in a way that is in keeping with the universal moral and ethical values that accord with the present time. Only in this way can the new challenges being raised by medical and bioethical questions, human rights, gender equality, environmental degradation, and freedom of religion and political thought be met.

Adherents of both approaches largely agree that certain essential aspects of the Islamic creed/dogma ought to remain constant, unchanging, and immutable regardless of time and location. Moreover, they acknowledge the existence of a specific separation among religious rituals (*ʿibādāt*), the belief system (*ʿaqīdah*), and explicit injunctions on the one hand,[6] and on the other human interrelations and social affairs (*muʿāmalāt*), which are historically and socially conditioned and thus relative or contingent. In general, the former are constant, immutable, essential, and trans-historical rulings that leave little or no room for contextualization or creative reinterpretation when faced with novel and unexpected contingencies. But the latter are open to public negotiation in a space that accommodates civic pluralism. In theory, however, there is nothing to prevent one from also considering an act of worship as entirely variable and open to negotiation, provided that one is certain (*yaqīn*) of having discovered its efficacious cause (*ʿillah*), thereby paving the way for rational deliberation.

Classical jurists define ijtihad as the process of discovering a new legal ruling on the basis of a particular set of principles and legal theory after having exerted oneself to the maximum extent possible. This undertaking is restricted to that area in which no explicit and unambiguous decree can be derived from the clear-cut source texts, and is invoked only to resolve issues by offering solutions that are only highly probable (*ghalabat al-ẓann*) as opposed to certain (*yaqīn*). This effort remains a perpetual collective obligation (*farḍ kifāyah*) upon the entire community, especially in the Shiʿi and Hanbali schools of thought. The community must always have enough qualified jurists to shoulder this obligation because it is a social necessity, as is the existence of enough qualified professionals in other fields to address society's needs.

Historically, ijtihad has accommodated a plurality of views on the basis that each qualified jurist does his best, via his own efforts along with consulting different sources as well as other prominent teachers and jurists, to derive a legal ruling that would remain a considered opinion subject to error and revision. The Shiʿi school deemed the transition from certainty to probability to be necessary so that it could deal with new contingencies and societal changes that were not covered in the texts and occurred during the infallible Imam's occultation. This prompted its jurists, from the time of al-Muḥaqqiq al-Ḥillī (d. 1277) onward, to accept ijtihad with a clear-cut epistemological distinction between certainty and probability. In other words, no legal ruling could ever be considered certain, regardless of the amount of human exertion expended, because no ordinary human being is infallible. This understanding opened up the scope for the exponents of natural ethics with Muʿtazilite leanings to argue that the intellect (*ʿaql*), like the traditional revelatory sources (*waḥy* and *naql*), can be called upon to determine one's religious responsibility, even though this would produce only a probable outcome. There would be no difference between a probability derived from scriptural or transmitted sources (*ẓann naqlī*) and one derived from the intellect (*ẓann ʿaqlī*) as regards determining the public welfare or issuing a legal ruling.

Introducing other disciplines, such as ethics, theology, and modern sciences, complicates the issues even further and warrants a collective (*ijtihād jamāʿī*) and multidisciplinary process to derive new legal rulings. Those who undertake it must consult with experts in the relevant fields and pay serious attention to their advice.[7] Tariq Ramadan has proposed a further step, "transformation reform" (in contrast to "adaptation reform"), in which the specialists and context scholars (*ʿulamā' al-wāqiʿ*) and jurists (*ʿulamā' al-nuṣūṣ*) are equal partners in formulating ethical norms and legal opinions.[8] Abdolkarem Soroush chimes in that the contemporary religious scholars' most important obligation is to "make the fundamentals (*uṣūl*) of religion [divine law] compatible with the fundamentals of the new world and not to seek out ways to make the secondary (*furūʿ*) aspects of religion compatible with the secondary aspects of the new world," because the new world is not merely a larger and magnified form of the old world.[9] In the words of Egyptian jurist Jasser Auda:

> Without incorporating relevant ideas from other disciplines, research in the fundamental theory of Islamic law will remain within the limits of traditional literature and its manuscripts, and Islamic law will continue to be largely "outdated" in its theoretical basis and practical outcomes.[10]

All ijtihad must be based upon the primary sources. For Shiʿi law, these are the Qur'an, the authentic Sunnah of the Prophet and the twelve infallible guides, consensus (*ijmāʿ*), and reason (*ʿaql*).[11] However, only the first two qualify as demonstrative and certain sources that can stand on their own. Shiʿi jurists do not regard consensus as an independent source, unlike their Sunni counterparts who assert that it is "[t]he only binding and unassailable authority that could ratify a doctrine in the name of Islam as a whole."[12] In Shiʿism, any *ijmāʿ* is valid not because of the jurists' consensus, but because of the deduction that the infallible Imam of that time was a party to endorsing it. Thus, *ijmāʿ* represents a way to discover the infallible Imam's opinion, for only his endorsement validates and ensures its certainty. In addition, Shiʿi legal methodology has limited the scope for analogical reasoning (*qiyās*) because it is considered to produce, in general, only a conjectural ruling. In order for it to be valid, the efficacious cause (*ʿillah*) must be explicitly stated (*qiyās jalī*) and not subject to multiple readings, as is the case with hidden analogy (*qiyās khafī*). The Imam thus occupies a central and pivotal position in Shiʿism. During the Twelfth Imam's prolonged occultation, it is argued, some of his authority is transmitted to those jurists who strive to resolve contemporary challenges but can never attain certainty in their rulings.

The epistemological and ethical foundations that underpin legal thinking depend upon the theology adopted. Debate over the nature of legal validity and its relationship to the normative authority of law as law has been dominated by two rival schools of thought: the Muʿtazilite (ethical objectivism) and the Ashʿarite (theistic subjectivism). The Maturidite school of thought can be situated somewhere between the two, but leans more toward Ashʿarism, which maintains that the divine law's authority flows not from the wisdom, justice, or reasonableness of God's commands, but rather from the fact that they are God's commands and therefore expressions of His will, coupled with His supreme power over us. "He cannot be called to account for anything He does, whereas they will be called to account" (Qur'an 21:23). In other words, prior to revelation there is an amoral space and thus no moral valuation can be assigned to an act based upon reason or its inherent nature. In the absence of a proof text, "one is left in a state of suspended judgment (*tawaqquf*)"[13] because reason has no ontological authority.

This conclusion, according to Anver Emon, is accurate but incomplete in its analysis because Ashʿarite scholars were forced to render decisions on issues that had no proof text by assuming that nature is a constant good only due to God's grace (*faḍl*) – instead of divine justice – that could be altered at any time by His Will and Power in order not to compromise God's omnipotence.[14] This enabled them to advance the role of reason, though only as a secondary source, in deriving legal rulings – provided that rigorous conditions were attached to the legal ruling in question where the role of reason was very limited in scope, and that it was understood that the ruling was neither authoritative nor determinate.[15] Emon refers to them as "Soft Naturalists" in contradistinction to "Hard Naturalists," whose "conception of nature as a bounty to humanity is fixed and not vulnerable to a divine 'change of mind.'"[16] The latter, known as the Muᶜtazilites, accorded to reason the capacity to discover universal moral and ethical values on the basis that "nature is invested with a presumptive normativity that stems from God's purposeful creation of nature for human benefit."[17] They argued that, based upon divine justice and wisdom, God's decree has to have a moral underpinning, for His acting without an objective (*gharad*) would constitute an act of futility (*ᶜabath*) and thus deficiency, which would invite blame (*dhamm*).

In their epistemic formula, reason, which has ontological authority as a source of law, can determine legal judgments or ordinances in those areas that fall within the "lacunae"[18] for which no legal or moral valuation has been prescribed. Judgment does not have to be suspended on the grounds of exercising caution, because the underlying premise is that scripture or revelatory texts do not provide legal decrees to cover each and every potentiality until the end of time.[19] Rather, they provide general principles and values, as well as a coherent epistemology that can be employed while keeping the new contexts and circumstances in mind.[20]

The Shiᶜis' adoption of some aspects of the Muᶜtazilites' rationalist -naturalist theology accorded to reason the ability to discover universal moral and ethical values. In addition, they regard the spheres of reason and revelation as correlative, as opposed to mutually exclusive. Based on this outlook, God cannot permit an immoral and unethical act, or declare prohibited or permissible an act that, from a rational ethical perspective, should be mandatory. However, God would be entitled to designate acts as prohibited or obligatory so long as they rationally belong to the permissible (*mubāḥ*) category. Thus, the Shiᶜis are better situated to engage in robust ijtihad (fresh intellectual exertion) in order to deduce legal/ ethical judicial decisions via reliance on reason-based deliberation and on the revelatory texts' general principles, instead of opting to err on the side of caution. In the recent past, Sunni Islam has experienced a gradual theological evolution from a position of strict determinism to one in which the human being becomes the owner of his/her acts and, as a result, can be held accountable. This is also reflected in the legal tools and devices incorporated under *adillah ʿaqliyyah* (rational evidence), such as *qiyās*, *istiṣlāḥ* (public benefit, especially *maṣāliḥ mursalah*), *istiḥsān* (juristic preference), and *ʿurf* (customary usage) to demonstrate an organic relationship between law and ethics. Thus there has been a significant widening of the scope of ijtihad in Sunni Islam to tackle modern challenges by resorting to the concept of the aims and objectives of the Shariʿah and public interest (*maṣlaḥah*).[21]

Shortly after the success of the Iranian revolution in 1979, Ayatollah Ruhollah Khomeini (d. 1989) became acutely aware that the traditional ijtihad's paradigm, which he had always strongly advocated, could not address the many new issues that were cropping up as a result of running a modern state. He therefore strove to expand the scope of the supreme jurist-ruler's authority by introducing the theory of *maṣlaḥah* as an active component in making state decisions. Even then, however, he couched his innovative ideas in such a manner that the traditionalists would not take exception to them.[22] In January 1988 he invoked *maṣlaḥah* as the guiding principle in resolving all state issues:

> The government is empowered to unilaterally revoke any shariʿa agreements which it has concluded with the people when these agreements are contrary to the interests of the country or Islam. The government can also prevent any devotional [*ʿibād*, from *ʿibādāt*] or non-devotional affair if it is opposed to the interests of Islam and for so long as it is so. The government can prevent Hajj, which is one of the important divine obligations, on a temporary basis, in cases when it is contrary to the interests of the Islamic country.[23]

But since he provided no methodology, this approach can result in arbitrary legal rulings. The Expediency Discernment Council (*Majmaʿ-e tashkhīs-e maṣlaḥat*) was formed to deal with issues that the Assembly of Experts was consistently rejecting as incompatible with Islamic law.

The concepts of *maṣlaḥah* and *maqāṣid al-sharīʿah* were adopted from Sunni jurisprudence in the recent past, especially by Ayatollah Khomeini, whose novel approach to ijtihad relied heavily upon *maṣlaḥah.* One outcome of this has been, in essence, the appearance of a jurisprudence of public welfare (*fiqh al-maṣlaḥah*) that could override scriptural authority and justify almost anything based upon the loosely applied principle of *maṣlaḥah.*[24] Such importations run the risk of providing only partial, patchy, and petty formal modifications to existing legal rulings if they are motivated primarily by pragmatic considerations. In such a case, therefore, it is quite possible that they will be incompatible with the existing framework and theoretical apparatus and thereby result in only formal or marginal ethical coherence. It remains an open question whether all of the above-mentioned juridical devices and legal maxims can function harmoniously within the framework of traditional ijtihad, which focuses only on secondary (*furūᶜ*) principles, without first introducing changes into the existing fundamentals and primary sources (*uṣūl*) of Shiᶜi legal theory.[25]

Mohsen Kadivar, a Shiᶜi jurist and research professor at Duke University, makes the following arguments: (1) structural ijtihad provides a coherent framework in which theology and ethics are reconstructed so that the intellect and other sciences, such as cosmology and anthropology, are given a more expansive role in ethical decision-making; (2) the attribute of justice is viewed as extra-religious and thus can vary depending upon the society's maturity: "Human beings define justice on the basis of experience and collective and historical reason"[26]; (3) justice is considered to be in harmony with egalitarian justice, in contrast to deserts-based justice (*al-ᶜadāla al-istiḥqāqiyyah*), or one can say that justice is in agreement with fundamental equality in contrast to proportional equality; (4) social, economic, political, and cultural conditions and circumstances are taken into account when revising a legal ruling if a "reasonable" person would judge it to be unjust, even if explicit textual evidence in the Qur'an or the Sunnah validates the previous ruling; (5) precedents and past consensus are not sanctified; (6) and the revelatory texts are to be read with an appreciation that some of the legal rulings, viewed as unjust today due to having been formulated within a different historical and social context, were meant to be temporary and therefore are based upon the principle of gradualism and an earlier notion of justice. In addition, structural ijtihad adopts a critical approach and re-reads the sources (*uṣūl*) of Islamic legal theory, consensus, Hadith literature, and legal rulings through a lens of ethics, egalitarian justice, modern science, reasonableness, and Islam's ultimate goals.[27]

Kadivar espouses the view that tinkering with existing traditional ijtihad within the realm of secondary principles by making petty formal readjustments or invoking various juridical devices (i.e., *maṣlaḥah, zamān, makān, ḍarūrah, ḍarar*, or *ḥājah*), all of which are highly subjective and relativistic in the absence of a rigorous methodology, cannot resolve modern challenges.[28] At times, jurists have resorted to loopholes and stratagems to make rather dubious and highly questionable acts lawful.[29] In Kadivar's estimation, only foundational ijtihad and the reconstruction of Islamic thought can resolve the challenges raised by modern medicine and bioethics, human rights, gender equality, environmental degradation, freedom of religion and political thought, and similar contemporary realities.

In the case of traditional ijtihad, a change in a legal ruling can be induced by various factors (e.g., a different time, place, and custom) that produce a new situational context (*mawḍūʿ*) and subject that warrants a new ruling. But in the foundational model, ethics and modern sciences, along with anthropology, hermeneutics, egalitarian justice, and other contemporary disciplines, could dictate a change in the ruling without any change having occurred in the subject's essence or situational context. For instance, the financial compensation awarded to a Muslim in relation to a non-Muslim, or to a free man in relation to a free woman, is amended to make it equivalent and on par, as opposed to the traditional ratio of 2:1 in favor of men. This new ruling is based upon the contemporary principle of fundamental equality under the rubric of egalitarian justice, while the subject matter and the situational context could remain the same as before.

More importantly, the foundational paradigm would allow a legal ruling to be revised even in cases where there is textual proof but no indication of whether it is a provisional or a permanent injunction, if doing so is warranted on account of egalitarian justice, ethics, and the principle of gradualism. For instance, the Qur'an states that a woman's testimony is half that of a man's (2:282) and that a man inherits twice as much as a woman (4:11 and 176), that penal laws call for flogging the guilty person and cutting off a thief's hand (24:4-5 and 5:38), that a non-Muslim's testimony is inadmissible, and that protected minorities (*dhimmī*) living in an Islamic state are to be accorded an inferior status (9:29).

Kadivar argues that it is time to initiate a radical departure from traditional ijtihad and thereby move toward a new foundational ijtihad, one that has its own sources and principles and is based upon a new theology and an ethical theory gleaned from the Qur'an. Abdolkarem Soroush has argued that "Because religious jurisprudence [fiqh] is nourished by theology [*kalām*], the extrareligious foundations of these rules must be clearly critiqued and scrutinized"[30] or, in other words, it is necessary to engage in a discourse on the philosophy and ethics of jurisprudence (*falsafat al-fiqh*).[31] And yet those who seek to develop it must keep in mind, as Fazlur Rahman astutely pointed out, the situational character of the Qur'an, for it "consists of moral, religious, and social pronouncements that respond to specific problems in concrete historical situations."[32] This holistic approach should provide legal rulings that are in harmony with both legal and ethical theory, instead of projecting inconsistency and incoherence between the jurist's legal edict and the legal methodology employed. One example of this problem is the many dissenting legal opinions issued by Ayatollah Yousef Saanei. Although compatible with the contemporary universal human rights discourse, they do not modify the pre-set assumptions and theoretical framework of traditional ijtihad. Thus it is hard to view his legal rulings as having emerged from the traditional ijtihad paradigm.[33]

Ayatollah Mostefa Mohaghegh Damad provides a number of startling examples of edicts generally accepted by jurists as conforming to the divine law on the basis of the traditional ijtihad paradigm, even though they are in stark conflict with universal ethical and moral values. In his estimation, such scenarios should be impossible because ethics (*akhlāq*) is supposed to be superior to and govern legal rulings (*al-aḥkām al-sharʿiyyah*).[34] In other words, ethics should be primary (*aṣl*) and fiqh should be secondary (*farʿ*).

Example 1: Under present-day ijtihad a man can divorce his wife on the grounds that she is too old and he wants to marry someone younger, even though she has no deficiencies, stood by him during challenging economic times, and suffered privations during the early phase of their marriage. At a moment's notice – be it day or night – he can inform her that she has been divorced and, after the waiting period (*ᶜiddah*), must leave the house with only the clothes she is wearing. In addition, she has to return those clothes upon reaching her father's house because they belong to the husband (i.e., were purchased from his property). Such a course of action, viewed as discouraged (*makrūh*) under the existing traditional paradigm, cannot be punished. According to Ayatollah Mohaghegh Damad, however, such an act would invite God's wrath and fury. In the words of his grandfather Shaykh Abdolkarem Ha'iri (d. 1937): "A person can be regarded as 'just' from the perspective of jurisprudence (fiqh) and at the same time be more merciless than Shimr b. Dhī al-Jawshan (the reported assassin of the third Shiᶜi Imam, Ḥusayn b. ᶜAlī, on the plains of Karbala, Iraq in 680 CE)."[35]

Example 2: A majority of jurists agree that a man can marry a still-nursing female infant if her father agrees. After signing the marital contract, the husband has the right to satisfy all of his sexual desires, except that of sexual intercourse.[36] This legal ruling is in perfect harmony with the present-day paradigm of ijtihad but is contrary to human conscience and ethics which now view such an act as criminal, lewd, ugly, and perverted. According to Ayatollah Mohaghegh Damad, if ethics were supreme and regulated the divine law, then such an unwholesome and abhorrent act could never be legitimized as a proper legal ruling.[37]

Example 3: According to Muḥammad Ḥasan Najafi (a.k.a. Ṣāḥib al-Jawāhir; d. 1850), a master can sell his female slave immediately after she delivers his child. He can even do this on the day that she gives birth and take the child away from her. He adds that there is no divine legal ruling on this matter, but nonetheless it is considered permissible due to its having attained consensus (*ijmāᶜ*).[38]

Many similar examples can be added to this list of *sharᶜī* legal rulings vs. ethics: the husband's right to prevent his wife from leaving the house even if her father is on his death-bed or to attend his funeral service; the formula for purifying unlawful money by paying *khums* (one-fifth) on the total sum to make the remaining four-fifths pure and lawful;[39] contracting a temporary marriage (*muṭʿah*) with an almost unlimited number of women simultaneously (no limit is specified) as long as he can support them; gossiping and backbiting about Sunnis because they are not regarded as "just" since they reject the infallible Imams; permission to steal from unbelievers so long as there is minimal risk of being caught because in this situation, the image and visage of Islam would be tarnished; the many instances in which one is allowed and, at times, required to lie under the guise of doing so for the sake of greater welfare (*maṣlaḥah*); treating the officially recognized religious minorities as inferior and requiring them to pay the poll tax (*jizyah*) to the Muslim authorities while in a humiliating posture; and the widow's share of inheritance from her husband being one-eighth, irrespective of his having one or more wives, such that if he had four wives at the time of his death each one would receive only 1/32 of his moveable and liquid assets (excluding land, but not the value of structures).

Ayatollah Ali Sistani, an eminent Shiʿi jurist residing in Najaf, Iraq, and a source of emulation (*marjaʿ*) for a substantial number of Shiʿis, has issued rulings in the areas of medical ethics and bioethics that would be construed as unethical and, as such, impossible under foundational ijtihad, which prohibits religion-based discrimination and considers everyone entitled to human rights by virtue of being a human being under the rubric of egalitarian justice.[40] According to Sistani, a Muslim does not have to provide CPR to a non-Muslim patient; however, no effort must be spared to resuscitate a Muslim patient. He has issued similar rulings concerning brain-dead patients and patient care. For example, any life-supporting devices can be removed from a non-Muslim patient, but never from a Muslim patient.[41]

These examples show the importance of reconciling Islamic legal rulings with an Islamic ethic. There is a wide spectrum of views on what constitutes Islamic ethics and its relationship to Islamic law. This spectrum ranges from Kevin Reinhart to Ayatollah Jaʿfar

Sobhani. The former holds that Islamic law and ethics are organically intertwined and writes: "Among the Islamicate intellectual disciplines, only Islamic law is both practical and theoretical, concerned with human action in the world, and (strictly speaking) religious. In this sense, Islamic law and legal theory must be the true locus of the discussion of Islamic ethics."[42] He adds that "Islamic law is not merely law, but also an ethical and epistemological system of great subtlety and sophistication."[43] In his estimation, scholars have failed to meticulously study and appreciate the interconnectedness of law and ethics because of the complexity of legal works and the daunting task of deciphering their contents.

At the other end of the spectrum, Ayatollah Sobhani represents the accepted view of jurists that the intellect is the source of ethics, whereas revelation is the source of Islamic law. He contends further that the gulf between them is akin to that between philosophy and divine law,[44] for the latter provides guidance for regulating individual and social life and, in the process, attaining God's pleasure and gaining proximity to Him.[45] Ayatollah Mohaghegh Damad concurs that Islamic law, which has historically relied almost exclusively upon revelation and traditional accounts, has paid scant attention to ethical deliberation. He makes a persuasive case that Muslim scholars have historically distinguished law from Aristotelian ethics. The former was concerned with those human actions that relied upon revelation for rulings, whereas the latter dealt with the inner aspects of a human being (i.e., the cultivation of such virtues as courage and patience, and the removal of such vices as jealousy, hate, and arrogance). The logical conclusion of such a division is, according to him, that societal ethical norms and values have no place in a religion that has a divine law because jurists do not concern themselves with ethics in their legal deliberations. To provide some shock value to his assertion, he says: "A religion that has no divine law can possibly have ethics, but one that has divine law, such as Islam and Judaism, would be void of ethics."[46]

Such a view strips Islamic law of an ethical dimension that has always been integral to it. For example, in present-day jurisprudence, an act of worship is valid only if the doer expresses the intention (i.e., doing it for the sake of seeking proximity and nearness to God) for its performance. That intention is considered necessary only at the beginning and its continuity is not required for validity, but for an act to acquire the maximum ethical value the intention would have to remain valid throughout the period of its performance. A similar contrast is evident in the realm of *muʿāmalat,* wherein an act only has to be properly executed, irrespective of the intention, in order to be considered valid from the perspective of present-day Islamic law. Without the proper intention, however, such an act would be considered void of ethical value in an ethical paradigm, wherein the given act is to be evaluated according to the purity of the actor's intention.

The Qur'an itself is permeated with an ethos in which law and ethics are organically intertwined to such an extent that even immutable and unchanging aspects of law, like the ritual prayers and fasting in the realm of acts of worship, are co-joined with an ethical imperative: "Keep up the prayer: prayer restrains indecent and immoral behavior" (29:45) and "You who believe, fasting is prescribed for you, as it was prescribed for those before you, so that you may be mindful of God and morally vigilant" (2:183).

A reading of the Qur'an makes it crystal clear that the cornerstone for establishing a virtuous society is the upholding of justice, equity, and fairness (*ʿadl* and *qisṭ*) in all of their dimensions. This recurring theme is emphasized with great intensity and is second only to the doctrine of radical monotheism (*tawḥīd*): "O Believers! Be resolute in your allegiance to God, staunch witnesses for justice. On no account let hatred against any people cause you to swerve from dealing justly. Be just (*iʿdilū*): that is nearest to piety and God-consciousness (*huwa aqrabu li al-taqwā*)" (5:8) and "O you who believe! Stand out firmly for justice, as witnesses to God, even as against yourselves, or your parents, or your kin, and whether it be (against) rich or poor: for God can best protect both. Follow not the lusts (of your hearts), lest you swerve, and if ye distort (justice) or decline to do justice, verily God is well-acquainted with all that ye do" (4:135). Divine justice is rooted in divine wisdom, which is applicable to all times and all people. Majid Khadduri notes that "in the Qur'an there are over two hundred admonitions against injustice expressed in such words as *ẓulm, ithm, ḍalāl,* and others, and no less than almost a hundred expressions embodying the notion of justice, either directly in such words as *ʿadl, qisṭ, mīzān*, and others as noted before, or in a variety of indirect expressions."[47] This moral religious principle has been emphasized repeatedly to underscore its centrality in the Qur'an and in the traditions. The Qur'an calls for this value system of justice to prevail in all spheres, be they political, theological, philosophical, ethical, legal, international, social, or otherwise. Thus, irrespective of whether the "other" shares the same religious worldview, a Muslim cannot compromise the normative value of justice.

Another core value taught by the Qur'an and the Prophet is the dignity of humanity. Both assert that all human beings were created by God and are creation's most dignified member because only they have been endowed with reason, conscience, freedom of choice, and accountability. In their capacity as God's deputy on Earth, they are mandated to actualize divine attributes: "We have honored the sons [and daughters] of Adam [and Eve]; provided them with transport on land and sea; given them for sustenance things good and pure; and conferred on them special favors, above a great part of Our Creation" (17:70); and "We have indeed created humankind in the best of molds" (95:4). Thus, God has endowed every man and woman with dignity and honor, which means that no one has the right to disrespect and dishonor anyone else. In fact, differences in cultures and faith are integral parts of the divine plan to enhance mutual recognition and respect (*li taʿārafu*, Qur'an 49:13). Protecting this dignity and honor extends even to the battlefield, as is clear from the extensive literature on the moral and ethical treatment of one's enemies while engaged in a just war and self-defense.

The core value of each individual's equality with all other individuals is the recurring theme that all people are created from a common source and origin and have been invited by the same Creator to excel in performing righteous deeds and exemplifying divine attributes in their dealings with each other and the Creator: "O humanity! We created you from a single (pair) of a male and a female, and made you into nations and tribes, that ye may know each other. Verily the most honored of you in the sight of God is (he who is) the most righteous and God-conscious of you…" (49:13). Thus, no one can claim superiority based upon such man-made distinctions as gender, race, ethnicity, economic status, education, school of thought, and other artificial and biased criteria. Before dispatching Malik al-Ashtar to Egypt as his governor, ʿAlī composed for him an epistle that stressed the universal equality of all human beings: "Infuse your heart with mercy, love and kindness for your subjects. Be not in face of them a voracious animal, counting them as easy prey, for they are of two kinds: *either they are your brothers [and sisters] in religion or your equals in creation.*"[48]

The Qur'an affirms the self-evident moral precept of the sanctity of human life: "And if anyone saved a life, it would be as if he [she] saved the life of the whole world" (5:32). Every life has been inspired with the divine breath and therefore deserves to be respected and honored: "And we breathed into him [her] of our own spirit" (38:72). As a consequence human beings are creation's most exalted members and therefore even the angels were commanded to bow down to them. All of them did so but Satan, who was overcome with the fatal spiritual disease of pride, arrogance, and self-conceit. Not only does the Qur'an categorically proclaim the sanctity of human life, but it also does the same for all of creation by prohibiting gratuitous destruction and enjoining environmental ethics.

Another prized value is celebrating diversity and not passing judgments about the salvific claims of others: "Had your Lord wished, the whole of mankind would have believed in Him. (Muhammad), do you force people to have faith?" (10:99). Only God, the final and sole arbiter, can resolve such disputes; our job is "to compete with one another in good deeds, for God is the final goal for all of you, and it is He who will clarify for you those things about which you now argue" (5:48, 2:148, and 23:61). A famous hadith attributed to the Prophet states that his community will splinter into seventy-three sects after his death and that only one of them will attain salvation (*al-firqah al-nājiyah*); however, this hadith has, beyond a shadow of a doubt, been fabricated and falsely ascribed to the Prophet because its chains of transmission are weak and such particularistic loyalties and exclusionary claims clearly violate the Qur'anic worldview. This is why we see intolerance not only between Muslims and the "other," but also among Muslims: Sunni vs. Shiʿi, Akhbari vs. Usuli, Sufi vs. other Muslims, theologians vs. mystics, traditionalists vs. reformists, and so on. It is not uncommon for each group to issue fatwas of *takfīr* (unbelief) against each other. Therefore, Muslim scholars and jurists need to promote a theology of inclusion and toleration that accords with the hadith that the Prophet stood up when a casket was being carried to a cemetery to show respect for the deceased person. When his Companions told him that the deceased was a Jew, thereby implying that such respect was unnecessary, he rebuked them, "Did he not have a soul?"

Those jurists who prioritize the Qur'anic teachings and Prophetic practices regarding essential ethical and moral norms, and who subject their deduced legal decrees to these ethical standards, would do well to bridge the gap and reduce the tension between legal rulings and ethical imperatives. Proponents of structural ijtihad have argued that it is by definition impossible for a decree to be regarded as "Islamic" and at the same time be unethical and immoral by the standards of society (*al-akhlāq al-ijtimāʿiyyah*). A Just, Wise, and Self-Sufficient God would not mandate His creation to act in a manner that is contrary to universal moral and ethical norms and values, all of which are derived from a source that is outside of and independent of religion.

Traditional ijtihad attempts to address contemporary challenges by invoking legal maxims and juridical devices as well as by undertaking an exhaustive search for analogous precedents in the revelatory sources or the pre-modern era even if these are non-existent, tenuous, or far-fetched. Another strategy is to creatively reformulate a precedent in order to give it a semblance of similarity to the new issue so that the new legal ruling can, potentially, be rationalized.[49] This results in a piecemeal, haphazard, and unsystematic application that seeks to provide temporary relief and dispensation in the absence of any theoretical grounding or epistemic coherence. Such a process does not subject the legal theory's foundations to any philosophical critique or interrogation; instead, it operates within the existing traditional ijtihad framework based upon the statement attributed to Imam Jaᶜfar al-Ṣādiq (d. 765) and Imam ᶜAlī al-Riḍā (d. 818): "It is for us to set out the foundational principles (*uṣūl*) and for you [the learned] to derive secondary (*tafrīᶜ*) outcomes."[50] As such, it lacks a coherent method and is, in many respects, quite subjective and arbitrary. Consequently its opponents call for a radical paradigm shift away from traditional ijtihad to what Kadivar proposes as structural or foundational ijtihad.

This proposed model attempts to provide a coherent framework in which theology and ethics can be reconstructed and thereby give the intellect (*ᶜaql*), ethics, and modern sciences a larger role in ethical decision making under the rubric of justice. In this framework, justice is viewed as extra-religious and in harmony with egalitarian justice, in contrast to a deserts-based justice. The interplay of foundational principles, theology, ethics, intellect, epistemology, linguistics, anthropology, modern sciences, history, and egalitarian justice is an attempt to reconstruct Islamic thought and legal theory. In essence, one can say that foundational ijtihad presents societal ethics as the arbiter that determines whether the deduced juridical legal ruling is acceptable or not because, by definition, God cannot legislate that which is unethical and immoral. Moreover, the recurrence of *maᶜrūf* (i.e., action morally approved by society) in the Qur'an without providing any specificity is additional proof that the human intellect, in collaboration with modern sciences and critical thinking, can discover universal ethical norms and values. In other words, *akhlāq*, *ᶜaql*, critical thinking, and the soft and hard sciences would have priority and preference over fiqh, *waḥy*, *naql*, and precedents. This is most definitely not the case in the traditional model.[51] To put it another way, "*ijtihad* itself is in need of another *ijtihad*."[52]

NOTES

1. *Muḥammad b. Yaʿqūb b. Isḥāq al-Kulaynī, al-Kāfī* (Arabic with Persian commentary and translation. (Ed.), Ali Akbar Ghaffari (Tehran: Dār al-Kutub al-Islāmiyyah, 1968), vol.1, p.58, hadith no.19.
2. Muḥammad Ḥusayn Faḍl Allāh, *al-Faqīh wa al-Ummah: Ta'ammulāt fī al-Fikr al-Ḥarakī wa al-Siyāsī wa al-Manhaj al-Ijtihādī ʿinda al-Imām al-Khumaynī* (Beirut: Dār al-Malāk, 2000), p.247.
3. The term *feqh-e pūyā* (dynamic fiqh), in contradistinction to *feqh-e sonnatī* (traditional fiqh), became current soon after the Iranian revolution. It was an acknowledgment that traditional ijtihad could not address contemporary societal issues and, as such, the legal methodology needed to be reformed. Although the concept remained vague and unused by eminent Shiʿi jurists it did enjoy some popularity among journalists. Within a decade, it had almost disappeared from the general discourse on legal reform.
4. Mohsen Kadivar, 'Revisiting Women's Rights in Islam: "Egalitarian Justice" in Lieu of "Deserts-based Justice"', in Ziba Mir-Hosseini, et al., *Gender and Equality in Muslim Family Law: Justice and Ethics in the Islamic Legal Tradition* (London: I.B. Tauris, 2012), pp.213–34.
5. Similarly, in Sunni Islam the arbitrary patching up of views (*talfīq*) and invoking choice (*takhayyur*) indicates the need to find innovative ways of addressing new challenges and reflects the need for a radical reform in the *uṣūl*.
6. Kadivar includes marriage, food, and drink in the first category of the immutable and unchanging, because the human intellect cannot, with any degree of high probability or certainty, fathom the wisdom behind their legal injunctions. Similarly, acts of worship belong to the same category because human reasoning cannot discover the wisdom behind their nature and form (e.g., why one must perform two units of prayer in the morning [*fajr*] and three at sunset [*maghrib*]), http://kadivar.com/?p=10158. See also Anver Emon, *Islamic Natural Law Theories* (Oxford: Oxford University Press, 2010), p.163.
7. Mohammed Ghaly, 'The Beginning of Human Life: Islamic Bioethical Perspectives', *Zygon* 47(1) (March 2012), p.177.
8. Tariq Ramadan, *Radical Reform: Islamic Ethics and Liberation* (New York: Oxford University Press, 2009), p.121.
9. Abdolkarem Soroush, *Bast-e Tajrobeh-ye Nabavī* (Tehran: Enteshārāt-e Ṣirāṭ, 1999), p.157.
10. Jasser Auda, *Maqasid al-Shariah as Philosophy of Islamic Law* (London and Washington: IIIT, 2008), p. xxvi.
11. Ayatollah Muhammad Sadeghi Tehrani (d. 2011) provides a scathing critique of the existing Shiʿi model of ijtihad. According to him, it claims to follow the Qur'an and the Sunnah, but in reality prioritizes the intellect, consensus, past precedents, famous rulings, and suspicious hadith reports. Due to this weak

foundation, Shiʿi jurists are required to qualify their rulings with the following terms: *aḥwat* (precautionary), *aqwā* (the stronger opinion), *fi-hi taraddud* (there is indecisiveness on the issue), and *taḍāḍ* (contradiction). Sunni Islam, he argues, has emphasized analogy, consensus, juristic preference (*istiḥsān*), and public welfare (*istiṣlāḥ*). He offers one example: the temporary suspension of Friday prayers while the infallible Imam is in occultation, even though the Qur'an is categorically clear that once the call to this prayer is made all Muslims must hasten to the prayer (62:9). See Muhammad Sadeghi Tehrani, *Feqh-e pūyā va feqh-e sonnatī, feqh-e pūyā, va feqh-e basharī* (Tehran: Omid-e Fardā, 2005), pp.22–27.

12. Sherman Jackson, *Islam and the Problem of Black Suffering* (New York: Oxford University Press, 2009), p.9.
13. Emon, *Islamic Natural Theories*, p.20.
14. Ibid., pp.90–91.
15. Ibid., pp.93–94, 121, 130–31, 136–37, 146, 167, and 203.
16. Ibid., p.40.
17. Ibid., pp.26–27.
18. This is analogous to the Sunni concept of *al-maṣāliḥ al-mursalah* (seeking the public good by using extra-revelatory sources when the revelatory texts are silent).
19. Mohammed Mojtahed Shabestari, *Naqdī bar Qerā'at-e Rasmī az Dīn* (Tehran: Tarh-e now, 2002), pp.346–47.
20. A common example provided is the analogy between the Qur'anic concept of consultation (*shūrā*) and parliamentary government.
21. The apparent tension between the Ashʿarite theology of ethical voluntarism and the derivation of Islamic law for issues that lack a proof text can be ameliorated in light of Emon's thesis of "soft natural law theory." For instance Mohammad Hashim Kamali, an exponent of Ashʿarite theology, is able to incorporate a very limited role for reason and rational inquiry in the legal deduction process: "The *ḥukm* must be rational in the sense that the human intellect is capable of understanding the reason or the cause of its enactment, or that the *ʿillah* is clearly given in the text itself." Mohammad Hashim Kamali, *Principles of Islamic Jurisprudence* (Cambridge: The Islamic Texts Society, 2003), p.270. "Imam Mālik has added two other conditions to the foregoing, one of which is that the *maṣlaḥah* must be rational (*maʿqūlah*) and acceptable to people of sound intellect." Ibid., p.359. At the same time, he is able to argue, "… Islam's perspective on good and evil (*ḥusn wa qubh*) which are, in principle, determined by divine revelation. Thus when God ordered the promotion of *ma'rūf*, He could not have meant the good that reason or custom decrees to be such, but what He enjoins." Ibid., p.370. Or "From an Islamic perspective, right and wrong are determined, not by reference to the 'nature of things', but because God has determined them as such." Ibid., p.323.

22. Ruhollah Mousavi Khomeini, *Ṣaḥīfe-ye Nūr* (Tehran: Sāzemān-e Madārek-e Farhangī-ye Enqelāb-e Eslāmī, 1990), vol.21, p.98.
23. Quoted in Chibli Mallat, *The Renewal of Islamic Law* (Cambridge: Cambridge University Press, 1993), pp.90, 91, and 92.
24. Abdulaziz A. Sachedina, *Islamic Biomedical Ethics: Principles and Application* (Oxford: Oxford University Press, 2009), p.215.
25. Shabestari, *Naqdi*, pp.468–69.
26. Kadivar, 'Revisiting Women's Rights in Islam', p.223.
27. Ibid., pp.213–34.
28. Wael Hallaq delineates four trends in Sunni Islam that have emerged in response to modernity: (1) secularism, which advocates the complete abandonment of Islam; (2) a return to the pure and pristine teachings of the Qur'an and the Prophet, which is sponsored by the Wahhabi movement, (3) "religious utilitarianism," which relies heavily on the concept of public interest (*maṣlaḥah*) and necessity to either revise previous juridical rulings or provide new ones for fresh contingencies (Hallaq views both of these as highly subjective and arbitrary); and (4) "religious liberalism," which realizes that every text originates in a context as opposed to a vacuum, and affirms that a changed context demands new rulings derived by applying universal principles in a particular context. Wael Hallaq, *A History of Islamic Legal Theories: An Introduction to Sunni Usul al-Fiqh* (Cambridge: Cambridge University Press, 2004), pp.207–54.
29. Naser Makarim Shirazi, *Ḥīleh-hā-ye Sharʿī* (Qum: Madrasat al-Imām ʿAlī b. Abī Ṭālib, 2006).
30. ʿAbdolkarim Soroush, *Reason, Freedom, & Democracy in Islam: Essential Writing of 'Abdolkarim Soroush*, transl. Mahmoud Sadri and Ahmad Sadri, (New York: Oxford University Press, 2000), pp.128–29.
31. Abu al-Qasim Fanaee, *Din dar Tarazu-ye Akhlaq* (Tehran: Enteshārāt-e Ṣirāṭ, 2007); Mostefa Malekiyan, *Jastarhayi dar ʿAqlaniyyat va Maʿnaviyyat* (Tehran: Nashr Negah-e Muʿasir, 2002), pp.446–86.
32. Fazlur Rahman, *Islam & Modernity* (Chicago: The University of Chicago Press, 1982), p.5.
33. Saanei negates the legal distinction between Muslim and non-Muslim, man and woman, and free and slave while employing the traditional model. This is in direct conflict with its bases and premises, which are considered fixed and eternal.
34. Mostefa Mohaghegh Damad, 'Goft va gu', in *Monāsebat-e Akhlāq va Feqh dar Goft va gū-ye Andishvārān* (Interviewer: Mohammed Hedayati) (Qom: Tablighat-e Eslami, 2014), p.274.
35. Ibid., p.277.
36. Ruhollah Khomeini, *Taḥrīr al-Wasīlah* (Qum: Daftar-e Enteshārāt-e Islāmī, 2008), vol.3, p.431.

37. Ibid.
38. Ibid., p.276.
39. Abdulaziz A. Sachedina, 'Gof va gu', in *Monāsebat-e Akhlāq va Feqh*, pp.172–73.
40. Kadivar, 'Revisiting Women's Rights in Islam', p.223.
41. Liyakat Takim, *Shiʿism in America* (New York: New York University Press, 2009), p.167.
42. A. Kevin Reinhart, 'Islamic Law as Islamic Ethics', *Journal of Religious Ethics* 11(2) (Fall 1983), p.186.
43. Ibid., p.187.
44. Ja'far Sobhani, 'Kholāseh-ye goft va gūhā-ye akhlāq va feqh,' in *Monāsebat-e Akhlāq*, p.61.
45. Ibid., p.62.
46. Damad, 'Goft va gu', in *Monasebat-e Akhlaq*, p.275.
47. Majid Khadduri, *The Islamic Conception of Justice* (Baltimore: The John Hopkins University Press, 1984), p.10.
48. Abdulaziz A. Sachedina, *Islamic Roots of Democratic Religious Pluralism* (New York: Oxford University Press, 2001), p.110.
49. Ebrahim Moosa, 'Interface of Science and Jurisprudence: Dissonant Gazes at the Body in Modern Muslim Ethics', in *God, Life, and the Cosmos: Christian and Islamic Perspectives*. (Ed.), Ted Peters, et al. (Hants, UK: Ashgate, 2002), pp.341–46.
50. Muhammad Ebrahim Jannati, *Taṭavvor-e Ejtehād dar Howze-ye Estenbāṭ* (Tehran: Amir Kabir, 2007), vol.1, pp.151–52.
51. Sachedina, 'Gof va gu', p.173.
52. Soroush, *Reason, Freedom & Democracy in Islam*, p.29.

4

The Application of *Maqāṣid al-Sharīʿah* in Islamic Chaplaincy

Kamal Abu-Shamsieh

ABSTRACT: Healthcare professional chaplains provide spiritual care to religiously and culturally diverse patients, while religious leaders, especially Christian, receive spiritual care education in seminaries and training in healthcare institutions to provide spiritual care to all patients. Patients communicate with faith leaders prior to or during hospitalization, or upon discharge, to receive the sacraments of the sick. The scope of Islamic spiritual care services and the understanding of the theological foundation of Islamic chaplaincy remain in their infancy, despite the emergence of Islamic chaplaincy training programs and professional associations in the United States. In Muslim countries, chaplaincy is non-existent, an underdeveloped field, or misunderstood, despite the rich Islamic tradition of caring for the soul, seeking care, healing, worship obligations, the legal-laden affairs of Muslims during sickness, and the ethics of care. This paper addresses the reciprocity of Islamic law and ethics in Islamic chaplaincy, and how the theory of *maqāṣid al-sharīʿah* is key to the development of an Islamic spiritual care methodology for care of the spiritual, emotional, relational, and religious needs of diverse Muslims, including non-practicing Muslims, and non-Muslims. The understanding of the foundation of Islamic chaplaincy requires articulation of an Islamic theology based on *tawḥīd*, the Oneness of God. In addition, the scope of services and the manner in which they are delivered are impacted by the goals of *maqāṣid al-sharīʿah*, Islamic jurisprudence, and the *qawāʿid al-sharīʿah* principles of ethics. Hence, Islamic spiritual care services follow the Sunnah of

Prophet Muhammad in offering spiritual care services guided by an understanding of Shariʿah that is theologically sound, scientifically evidence-based, and legally-ethically patient-centered, all within the general guidelines in the Qur'an and the Sunnah.

This paper grounds Islamic chaplaincy and spiritual care within the Islamic legal and ethical theory of *maqāṣid al-sharīʿah* and makes *ḥifẓ al-dīn*, preservation of religion, the goal of chaplaincy as a way to provide religious support to all patients, Muslim and non-Muslim. The positioning of Islamic chaplaincy within the legal and ethical domain will set the stage towards the development of a universal theory of Islamic chaplaincy, its services, and its purposes. A Muslim chaplain is bound by professional guidelines, including hospital regulations, and by the boundaries of Shariʿah. To this extent, the rendering of Islamic chaplaincy services seeks the higher *maqāṣid* of the Shariʿah in establishing justice (Qur'an 4:135), eliminating prejudice (5:8), and alleviating hardship (2:185), in a manner following the example of the Prophet Muhammad of being *raḥma* (compassion) and offering *hudan* (guidance). Thus, Islamic chaplaincy is deeply rooted in the fulfillment of *maṣlaḥah* benefits including essential (*darūriyyāt*), complementary (*ḥājiyyāt*) and desirable benefits (*taḥsīniyyāt*). To accomplish this task, a Muslim chaplain serves as a guide, a counselor, and a teacher providing support and empowerment, out of love and the bonds of faith and humanity, to orient individuals towards God. In addition, a Muslim chaplain may facilitate services, without abandoning patients, in contexts where what is being asked contradicts the Shariʿah.

Introduction

The interconnectedness of faith and action creates opportunities for growth and reflection, both personal and communal. As a healthcare chaplain, I offer spiritual care services to Muslim and non-Muslim patients, conduct spiritual care assessment, and reflect with patients and families. Patients often struggle with discernment about what is going on, why something is happening to them, how to figure out what ought to happen, or how to plan in response to their ever-changing situation, all within the boundaries of Shariʿah. My Ph.D. project aims to explore the connection between Islam as a faith, its theology, and its legal-ethical theory, and it examines how faith and Shariʿah impact the actions and practices of Muslims, and vice versa. I adopted practical theology as the methodology to describe how illness and healthcare contexts impact Muslims' religious practice and understanding of their faith. What impacts the belief of Muslims? What guides Muslims to know what they ought to do? Why should Muslims act? And what criteria do Muslims employ to figure out what to do in response to life experiences? In this paper; however, my aim is to understand the connection between Islam, its theology, its practices, and the actions of Muslims. I will briefly describe the sources and purposes of Shariʿah and introduce the theory of *maqāṣid al-sharīʿah*. In addition, I will briefly describe the interconnectedness between Islamic law and ethics, and introduce the major Islamic legal maxims that impact the work of the chaplain and the practices and services offered to patients. As a result, I hope to present a better idea of what Muslims are allowed to do, the role of the context in deciding how Muslims act, and the role of Shariʿah in shaping Islamic chaplaincy.

Islam is a faith that requires its adherents to declare their belief, follow the commands of God, and act accordingly. Muslims encounter various life situations which require resources to help guide to what is good and what one ought to do. Action (*ʿamal*) is a central focus of Islamic theology, and Muslim jurists focused their attention on understanding action and practice.[1] The study of action requires an interdisciplinary approach to Islamic law and ethics in order to understand how these disciplines influence one's actions and each other. I will therefore discuss the sources of Islamic law and ethics, the purposes of Islamic law (*maqāṣid al-sharīʿah*), and legal maxims (*qawāʿid fiqhiyyah*), all of which guide and influence Muslims in every facet of daily life. I will present highlights of the works of scholars who impacted the *maqāṣid* discourse such as Ibn ʿAshur, Imam al-Ghazālī and Imam al-Juwaynī, and I will examine the consequences of human action and inaction for interpersonal, intrapersonal, and divine-human relationships. I will argue that the theory of *maqāṣid* presents a simplified framework for scholars and lay individuals to further understand what God meant in revealing the Shariʿah, and how its legal and ethical standards impact and define human responsibilities, shape morality and character, and influence relations among people.

Sources of Shariʿah

There are two sources of Shariʿah, revealed and deconstructed. The revealed sources are the Qur'an and the Prophetic Tradition (Sunnah), and are considered the primary sources of Shariʿah. The two other sources are scholarly deconstructed literary theory and hermeneutics utilizing juristic methods of analytical reasoning (*qiyās*) and scholarly consensus (*ijmāʿ*) in Sunni jurisprudence. The consensus of the community was adopted despite serious challenges regarding what such consensus meant, the scope of the issues in question, and the qualification of those consenting.[2] Analogical reasoning (*qiyās*) is a common scholarly method of reaching a juristic ruling (fatwa) and remains a valid methodology for formulating laws despite the emergence of rulings inconsistent with Islamic precepts.[3] Khaled Abou El Fadl has highlighted the significance of the Qur'an as the immutable and literal word of God, revealed, memorized, orally transmitted, and eventually collected and put into writing at the time of the Companions after the death of the Prophet (d. 10/632).[4] *Qiyās* was described as the "balance of the minds" because it seeks to establish a balance between two issues in a just manner. Hence, the Qur'an recognized that the task of people is to "seek guidance for an Islamic life on issues where the commands are not explicit or appear to conflict."[5] In such cases, one would not find a rational methodology other than an analogy (*qiyās*).

The knowledge of Shariʿah is interdisciplinary and inseparable from other Islamic disciplines; hence, the scope of Shariʿah includes the corpus of divine rulings ordained for humanity and encompasses all their affairs, religious and societal, for the purpose of leading people to happiness, justice, and salvation. *ʿAqīdah* means to tie tightly, and designates Muslim belief; it is encompassed by the Shariʿah, and serves as the knot of faith upon which other disciplines are built. Al-Zarqa has defined Shariʿah as the collection of divine commands and practical rulings that are obligatory for Muslims to follow in order to reform and mend affairs (*iṣlāḥ*) in society.[6] Kamali has considered Shariʿah the verbatim embodiment of the commandments of God embracing His commands, prohibitions, guiding principles, and narratives; it is addressed to humanity through revelation to achieve salvation following the Qur'an and the Sunnah.[7] Sunnah is the application of Shariʿah and is considered the way of life by which Prophet Muhammad embodied Shariʿah in what he said, did, silently approved of, or disapproved of. The Sunnah was reported in the literature and ultimately canonized in books of Hadith.

The Purposes of Shariʿah

Shariʿah is derived from the root *sh-r-ʿ* and is best known for being a road (*shāriʿ*) or path to water. Shariʿah is often used interchangeably with Islamic law, yet it encompasses the law and leads towards well-being and goodness. Khaled Abou El Fadl has defined Shariʿah as God's eternal and immutable law – the way of truth, virtue, and justice. Shariʿah was revealed to prophets and has been described as a vital path to the survival of humanity, and an inclusive way of life that is available for Muslims and non-Muslims alike.[8] Ibn al-Qayyim has described Shariʿah as the structure upon which Islamic law was constructed for the purposes of protecting the best interests of God's servants both in this world and the next:

> The law is pure justice, pure mercy, pure benefit, and pure wisdom. Hence, anything which embodies injustice rather than justice, cruelty rather than mercy, harm rather than benefit or folly rather than wisdom does not originate from the Law even if it happens to have been interpolated therein by means of interpretation.[9]

The higher objective of the theory of *maqāṣid* is ultimately safeguarding the interests that God, the Lawgiver, intended for humanity. The jurists research the primary sources of Shariʿah when they encounter an issue that requires a legal ruling. The initial stage towards issuing a juristic opinion includes the return to the primary sources to search for a proof (*dalīl*) that will serve as a precedent for how to respond to the matter in question. The jurists apply legal methods and utilize their Islamic knowledge to enhance their human understanding (fiqh) of the disciplines of Shariʿah. In addition, jurists emulate (*taqlīd*) the teachings of previous scholars and revive their heritage or engage in innovative legal determinations (ijtihad).[10] The discipline of fiqh is the knowledge derived through ijtihad to comprehend the legal ruling of Shariʿah as derived from its detailed evidence in the source.[11] The heritage contains the collection of judicial opinions given by jurists of various schools of theology in the past fourteen centuries for the application of Shariʿah. The various life questions that are not directly addressed in the revealed sources often require seeking a juristic opinion (fatwa). The jurist (*muftī*) addresses each question on its own and issues the non-binding fatwa.[12]

People seek legal rulings based on their own Shariʿah, as God intended diversity in the divine laws. The Qur'an states that if God willed, He would have created humanity as one community.[13] The monotheistic Abrahamic religions, Judaism, Christianity, and Islam, all received different kinds of divine Shariʿah.[14] The Old Testament (Torah) revealed to Prophet Moses (Mūsā) ordained specific laws for the Children of Israel for a unique time and specific location. The revealed Gospel (*Injīl*) revealed to Jesus (*ʿĪsa*) focused on moral reforms and character building; however, Christianity lacked a legal system or Shariʿah. As a result, the revealed Shariʿah brought forth a comprehensive and universal legal and ethical system, irrespective of time and location. Hence, Islam is viewed as a way of life, as Shariʿah prescribes the basic principles of faith and life. To achieve comprehensiveness in all facets of life, Shariʿah brought forth laws for daily practice, flexibility, and leniency to suspend the implementation of laws temporarily or to adjust practice during illness or to make accommodations due to necessity or hardship. Hence, the laws of Shariʿah allow for certain variations in accordance with the contexts, environment, and societal changes. Qur'an 45:18 describes Shariʿah as protector of the basic principles of justice and equity; the purpose of faith is to lead to the stream of water, an indispensable element for all organic life. Shariʿah denotes a system of laws, both moral and practical, which shows man the way towards spiritual fulfillment and social welfare:[15]

> [Shariʿah refers] to any other group of people bonded by a common set of beliefs or convictions. [… It] refers to the broad concept of the all-inclusive and total path to and from God, which equated, by necessity, to the path leading to and resulting from social goodness (*ma'ruf*) and moral goodness (*husn*). […] Shari'ah does not necessarily denote a positive set of divine commands which humans must comply with, but rather denotes the ultimate good God desires for human beings.[16]

Several scholars attempted to understand the wisdom behind the divine revelation and the commands embedded in the scriptures. Ibn ʿAshur concluded that the purposes of the law are to preserve order, achieve benefits and prevent harm or corruption, establish equality among people, restore reverence for the divine law and empower the community (Ummah).[17]

The process of achieving knowledge resulted in a diversity of opinions among Muslim scholars and gave birth to the various schools of Islamic law (*madhhab*) which were reduced later to Sunni and Shiite schools of Islamic law. For example, the Ḥanafite school was named after Imam Abū Ḥanīfah (d. 767) and classified laws according to three distinctive categories: worship (*ʿibādāt*), civil transactions (*muʿāmalāt*), and punishments (*ʿuqūbāt*). Each category was further divided into sections that address the specifics of each field. Prayer, for example, was classified as part of *ʿibādāt* and was further divided into main headings such as cleanliness (*ṭahārah*), obligatory prayer (salah), or fasting (*ṣawm*).[18]

The Theory of *Maqāṣid al-Sharīʿah*

The term purpose (*maqṣad*, pl. *maqāṣid*) is derived from the root *q-ṣ-d* which means to approach something with straightforwardness, free of bias or tilting. Theologians elaborated on what was meant by *maqāṣid* instead of defining it. Youssef al-ᶜĀlem viewed *maqāṣid* as benefits that believers earn in this life and the Hereafter by maximizing benefits or removing harm. Ibn ᶜAshur described the overall purposes of the *maqāṣid* as preserving the social order of the community and ensuring its healthy progress, wellbeing, and righteousness.[19] Al-Fasi focused on the hidden truths that God placed in each ruling.[20] Al-Qaradawi examined the text to know what actions the *maqāṣid* aimed for, and what is prohibited or allowed that might yield benefits to individuals or the Ummah. Ahmad al-Raysouni saw *maqāṣid* as purposes revealed in the Shariᶜah for the benefit of the faithful. Shariᶜah has presented the divine master plan for humanity, including belief in the Oneness of God (*tawḥīd*) and a prevention system of rewards and warnings to maximize benefits (*maṣlaḥah*) and avoid harm (*ḍarar*), all to steer humans toward success and salvation in the material world and the Hereafter. Hence, just acts are promoted and deemed in line with the purposes of Shariᶜah, whereas injustice is irreconcilable and amounts to a fundamental betrayal of Shariᶜah.[21]

Muslim jurists contributed to the development of the benefit-based theory of *maqāṣid* over an extended period of time. Imām al-Ḥaramayn al-Juwaynī (d. 1085) established a framework to set priorities for actions, based on the prevalent themes within the sacred texts, for the use of jurists and individuals alike. Al-Juwaynī underscored the significance of acquiring knowledge of the Shariᶜah rulings (*al-aḥkām al-sharᶜiyyah*), and divided the purposes of divine revelation into three basic categories: (1) the protection of the essential benefits of faith, life, intellect, lineage, and property, classified as necessities (*ḍarūriyyāt*) for which there is dire need; (2) the facilitation of the provision of basic needs (*ḥājiyyāt*) which seek to remove severity and hardship in cases of public need but aren't elevated to the level of necessity, such as the need to have a home rental agreement where the absence of a contract is a hardship but not a threat to the very survival of normal order; and (3) the provision of embellishments (*taḥsīniyyāt*) which are desirable for the refinement and perfection of the customs and conduct of the people.[22] Imam al-Ghazālī (d. 1111), a student of al-Juwaynī, contributed to the *maqāṣid* discourse in his book *al-Mustaṣfā min ʿIlm al-Uṣūl*[23] and expanded on the work of al-Juwaynī. He highlighted the category of *ḍarūriyyāt*, a category of utmost necessity, to preserve what God intended for humanity to preserve: religion (*dīn*), life (*nafs*), property (*māl*), mind (*ʿaql*), and offspring (*nasl*). The divine goals for humanity, according to al-Ghazālī, are to achieve happiness and closeness to God by following Shariʿah which will lead the faithful to salvation in the eternal life hereafter.[24]

Shariʿah: Law and Ethics

The theory of *maqāṣid* is interdisciplinary and includes the study of various Islamic disciplines such as hermeneutics of the Qur'an and Tradition, exegesis (*tafsīr*), lawmaking (*tashrīʿ*), ethics (*akhlāq*), and sub-fields such as the fundamentals of Islamic law (*ūṣūl*).

An interdisciplinary study of law and ethics can be pursued through the lens of *maqāṣid*, explaining processes, defining disciplines, and embarking on the goal of integrating the disciplines, all for the purpose of reaching a more comprehensive understanding of the divine goal for humanity. Such interdisciplinary study can be defined as "a process of answering a question, solving a problem, or addressing a topic that is too broad or complex to be dealt with adequately by a single discipline, and draws on the disciplines with the goal of integrating their insights to construct a more comprehensive understanding."[25] Including Shariʿah in one's definition of ethics frames the moral behavior of individuals as acts of obedience or disobedience to the moral theology of Islam. Ethics is a field that is rooted in law, and does not function as an independent discipline.

Prayers are one form of worshipping God, and are classified as an obligation where their fulfillment is both a legal and an ethical divine command. The Qur'an instructs believers to establish the prayers following a formula demonstrated by the Prophet. The fulfillment and neglect of prayers are judged in accordance with a legal scale that specifies rewards or punishments for each act or omission. But they also carry ethical significance, as is evident from the description of prayer as a source of immunity. Qur'an 29:45 claims that prayers keep one away from indecency and evil, and that hearts will enter into tranquility as a result of the act of remembrance of God in prayer. George Hourani suggests that the relation between ethics and Shariʿah is one of mutual influence: the Shariʿah defines ethics, but ethics is the base of jurisprudence:

> The relation between ethics and divine law in Islam is usually stated in the reverse direction: that the whole range of ethics was absorbed into the Shariʿah, so that all conduct was judged as obedience or disobedience to divine law. This is true in a formal sense that normative ethics was worked out in legal books and judgments. But we may equally observe that the purpose of the vast legal structures was ethical in a modern sense. The relation may be proved by the evidence of several legal principles, fictions, and practices which broke out of the strict mold of classical theory in order to accommodate the demands of justice and public interest. An example is the Malikite principle of *istiṣlāḥ*, "consideration of public interest", which may be used in preferring one interpretation of the Shariʿah to another.[26]

Islamic morality and faith are inseparable. The term *khuluq* describes the character and the innate disposition (*fiṭra*) of human beings. The Qur'an described the life of the Prophet as a sublime way of life,[27] while Hadith elevated ethics by declaring that the best virtue humans can achieve is good character (*khulq ḥasan*).[28] Nonetheless, Islamic ethical theory is broad and deals with a wide range of ethical virtues, among them the virtues of honesty or empathy. Islamic ethics can be narrowed down to focus on sub-disciplines such as bioethics, the ethics of family and marriage, and the ethics of charitable contributions. Muslims, especially those who live as minorities in diverse communities and those in hostile environments, are continuously being challenged to remain within the boundaries of what Shariʿah considers legal, ethical, prohibited, or permitted. Muslim jurists expounded on the revealed sources of Islam to establish parameters to help discern and define virtues (*akhlāq*), juristic preference (*istiḥsān*), public interest (*maṣlaḥah*), while following the divine requirements of commanding what is good (*maʿrūf*) and forbidding what is bad (*munkar*).[29] The boundaries of legal and ethical behavior were often so well defined that Muslims were unanimous in their interpretations, or there was very little room for disagreement. For example, the Qur'an instructed Muslims on what is prohibited[30] and commanded them to avoid prohibited things such as fornication, consumption of wine and pork, and incest, just to name a few. In other circumstances, the ethical commands were generalized and allowed for differences of opinion about what is right and wrong, what constitutes the best *maṣlaḥah*, considerations of public interest (*istiṣlāḥ*), or juristic preference (*istiḥṣān*). Differences among the scholars were shaped by their diverse methods of interpretation, or by the cultures and customs of the communities where Muslims resided.

Islamic Legal Maxims

The Islamic legal maxims (*al-qawāᶜid al-fiqhiyyah*) helped in providing simple statements of what is legally lawful and ethical. The term *qāᶜidah* was mentioned in Qur'an 2:127 to refer to foundational structures. In general, a legal maxim may refer to a general case where it connects and influences various parts, branches, or sub-cases. Its influence may extend to other disciplines and impact numerous legal rulings. The legal maxims are often very succinct statements, easy to remember, universal, and comprehensive. Scholars and individuals may utilize the maxims and apply them to other cases and life experiences.

The sources of the legal maxims are the Qur'an, Sunnah, and scholarly efforts or ijtihad. The Qur'anic-based legal maxims were constructed from verses that affirmed general principles, the flexibility of Shariᶜah, or its universality. The maxims respond to needs irrespective of time and location. For example, the legal maxim of hardship was constructed based on Qur'an 2:185, which states "God wills that you shall have ease, and does not will you to suffer hardship." The constructed legal maxim mirrored the Qur'anic verse and states "hardship begets facility."[31] The Sunnah-based maxims captured the hadith of the Prophet Muhammad, and contained brief and rich statements that described the essence of Shariᶜah. For example, the legal maxim of intention[32] mirrored the hadith which states, "Actions are to be judged by their intentions."[33] The ijtihad-based maxims were constructed from non-revealed sources following a process of deduction by scholars. The sources of the ijtihad-based maxims are legal precedents in Islamic legal rulings, logic, reasoning, and rules of the Arabic language. The *qawāʿid* vary in their universality, comprehensiveness, and acceptance by the various schools of thought. There are five normative legal maxims that are universal in their application and influence over all Islamic disciplines. The maxims address foundational themes such as harm, intention, hardship, certainty, and customs.

The maxim of harm (*al-ḍarar yuzāl*) states that injury must be removed.[34] The scope of the legal maxim of harm (*ḍarar*) can be far reaching, beyond the traditional definition of avoidance of inflicting harm. The reading of the legal maxim of harm and its application in the field of Islamic bioethics renders nonmaleficence a universal principle that works to remove three kinds of legal harms: explicitly inflicted harm, harm inflicted without due justice or not based on legally prescribed punishment,[35] and harm that might befall the [healthcare] provider during the course of treating others. Self-inflicted harm was addressed in Qur'an 2:188 and 4:29; the verses cautioned against "eating up property unless by mutual consent." The call to refrain from harming others was derived from Qur'an 2:229 and addressed matters related to familial discord and spousal relations. In the verse, the terms of divorce were discussed: the parties should either hold together on equitable terms or separate with kindness. The far-reaching understanding of the removal of dependent harm in Qur'an 2:233 protects the mother against injustice and harm on account of her child, born or unborn. On the other hand, Hadith expanded the understanding of avoidance of harm by explicitly advocating against inflicting harm or reciprocating it. The Prophet Muhammad said, "Anyone who causes harm, God will do harm to him and anyone who causes hardship to people, Allah will do the same to him." Therefore, the comprehensiveness of Islamic ethics in regards to the removal of harm extends its reach to minimizing harm as it occurs and preventing further harm from occurring, against victims and perpetrators alike.

The removal of harm is both an ethical and legal obligation, and a priority that can be achieved in different ways. To begin with, harm must be prevented from appearing as much as possible prior to its occurrence. The legal maxim of blocking the means (*sadd al-dharā'iʿ*) can be applied to prevent harm from occurring as a result of employing legal and ethical means that may lead to an unethical result. In addition, the removed harm must be the greatest harm and cannot be achieved by inflicting a similar harm in the course of removing the current harm. Therefore, the principle of the lesser of the two evils is compatible with the Islamic understanding of ethics, and a greater harm can be removed by a lesser harm. Hence, the legal and ethical obligation begins with repelling an evil, which is a priority that supersedes the securing of benefits when there is a choice between maximizing benefits and preventing or removing harms.

The maxim of intention is articulated by a brief statement and states that actions are judged in accordance to their intentions (*al-umūr bi-maqāṣidihā*).[36] The Qur'anic base for the maxim appears in Qur'an 3:145 which states, "And if one desires the rewards of this world, We shall grant him thereof; and if one desires the rewards of the life to come, We shall grant him thereof; and We shall requite those who are grateful [to Us]." In the Hadith, Prophet Muhammad said, "Deeds are judged by intentions and every person is judged according to his intentions."[37] The actions of the individual, good and evil, are judged by God based on the intentions behind them. The judgment of intentions is based on a few categories. The Qur'an addresses the intentions of the heart when considering a pardon for committed mistakes:

> [As for your adopted children,] call them by their [real] fathers' names: this is more equitable in the sight of God; and if you know not who their fathers were, [call them] your brethren in faith and your friends. However, you will incur no sin if you err in this respect: [what really matters is] but what your hearts intend, for God is indeed forgiving and a dispenser of grace![38]

In addition to intentions, the judgment of actions is also determined based on whether one carried out the thoughts one had or not, and whether the act resulted in harm to others or not.

Individuals may receive rewards when they have evil thoughts but refrain from carrying them out. On the other hand, punishments for intentions to cause harm may be decided by determining whether the harm was intentional, unintentional, accidental, or incidental. In devotional acts, an individual may be judged based on the intentions behind the good act. For example, rewards vary for those who search for a lost item with the intention to return it, to keep it, to return it with the intention of receiving a gift, to receive praise, or to gain recognition. The intentions give rise to the meanings of words, which are not determined simply by the words and how they are articulated. The legal maxim of intentions creates a real opportunity for engagement to get to know people at the core and intimate levels.

Intentions alone are insignificant in the presence of harm or its consequences. According to Ibn ʿAshur, the dual purpose of Shariʿah is to fulfill goals for people in society and simultaneously to avoid hardship or burden, whenever that combination is possible. The removal of harm is considered the prime purpose and supersedes any other benefit. Hence, the application of the legal maxim of harm protects patients and spiritual care providers alike, as one weighs benefits against harm. The following case represents an actual scenario that took place in a medical facility:

> Sameer is an adult Muslim patient who was diagnosed with leukemia and required chemotherapy, blood transfusion and stem cell transplant. As a result of having a suppressed immune system, Sameer was admitted to the intensive care unit. His physician decided to restrict visitations as a precaution, and a warning sticker was placed on the door prohibiting visitors except for immediate family members. In addition, visitors who had cold symptoms were not allowed to visit the patient. One of Sameer's friends was very concerned about Sameer's poor prognosis and decided to visit his friend. Upon reaching the nurses' station, the friend identified himself as a brother of Sameer and was allowed access.

In the case above, no one can doubt the noble intentions of care, concern, and compassion of Sameer's friend. However, intentions in such circumstances are secondary to the harm that the visit can lead to. The legal maxim of harm made it prohibited to endure and reciprocate harm, thus preserving the interests of both. In this case the harm outweighed the benefits of the visit, and unnecessarily jeopardized the essential purpose of preserving life. Similarly, visits that place visitors in harm's way must be delayed or canceled unless effective precautionary measures are in place. For example, if a patient is diagnosed with Ebola, restrictions must be imposed on who can have contact with such patients, as the community at large will be placed in harm's way.

The legal maxim of hardship (*al-mashaqqah tajlibu al-taysīr*)[39] stipulates that the existence of a hardship begets facility, relief, and ease (*taysīr*). Necessity (*ḥājah*) is the trigger for implementing this maxim, which seeks to lighten the burden. In the existence of a necessity, the call for relief might call for leniency (*rukhṣah*), a legal tool that allows for the temporary disregard of rules in exceptional circumstances if they will cause hardship. There are various instances in the Qur'an and the Sunnah that call for ease in the face of hardship. Fasting in the month of Ramadan while traveling or being sick represents a hardship, so breaking the fast is allowed. Qur'an 2:185 indicates that God wills that you should have ease, and does not will you to suffer hardship. Similarly, God does not burden any human being beyond his or her ability.[40] People may opt for endurance (*ʿazm*) and patience (*ṣabr*), but the legal and ethical responsibility is to seek relief and to benefit from the *rukhṣah* out of appreciation. In the Hadith it was reported that "God loves when [people] indulge in His *rukhṣah*."[41] Hadith also provided relief and a choice to fulfill religious duties by selecting the easiest lawful option available. ʿAisha, Mother of the believers and wife of the Prophet Muhammad said, "Whenever the Messenger of God was given a choice between two things, he would chose the easier one unless it was a sin."[42]

The legal maxim of hardship deals with the obstacles that result in hardship or the inability of the individual to perform a duty; hence its purview is the search for means and alternatives that enable the overcoming of hardships. For example, a traveling person may reduce (*qaṣr*) the prayers, combine them (*jamʿ*), delay them (*ta'khīr*), and/or advance them (*taqdīm*) to relieve the individual of any hardship or any obstacles to performing the prayers. The reasons for which the legal maxim of hardship may enact a *rukhṣah* are numerous, and among them are traveling, sickness, compulsion or persecution, forgetfulness, ignorance, difficulty, and incapacity. Determining the level of hardship matters, as a jurist will consider the impact of the hardship on the individual's ability to fulfill a duty in accordance with the duty's status as obligatory, recommended, permitted, frowned upon, or prohibited. The restrictions that rendered the utilization of *rukhṣah* lawful and valid expire when necessity no longer exists. In such cases, the excusable becomes unlawful and one reverts to the original prohibition. Leeway should be afforded in cases where difficulties appear to cause hardship. Necessity renders all prohibited things permissible, as long as one does not violate the right of others or cause new hardships in the course of removing current hardships.

The legal maxim of certainty (*al-yaqīn la yuzālu bil-shakk*)[43] specifies that in matters where certainty is the state of affairs, it cannot be displaced by doubt. The Qur'an addressed matters of certainty in reflections on creation. Qur'an 2:29 states, "He has created for you all that is on earth, and has applied His design to the heavens and fashioned them into seven heavens; and He alone has full knowledge of everything." Hence the legal maxim of certainty indicates that all things are considered permissible unless they are prohibited, as permissibility is the natural state. In addition, certainty is applied to matters of knowledge, truth, and superstition. Qur'an 10:36 states "For most of them follow nothing but conjecture: behold, conjecture can never be a substitute for truth. Verily, God has full knowledge of all that they do." In addition to the Qur'an, the Hadith mention aspects of certainty. The Prophet said, "That which is lawful is clear and that which is unlawful is clear, and between the two of them are doubtful matters."[44] Certainty and its rulings cannot be set aside by doubt. The legal and ethical impact of the maxim of certainty is evident in criminal cases, as priority is given to what is originally known over what is doubted: for example, every suspect is considered innocent until proven guilty.

The legal maxim of custom (*ʿurf*) states that custom is authoritative (*al-ʿāda muḥakammah*).[45] It appears in the Qur'an and Hadith.

The maxim admits into legal theory what is known to and practiced by people at a given time, and recognized and permitted by Shariʿah.[46] For example, Qur'an 3:19 prescribes spousal relations to be established on a footing of kindness (*ʿāshirūhunna bil-maʿrūf*). Kindness in this verse is referred to as the norm; hence, Shariʿah recognizes the *ʿurf* of kindness as the norm of spousal relations. In addition, Qur'an 7:199 recognized forgiveness (*ʿafū*) as the norm in relations, along with commanding what is known as right and turning away from what is unknown or wrong. In Qur'an 2:241, the Shariʿah used *ʿurf* as the foundation for setting the amount of alimony to be provided to divorcees as long as the custom was practiced and reasonable. In the Hadith, the maxim of custom was the foundation in what Ibn Masʿud narrated, "Whatever the Muslim saw as good is [considered] good by God, and whatever the Muslim saw as evil is evil according to God."[47]

A contemporary challenge to bioethics and Shariʿah is evident in the cultural pressure from families on physicians not to disclose a poor diagnosis to the patient and other family members. In other extreme cases, the patient is not told s/he is terminal and expiring out of fear of "upsetting" the patient. A study published in the *Journal of Medical Ethics* found that 36% of surveyed Muslim countries lacked codes in regards to disclosing terminal conditions to patients, 50% allowed concealment, while only 28% allowed disclosure. On the other hand, only one country mandated disclosure and one prohibited disclosure. Five codes were silent regarding informing the family, four allowed disclosure and five mandated/recommended disclosure. The Islamic Organization for Medical Sciences code was silent on both issues.[48] Non-disclosure is professionally and religiously unethical. A Muslim patient might attain salvation when affirming the creed of Islam at the last moments of life. In addition, patients have rights and duties that must be addressed prior to their death, and concealment at this stage of someone's life runs contrary to the *maqāṣid* of Islam. Finally, reflecting on one's life and death is a gift that may result in reconciliation and mending of relationships.

The authoritativeness of customs stems from their being widely carried out by a group of people or the community at large, and demonstrated through actions or abstinence, especially when the revealed texts of enacted laws are silent or absent. They must be acceptable to people of sound nature, with general or universal acceptance by a country or a particular generation. There are conditions that limit the scope of the legal maxim of customs. The agreed-upon practices or customs must not contradict a revealed text, they must be already practiced by society, and they must already have been in practice before the issue in questions arises.

All these legal maxims were derived from revealed sources or from induction for several purposes. The two most important goals are the removal of harm and the maximization of benefit. The removal of harm has been designated as a top priority and contains clauses for the prevention of harm prior to its occurrence, the minimizing of the degree of harm while it is happening, and the elimination of harm in the future. Maximizing benefit is a second priority where benefits are divided into categories based on the number of people benefiting from them and the means adopted to reach such benefits. There are five levels of benefit-driven actions, classified as necessity (*ḍarūrah*), need (*ḥājah*), benefit (*manfaʿah*), adornment (*zīnah*), and curiosity (*fuḍūl*).[49] As a result, Muslim ethics initially depends on Islamic theology and Islamic law for their determination. Similarly, Islamic ethics, and its sub-fields concerned with the ethics of war, commerce, or marital life, will continue to rely on Shariʿah and its sources for establishing ethical norms and judgements.

Impact of *Qawāʿid*

Faith in action is a divine command and an obligation that continuously appears in the Qur'an. Declaring faith and emulating the Prophet Muhammad have been organically connected and are labeled a "reciprocated act of love." Qur'an 3:31 states, "If you love God, follow me, [and] God will love you and forgive you your sins; God is Much-Forgiving and a dispenser of grace." Following the

Qur'an while neglecting the Sunnah is blameworthy, therefore, while fulfilling the command is rewarded and loved.

A spiritual care application of the purposes of the legal maxims begins with examining what it means to, and what is the process for, removing corruption (*mafsadah*), easing difficulty (mashaqqah), removing harm (*ḍarar*), and maximizing benefits (*maṣlaḥah*) in healthcare. The legal maxims might be helpful to a chaplain in determining what spiritual care services to provide, discerning what one ought to do or refrain from in response to a bioethics question, or taking an action to fulfill the immediate needs of a patient. The deployment of spiritual tools made available by the legal sources might help remove any intrinsic or extrinsic barriers to spiritual wellness, help patients preserve their religion (*ḥifẓ al-dīn*), or maximize benefits that may yield them success in this life and the hereafter.

The ethics of spiritual care lies in the fulfillment of the provider's obligation to advocate for the basic interests of patients such as offering competent healthcare, supporting the fulfillment of worship needs, or providing compassionate care and comfort at the end of life. However, the understanding of what is legal and ethical is not always clear. Robert Hefner suggests that hermeneutical understanding changes depending on the environment, time and location, despite the authenticity and authoritativeness of the Islamic sources:

> Muslim ethical understandings vary because the achievement of those understandings is contingent and conjectural. Ethical understanding is not hermetically sealed from the world but rather emerges from the efforts of real human actors who engage Islamic traditions even as they are involved in other life projects and influenced by other ethical norms. As a result, Muslims' understanding of sharia and ethics can change over time and can differ from and contradict those of other believers.[50]

The relationship between ethics and law might be seen as a matter of ethics being derived from legal theory, an opinion that is not supported by all scholars. However, what is the most significant element in the relationship between ethics and law? According to Tariq Ramadan, the priority for living an ethical life consistent with

Shariʿah is not merely a matter of conformity to a fixed and finished body of legal rules (*aḥkām*). The discernment of what is good requires the believers to also become knowledgeable of the higher purposes and aims of the Shariʿah. In addition, Ramadan suggests the development of empirical knowledge about society and nature is required to solve ethical problems in an empirically effective manner consistent with the full truth of the divine message.[51]

Islamic Ethics and Healthcare

The ethical challenges and practices of various settings make it necessary for spiritual care providers to gain knowledge of legally and ethically permissible and prohibited acts in healthcare. Chaplains and faith leaders, especially those who visit patients of a different faith or non-practicing patients, are expected to draw ethical, religious, and professional boundaries when visiting patients. They need to understand how the ethics of care is shaped by the legal sources, and vice versa. For example, the sacrament of anointing a Catholic patient can bring comfort to patients knowing they might achieve salvation. A Muslim chaplain is expected to understand the significance of such rituals and draw boundaries that prohibit a Muslim chaplain from anointing a Catholic patient.

Islamic ethics and especially biomedical ethics are of interest to physicians, academics, religious leaders, patients, and all those concerned with medical policies. One of the major challenges facing Muslims, especially in the United States, is access to legal and ethical resources to guide patients, family members, and medical professionals on bioethical decisions related to care for hospitalized Muslim patients. Lay Muslim patients and family members are often confronted with the need for an opinion on whether a medical procedure remains within the guidelines of Shariʿah. A devout Muslim may seek assurances from Muslim physicians and religious leaders, or search for fatwas to be assured the course of treatment does not violate Islamic teachings. The quest for an Islamic bioethics perspective often exposes layers of crisis experienced in a healthcare setting. Patients, families and healthcare professionals often encounter a shortage of bioethical material, a lack of scholarly published or peer-reviewed material, or a scarcity of trained religious leaders and scholars in the discipline of ethics. Furthermore, there is a crisis of authority: Muslim chaplains who often provide Islamic bioethics opinions are not trained as jurists, yet their recommendations profoundly influence patients and impact patients' quality of life or life expectancy.

The decision as to what is permissible in Islamic bioethics, and in decisions on a course of treatment, follows the process of reaching juristic opinions (fatwas). A jurist (mufti), in response to a legal or ethical question, searches in the sources of Shariʿah in preparation for issuing a fatwa. Bioethics cases are often considered in end-of-life care where Muslims and physicians discuss continuation of treatment, withdrawal, or downgrading of care. It is important to note that fatwas remain non-binding opinions, and that anyone can seek a second opinion. Nonetheless, the tradition of issuing juristic opinions is legally mandatory and is considered a collective responsibility (*farḍ kifāyah*), and in certain cases an individual duty (*farḍ ʿayn*) that a jurist must fulfill just like the obligation to establish the prayers.[52] Muslims also face the challenge of being divided politically and religiously. Scholars and lay Muslims may be classified as liberal, conservative, fundamentalist, or modern. This diversity creates room for "fatwa shopping," in which patients search for interpretations and understandings that support their philosophies or ideologies. In the course of my work as a healthcare chaplain, I witnessed numerous people who resorted to relatives, colleagues, and in some cases, religious leaders in local congregations to help them decide on bioethical cases:

> A devout Muslim couple recently welcomed their newborn daughter who was born at 34-week gestation. Upon delivery, the baby was in distress and gasping for air. The team made the decision to incubate the infant. Upon examining the newborn, it was determined the baby had short limbs. A geneticist and a genetic counselor examined the baby and decided the baby had a terminal diagnosis with a life expectancy of two months. The baby was diagnosed with a lethal genetic form of dysplasia, a genetic disorder that left the baby with short limbs and underdeveloped lungs. A

neonatologist treated the lungs for four days without success. The baby was unable to breathe independently. The baby was receiving fluids and the team was considering whether feeding was medically needed. The distressed parents were in shock and unable to decide whether to keep their child on the ventilator or seek additional invasive treatments to stabilize the newborn. The certainty of the diagnosis left the baby without any chance of recovery. The brain was not functioning and further treatment would subject the newborn to procedures that were unnecessary and would cause pain but yield no benefits. Would the removal of the breathing tube be justified per Shariʿah guidelines?

I encountered the above case recently, and it represents a manifestation of the challenges mentioned above. The couple sought support from a local Imam who had no official training in bioethics. The Imam advised the couple against removing the breathing tube. When I met with the couple as a chaplain, on the referral of the treatment team, the couple simply wanted to know what the Islamic legal and ethical guidelines were. I asked the attending pediatrician and the neonatologist to join me as I met with the couple. The physicians took their time to answer the couple's questions, especially about the certainty of the terminal condition as well as the health of the brain. The couple asked for additional time to decide. How was I to help the family? The terminal diagnosis was key in the discussion. First of all, I shared with the couple that the goal of Islam is to preserve the quality of life, not the longevity. Hence, the decision of the medical team to place the infant on a "Do Not Resuscitate" order was appropriate. Second, preserving the resources (*ḥifẓ al-māl*) allowed for downgrading or withholding treatment when the outcome of the treatment was futile. Instead of extubating the patient, I asked the neonatologist if it was appropriate to experiment whether the infant could breathe without support. The subspecialist agreed and observed the child. The baby breathed without support, with the exception of a few puffs of air, for 36 hours. At that point, I endorsed the medical opinion in favor of removing the breathing support and keeping the DNR order in place should the baby lapse later. The terminally ill patient was later discharged home and placed under the care of a pediatric palliative care physician.

The Ethical Discourse

The foundation of Islamic ethics is the principles, duties and rights of Islamic law, as well as the embodiment of virtues and the noble moral traits (*makārim al-akhlāq*), which are the yardstick by which every public benefit and each purpose of the *maqāṣid* is evaluated and judged. What is Islamic about ethics? The Islamic nature and identity of ethics stem from the universal framework of virtues and values that are derived from the revealed sources of the Qur'an and Sunnah, the rich tradition of the Prophet Muhammad, scholarly interpretations and hermeneutics of the revealed sources, and the biography of the Prophet. The process of discerning Islamic ethics depends on the ethical norms and the methods that scholars utilize based on logic, analogy and hermeneutics. The process of discerning what is ethical begins with discernment of what is legal. In addition, the process includes empowerment of the human agency to understand what ought to happen, which is exercised by scholars deploying tools for analogical reasoning or reaching for scholarly consensus. Ethical standards and means are avenues for theological discussions; topics such as the will of God and human actions, and reflections on the responsibility of humans to fulfill the divine plan for humanity, must be addressed as part of the ethics of healthcare and chaplaincy.

The existence of ethical concerns requires reaching various levels of certainty in efforts to discern right from wrong. The level of certainty varies based on the sources of knowledge and the processes used to reach it. There is textual certainty (*al-adillah al-samʿiyyah*) in which knowledge is reached through a search in the revealed texts and the application of scholarly hermeneutics. The Qur'an illustrates a level of firm authenticity (*qaṭʿiyyat al-thubūt*) where knowledge is provided by revelation and there is no room for scholarly opinions or disagreements. For example, Qur'an 112:1 states "God is one." The verse doesn't support different interpretations that contradict the oneness of God, and any such attempts will face rejection. Qur'anic verses, however, are not all the same in their level of revealed certainty. Certainty can also be reached intellectually (*al-dalālah al-*

ʿaqliyah). Such knowledge accommodates various interpretations and opinions based on human reasoning. In most bioethical cases, scholars aim to achieve the predominant likelihood of certainty (*ghalabat al-ẓann*), a level of near-certainty. In medical practices, a physician embarks on various differentials and tests to achieve a level of certainty in regards to the diagnosis, the effectiveness of the treatment, and the removal of harms and the maximization of benefits. In addition, the level of certainty impacts the *maqāṣid* considerations, which in turn may affect the course of treatment or be impacted by it.

The challenges faced by the couple with a newborn child mentioned above are related to the viability of human life, an issue that is foundational to medical ethics. Islamic medical ethics is organically connected to a wide spectrum of ethical teachings in the Qur'an and the Sunnah. Shariʿah is established based on the careful and flexible consideration of public benefit in all affairs, in both worship (*ʿibādāt*) and civic affairs (*muʿāmalāt*). The purpose of Islamic ethics is to lead ultimately to success and salvation, not only based on individual and communal benefit, but also on the prevention of harms within the ethical and legal boundaries of Shariʿah. Among the values and virtues to be considered are respect, compassion and the protection of the physical, mental and spiritual dimensions of human beings so as to remain in constant worship of God.

Compassion is a virtue connected to the parents' explicit deontological responsibility to treat their newborn with love and mercy. Similarly, tender care and respect is the mantra of how the interdisciplinary medical team should treat the parents and the newborn. The significance of compassion was elevated in the Hadith as compassion was assigned a legal value, and it was made a condition for the attainment of faith in a Hadith Qudsi: "None of you [truly] believes until he loves to have befall his brother what he loves for himself."[53] In addition, Islamic bioethics requires moderation, justice and balance in relations among people. The Qur'an has listed numerous references to moderation, among them the call to warn against following one's whims and desires.[54] The Qur'an commanded moderation in matters of faith and worship (*ʿibādāt*), and illustrated moderation as the divine plan for humanity.[55] Therefore, people were admonished against extremism in faith,[56] and the learned was described as the one who is most knowledgeable, most just, and most aware that nothing can come about unless the Almighty so wills. Moderation might be as simple as not insisting on enduring hardship when there are legal and ethical avenues for seeking ease. The utilization of the juristic tool of *rukhṣah* is a moderate approach to faith, while intentionally enduring hardship is a form of extremism.

Each case deserves careful examination and application of the legal maxims of intention, harm, hardship, and custom. What is the *ʿurf* that is customary and practiced among medical professionals regarding terminally ill patients for whom further invasive treatment will yield pain with no benefits? The admission of custom might not be accepted by all, and disagreement has arisen regarding the variations of customs according to their localities, the soundness of customary practices, and the cultural environment where they occur. Nonetheless, the legal maxim of custom emphasizes the importance of *ʿurf* and the actual societal conditions in the conduct of innovative legal determinations (ijtihad). In the above case, the parents are of Yemeni Sunni background, and supporting them required considering resources provided by scholars trained in the diverse Islamic legal schools (*madhhab*) and being aware of the differences (*ikhtilāf*). In the end, the course of action was impacted by the level of certainty expressed by physicians that the condition of the baby was terminal.

Conclusion

The innermost purpose of the divine revelation is to empower individuals to differentiate between right and wrong. To accomplish this task, God has endowed humans with the innate ability to be oriented towards what is right. The responsibility of humans is to develop their consciences in the ways God guides them, through knowledge and wisdom, to navigate the earthly environment. The collective responsibility of humans is to guide fellow humans to maintain a healthy human-divine relationship and to achieve individual and social harmony and happiness, moral and spiritual growth, and divine guidance. The best ways to cultivate these relationships may be discovered through several legal principles, fictions, and practices which break out of the strict mold of classical legal theory in order to accommodate the demands of justice and public interest.

God intended for humanity relief from hardship, and affirmed this in the revealed Qur'an and Hadith. The Prophet demonstrated leniency, as when he was offered a choice, he opted for the easier option, not imposing hardship in matters of worship, as long as his choice was free of any sin.

With the goal of promoting *maṣlaḥah*, scholars' aim is to identify matters that impose hardship and impact the realization of certain needs (*ḍarūriyyāt*). The existence of hardship calls for the use of various tools, including the resort to leniency (*rukhṣah*), to remove hardship in order to achieve necessities. Scholars have highlighted conditions for the utilization of *rukhṣah*, including the demonstration of a need (*ḥājah*), the existence of a hardship (*mashaqqah*), and its impact on an essential need (*ḍarūrah*).

Universal values and virtues are divine qualities that humans strive for in how they conduct themselves and how they treat others with love and mercy. Compassion, for example, was assigned a legal value and became a pre-requisite for attaining faith. This message was captured in a Hadith Qudsi included by Jamal al-Din Zarabozo in the *Commentary of the Forty Hadith*. The tradition of connecting altruism to faith was brought forth in the Hadith that says "none will truly believe until they love for others what they love for themselves."

God addressed societal and individual change, and encouraged reform that must first take place internally, and then within the environment, in order for individuals to adapt. However, the Qur'an frowned upon personal efforts to impose changes on the unchangeable principles of Shariʿah, and considered such attempts a disruption to the ethical and legal foundation and the principles of Shariʿah. Any changes to the foundation of Shariʿah to accommodate temporal needs will be rejected and labeled as compelling or coercing (*taṭwīʿ al-sharīʿah*). Islamic ethics was highlighted including the subdisciplines of ethics such as the science of morals (*akhlāq*), the science of virtue (*faḍīlah*), and Islamic biomedical ethics (*akhlāqiyāt ṭibiyyah islāmiyyah*). Shariʿah has illustrated the basics of legal and moral behavior and character within the framework of belief in absolute monotheism, in which God is knowledgeable and the source of all knowledge. Individuals would be judged based on their obedience or disobedience to the divine commands. The beginnings of ethics, similar to law, are rooted in the primary sources of Islam, the Qur'an and the Sunnah. George Hourani mentioned in *Reason and Tradition in Islamic Ethics* that ethics informs the rules of law and morality. The Qur'an has identified ethics in terms of attributes, character traits, and personal behavior. There are several personal attributes that God either loves or dislikes. The Qur'an listed that God dislikes aggression and corruption, and He loves those who act righteously, those whose hearts are purified, and those who are repentant. Hence, what is ethical and good must begin with being legally permissible. The roots of ethics are legal.

The theory of *maqāṣid* has provided a set of legal and ethical parameters for discerning what is legally good and ethically permissible. The legal and ethical standards of *maqāṣid* protect the five basic essentials and move towards adopting a Shariʿah-oriented policy (*siyāsat al-sharīʿah*) that would bring people closer to beneficence (*ṣalāḥ*) and away from corruption (*fasād*). Ibn al-Qayyim states that the ethos of Shariʿah is founded upon wisdom, the welfare of God's servants in this life and the afterlife, justice, mercy, benefit, and wisdom. Hence, abandoning justice for tyranny, mercy for cruelty, benefit for corruption, and wisdom for foolishness is not a part of Shariʿah.

The normative laws of Shariʿah have informed people's identity and practice and have provided ethical guidance. Muslim scholars, past and contemporary, have navigated the Islamic texts and provided ethical answers and juristic opinions. However, are the legal and the ethical rulings (*aḥkām*) in the primary textual sources set in stone, non-negotiable, or impossible to redefine? If so, people would only need the texts to discern what is Islamically good and how one should act in any given context. On the contrary, knowledge in not restricted, and ethical norms do not reside solely in the Islamic texts.

The universality of ethics is evident in other cultures, scriptures, and standards, so that no one religious community can claim a monopoly on ethics.

The study of ethics and law does not aim to depart from Shariʿah or abandon the texts. On the contrary, the aim is to create an environment to invite a conversation across all the disciplines that inform Islamic ethics, including moral theology, sociology, and anthropology, in order to reflect on the scholarly heritage and reexamine it. More importantly, the process can create opportunities for critical engagement with the intellectual tradition and scholarly authorities, and can provide conceptual clarity as to what constitutes ethics and how Islamic ethics is distinctive from others ethical theories.

Imam al-Ḥaramayn al-Juwaynī contributed to the development of *maqāṣid al-sharīʿah* and helped identify a scale by which one could measure the ethical and legal obligation of actions using variables such as benefit, harm, permissibility, rewards, and punishments. The individual's responsibility to adhere to divine commands was coded based on the degree of obligation to engage in an action or refrain from it. Actions were classified as obligatory (*farḍ* or *wājib*), recommended (*mandūb*), permitted (*mubāḥ*), reprehensible (*makrūh*), prohibited (*ḥarām*), authentic (*ṣaḥīḥ*), and negated (*bāṭil*), and these categories were defined in terms of the reward or punishment that would result for each action or inaction. The Qur'an states that God will reward those individuals who fulfill their obligatory and recommended acts, and will punish whoever neglects the obligatory acts. In addition, those who abstain from reprehensible and prohibited acts will be rewarded; those who carry out prohibited acts will be punished. Individuals may engage in permitted acts, and while the legality of actions may appear neutral and left to the discretion of the individual, God will allow individuals to act and will judge each according to his or her intentions, the harms that were removed, or the benefits that were produced.

REFERENCES

Abd-Allah, Umar F., 'Theological Dimensions of Islamic Law', in *The Cambridge Companion to Classical Islamic Theology* (Cambridge: Cambridge University Press, 2008), pp.237-57.

Abdulhameed, Hunida E., Muhammad M. Hammami, and Elbushra A. Hameed Mohamed, 'Disclosure of Terminal Illness to Patients and Families: Diversity of Governing Codes in 14 Islamic Countries', *Journal of Medical Ethics* 37 (2011), pp. 472–75.

Abou El Fadl, Khaled, *Reasoning with God: Reclaiming Sharīʿah in the Modern Age* (Lanham, MD: Rowman & Littlefield, 2014).

Abou El Fadl, Khaled, *Speaking in God's Name: Islamic Law, Authority and Women* (Oxford: Oneworld Publications, 2001).

Abu Shamsieh, Kamal, 'Barriers to Spiritual Care among Muslim Patients', Master's thesis, Hartford Seminary, 2012.

Abu Zahra, Muhammad, *The Four Imams: Their Lives, Works and their Schools of Thought* (London: Dar Al Taqwa, 2005).

Ahmad, Khurshid, and Khurram Murad, *Sayyid Abul A'la Mawdudi: The Islamic Way of Life* (London: U.K.I.M. Dawah Centre, 2012). Accessed October 21, 2015, https://ia601304.us.archive.org/29/items/MaulanaMaududi IslamicWay OfLife/Maulana_Maududi_Islamic_way_of_Life.pdf.

al-ʿAlim, Yusuf Hamid, *al-Maqāṣid al-ʿĀmmah lil-Sharīʿah al-Islāmiyyah* (Herndon: International Institute of Islamic Thought, 1991).

Al-Alwani, Jabir Taha, 'Towards a Fiqh for Minorities: Some Reflections', in *Muslims' Place in the American Public Square.* (Ed.), Zahid Bukhari, Sulayman Nyang, Mumtaz Ahmad, and John Esposito (Oxford: Rowman & Littlefield, 2004), pp.1-35.

Attiya, Gamal Eldin, *Towards Realization of the Higher Intents of Islamic Law* (Herndon: International Institute of Islamic Thought, 2007).

Auda, Jasser, *Maqasid al-Shariah as Philosophy of Islamic Law* (Herndon: International Institute of Islamic Thought, 2008).

Auda, Jasser, *Fiqh al-Maqāṣid* (Herndon: International Institute of Islamic Thought, 2008).

Fakhry, Majid, *Ethical Theories in Islam* (Leiden: Brill, 1997).

al-Fāsī, ʿAllāl, *Maqāṣid al-Sharīʿah al-Islāmiyyah wa Makārimuhā*, 5th edn. (Rabat: Dār al-Gharb al-Islāmī, 1993).

al-Ghazālī, Abū Ḥāmid, *Iḥyā' ʿUlūm al-Dīn*, vol.3. Accessed online May 26, 2014, http://www.al-mostafa.info/data/arabic/depot3/gap.php?file=i003417.pdf.

Hefner, Robert W., *Sharia Law and Modern Muslim Ethics* (Bloomington: Indiana University Press, 2016).

Hourani, George, *Reason and Tradition in Islamic Ethics* (Cambridge: Cambridge University Press, 1985).

Ibn ʿAshur, Muhammad al-Tahir, *Maqāṣid al-Sharīʿah al-Islāmiyyah* (Beirut: Dār al-Kitāb al-Lubnānī, 2011).

Ibn ʿAshur, Muhammad al-Tahir, *Treatise on Maqāṣid al-Sharīʿah*, trans. Mohamed El-Tahir El-Mesawi (Herndon: International Institute of Islamic Thought, 2006).

Ibn Ḥanbal, Aḥmad, *Ṣifat al-Fatwā wa al-Mustaftī* (Damascus: Islamic Office Publications, 1960).

Ibn al-Mulaqqin, *Tuḥfat al-Muḥtāj ilā Adillat al-Minhāj*, vol.1. (Makkah: Dār Ḥirā', 1986).

Ibn al-Najjār, Muḥammad, *Sharḥ al-Kawkab al-Munīr*, vol.4. (Saudi Arabia: Ministry of Islamic Affairs).

Ibn Qayyim al-Jawziyyah, *Iʿlām al-Muwaqqiʿīn* (Riyadh: Dār Ibn al-Jawzī, 2002).

IslamicCity, Qur'an Notes: Online commentary. Accessed November 1, 2016, http://www.islamicity.org/Qur'ansearch/shownote.asp?chap=45&note=18.

al-Juwaynī, ʿAbd al-Malik, *al-Waraqāt* (Riyadh: Riyadh University Manuscript, 1979). Accessed September 24, 2015, http://www.almostafa.info/data/arabic/depot/ gap.php?file=m010406.pdf.

Kamali, Muhammad Hashim, *The Dignity of Man: An Islamic Perspective* (Selangor: Ilmiah Publishers, 2002).

Kamali, Muhammad Hashim, *Moderation and Balance in Islam: The Qur'anic Principle of Wasatiyyah* (Kuala Lumpur: International Institute of Advanced Islamic Studies, 2010).

Kamali, Muhammad Hashim, *Sharīʿah Law: An Introduction* (Oxford: Oneworld Publications, 2008).

Lings, Martin, *Muhammad: His Life based on the Earliest Sources* (Rochester: Inner Tradition International, 1983).

Majallat al-Aḥkām al-ʿAdliyyah. Accessed November 12, 2016, http://www.moj.ps /images/majallatalhkam.pdf.

Mattson, Ingrid, *The Story of the Qur'an: Its History and Place in Muslim Life* (Malden: Blackwell Publishing, 2009).

Mawdudi, Sayyid Abul A'la, *The Islamic Way of Life* (London: Australian Islamic Library, 2012).

Ministry of Islamic Trust and Religious Affairs, *al-Mawsūʿa al-Fiqhiyyah*, vol.22. (Kuwait: Salasel, 1993).

al-Najjār, ʿAbd al-Majīd, 'al-Manḥā al-Taṭbīqī fī Maqāṣid Ibn ʿĀshūr', in *Sheikh Muhammad Tahir Ibn ʿAshur: Reform and Revival Issues in Contemporary Islamic Thought*. (Ed.), Fathi Hasan Makkawi (Herndon: International Islamic Institute of Thought, 2011), pp.219-45.

Nimer, Mohamed, *The North American Muslim Resource Guide* (New York: Routledge, 2002).

Al-Qaradawi, Yusuf, *The Lawful and the Prohibited in Islam* (New Delhi: Al-Minar Publishers, 1960).

Al-Raysuni, Ahmed, *Imam al-Shatibi's Theory of the Higher Objectives and Intents of Islamic Law* (Herndon: International Institute of Islamic Thought, 2005).

Repko, Allen, *Interdisciplinary Studies: Process and Theory*, 2nd edn. (Los Angeles: Sage Publications, 2012).

Sachedina, Abdulaziz, *Islamic Biomedical Ethics* (Oxford: Oxford University Press, 2009).

Stelzer, Stefen A., *'Ethics', in Classical Islamic Theology*. (Ed.), Tim Winter (Cambridge: Cambridge University Press, 2008), pp.161-79.

al-Tabrīzī, Muḥammad ʿAbd Allāh al-Khaṭīb, *Mishkāt al-Maṣabīḥ*. (Ed.), M.N. Albānī, 2nd edn. (Beirut: Dār al-Maʿrifah, 1400 AH / 1980).

al-Tabrīzī, Muḥammad ʿAbd Allāh al-Khaṭīb, *Mirqāt al-Mafātīḥ*, vol.9. (Beirut: Dār al-Kutub al-ʿIlmiyyah, 2001).

Watt, W. Montgomery, *The Faith and Practice of Al-Ghazālī* (Lahore: Ashraf Printing Press, 1963).

Zarabozo, Jamaal al-Din, *Commentary on the Forty Hadith of Al-Nawawi*, vol.1. (Denver: Dar al-Basheer, 2008).

al-Zarqā', Muṣṭafā Aḥmad, *al-Madkhal al-Fiqhī al-ʿĀmm*, vol.1. (Damascus: Dār al-Qalam, 2004).

al-Zuhaylī, Muḥammad Muṣṭafā, *al-Qawāʿid al-Fiqhiyyah wa Taṭbīqātuhā fī al-Madhāhib al-Arbaʿah*, vol.1. (Damascus: Dār al-Fikr, 2006).

NOTES

1. Umar F. Abd-Allah, 'Theological Dimensions of Islamic Law', in *The Cambridge Companion to Classical Islamic Theology* (Cambridge: Cambridge University Press, 2008), p.249.
2. Muhammad al-Tahir Ibn ʿAshur, *Maqāṣid al-Sharīʿah al-Islāmiyyah* (Beirut: Dār al-Kitāb al-Lubnānī, 2011), p.165.
3. Ibid, p.218.
4. Khaled Abou El Fadl, *Speaking in God's Name* (Oxford: Oneworld Publications, 2001), p.100.
5. George Hourani, *Reason & Tradition in Islamic Ethics* (Cambridge: Cambridge University Press, 1985), p.62.
6. Mustafa Ahmad al-Zarqa, *al-Madkhal al-Fiqhī al-ʿĀmm* (Damascus: Dār al-Qalam, 2004), vol.1, p.48.
7. Mohammad H. Kamali, *Shariʿah Law: An Introduction* (Oxford: Oneworld, 2008), p.19.
8. Khaled Abou El Fadl, *Reasoning with God: Reclaiming Shariʿah in the Modern Age* (Lanham, MD: Rowman & Littlefield, 2014), p. xxxii.

9. Gamal Eldin Attiya, *Towards Realization of the Higher Intents of Islamic Law* (Herndon: International Institute of Islamic Thought, 2007), p.14.
10. Abou El Fadl, *Speaking in God's Name*, p.xxxiv.
11. Kamali, *Shariʿah Law*, p.41.
12. Jasser Auda, *Maqasid al-Shariah as Philosophy of Islamic Law* (Herndon: International Institute of Islamic Thought, 2008), p.xxiii.
13. Qur'an 5:48.
14. Al-Zarqa, *al-Madkhal al-Fiqhī al-ʿĀmm*, p.47.
15. IslamicCity, Qur'an Notes, online commentary, http://www.islamicity.org/Qur'ansearch/shownote.asp?chap=45&note=18, accessed November 1, 2016.
16. Abou El Fadl, *Reasoning with God*, p.296.
17. Ahmed al-Raysuni, *Imam al-Shatibi's Theory of the Higher Objectives and Intents of Islamic Law* (Herndon: International Institute of Islamic Thought, 2005), p.xxii.
18. Kamali, *Shariʿah Law*, p.43.
19. Ibn ʿAshur, *Maqāṣid al-Sharīʿah*, p.91.
20. ʿAllāl al-Fāsī, *Maqāṣid al-Sharīʿah al-Islāmiyyah wa Makārimuhā*, 5th edn. (Rabat: Dār al-Gharb al-Islāmī, 1993), p.1.
21. Abou El Fadl, *Reasoning with God*, p.298.
22. Kamali, *Shariʿah Law*, p.125.
23. Muhammad al-Tahir Ibn ʿAshur, *Treatise on Maqāṣid al-Sharīʿah*, trans. Mohamed El-Tahir El-Mesawi (Herndon: International Institute of Islamic Thought, 2006), p.118.
24. Abū Ḥāmid al-Ghazālī, *Iḥyā' ʿUlūm al-Dīn*, vol.3, http://www.al-mostafa.info/data/arabic/depot3/gap.php?file=i003417.pdf, accessed May 26, 2014.
25. Allen Repko, *Interdisciplinary Studies: Process and Theory*, 2nd edn. (Los Angeles: Sage Publications, 2012), p.16.
26. Hourani, *Reason & Tradition*, p.1.
27. Qur'an 68:4.
28. Muḥammad al-Tabrīzī, *Mirqāt al-Mafātīḥ* (Beirut: Dār al-Kutub al-ʿIlmiyyah, 2001), vol.9, p.274, hadith no. 50789.
29. Qur'an 3:110.
30. Qur'an 2:173.
31. Kamali, *Shariʿah Law*, p.145.
32. *Majallat al-Aḥkām al-ʿAdliyyah*, article 2, http://www.moj.ps/images/majallatalhkam.pdf, accessed November 12, 2016.
33. Jamaal al-Din Zarabozo, *Commentary on the Forty Hadith of Al-Nawawi* (Denver: Dar al-Basheer, 2008), vol.1, p.91.
34. *Majallat al-Aḥkām al-ʿAdliyyah*, article 20.
35. Qur'an 5:32.
36. *Majallat al-Aḥkām al-ʿAdliyyah*, article 2.
37. Hadith no.1 in *Al-Nawawī's Forty Hadith*.

38. Qur'an 33:5.
39. *Majallat al-Aḥkām al-ʿAdliyyah*, article 17.
40. Qur'an 2:286.
41. Ibn al-Mulaqqin, *Tuḥfat al-Muḥtāj ilā Adillat al-Minhāj* (Makkah: Dār Ḥirā', 1986), vol.1, p.478.
42. Ministry of Islamic Trust and Religious Affairs, *al-Mawsūʿa al-Fiqhiyyah* (Kuwait: Salasel, 1993), vol.22, p.284.
43. *Majallat al-Aḥkām al-ʿAdliyyah*, article 4.
44. Zarabozo, *Commentary on the Forty Hadith*, p.375.
45. *Majallat al-Aḥkām al-ʿAdliyyah*, article 36.
46. Muhammad Ibn al-Najjar, *Sharḥ al-Kawkab al-Munīr* (Saudi Arabia: Ministry of Islamic Affairs), vol.4, p.449.
47. Muḥammad Muṣṭafā al-Zuḥaylī, *al-Qawāʿid al-Fiqhiyyah wa Taṭbīqātuhā fī al-Madhāhib al-Arbaʿah* (Damascus: Dār al-Fikr, 2006), vol.1, p.298.
48. Hunida E. Abdulhameed, Muhammad M. Hammami, and Elbushra A. Hameed Mohamed, 'Disclosure of Terminal Illness to Patients and Families: Diversity of Governing Codes in 14 Islamic Countries', *Journal of Medical Ethics* 37 (2011), pp.472–75.
49. al-Zuhaylī, *al-Qawāʿid al-Fiqhiyyah*, vol.1, p.285.
50. Robert W. Hefner, *Sharia Law and Modern Muslim Ethics* (Bloomington: Indiana University Press, 2016), p.3.
51. Ibid., 15.
52. Aḥmad Ibn Ḥanbal, *Ṣifat al-Fatwā wa al-Mustaftī* (Damascus: Islamic Office Publications, 1960), p.6.
53. Zarabozo, *Commentary on the Forty Hadith*, p.493.
54. Qur'an 38:26.
55. Qur'an 2:143.
56. Qur'an 4:171.

5

The Developmentalist Ethic in Islamic Charity: *Fiqh al-Zakāh* and the Applied Ethics of Muslim Charity Organizations in India

Christopher B. Taylor

ABSTRACT: Islamic ritual charity (zakah) is an increasingly prominent feature of Muslim social practice in India. At the same time, an important shift is occurring in zakah, even as awareness of it expands to more and more discursive arenas. I describe the emerging framework as a "developmentalist ethic" in Islamic charity. This shift to zakah as "development" is not merely the result of Western influence and imported NGO practices replacing authentic Islamic rituals, nor is it to be seen as the kind of inexorable rationalization of religion that the eminent sociologist Max Weber once identified. This shift in zakah ethics is a result of the diversity of ethical concerns already contained within Islamic ritual prescriptions, rather than an attempt to disregard them.

Islamic scriptures teach that charity is best given in secret. The Prophet Muhammad exhorted almsgivers, "Give from your right hand so the left will not know," a popular saying repeated to me numerous times in my one and a half years of field research in Lucknow, India.[1] Yet one steamy midsummer day I found myself sitting among a dozen Muslim almsgivers in a mosque in a bazaar of the old city neighborhoods of Lucknow, observing charity that was not so secret. These men were donors to an Islamic charity organization, and they watched as wares purchased with their alms – sewing machines, rickshaws, street-vendor carts – were distributed to needy unemployed Muslims. Women in black veils and men wearing beards and Islamic skullcaps approached the director of the charity organization, a *madrasah*-educated preacher, as he called them forward. The donors themselves handed out the items, posing for a photograph while frozen in the act of passing sewing machines to bemused burqa-clad women. The next day, I saw the distribution event in the local newspaper. During my research the aging preacher's sons launched his Facebook Page, expanding the audience for these charity activities.

These gifts of Islamic charity were far from secret. They were given in public, alms-takers' names were called, they were photographed along with donors, and the event was written up in the local news and even broadcast on the Internet. This is a far cry from the "left hand not knowing," as Bukhari recorded the words of the Prophet Muhammad. Yet scholars of Islamic law and ordinary Muslims alike in India are lauding such new organizations for reviving the Islamic ritual of almsgiving (zakah) to address Muslim poverty, even when they depart from older practices.

Islamic ritual charity is an increasingly prominent feature of Muslim social practice in India. A recent study by the Pew Research Center found that more Muslims give zakah worldwide (76 percent) than perform daily ritual prayers.[2] While the researchers did not survey Muslims in India (stating, by way of explanation, that "political" permission was not granted), Islamic almsgiving is a growing topic in public discourse in India as well. In my 18 months of dissertation fieldwork in 2012 and 2013 in Lucknow, India, the large capital city of the north Indian state of Uttar Pradesh, I collected data on these Islamic charities. They are growing in size and number. Existing charities' budgets are expanding. New charities are being founded. Ordinary Muslims are increasingly discussing zakah, debating questions such as whether the Muslim population is giving at mandated rates or not, how to calculate zakah on new forms of property like stocks, where to give zakah so that it reaches legitimately needy recipients, and so forth.

At the same time, an important shift is also occurring in zakah, even as awareness of it expands to more and more discursive arenas. I describe the emerging framework as a "developmentalist ethic" in

Islamic charity. Zakah is traditionally given within networks of kinship and locality with a focus on the donor and his or her obligation to give, but today in north India it is becoming a focus of Muslim organizations' efforts to alleviate poverty and promote "development." This shift to zakah as "development" is not merely the result of Western influence and imported NGO practices replacing authentic Islamic rituals, nor is it to be seen as the kind of inexorable rationalization of religion that Max Weber once identified.[3] Rather, as this essay will show, this shift in zakah ethics is very much the result of Muslims' search for moral guidance from the Shariʿah, not an attempt to disregard it.

Everyday representations of Shariʿah as "Islamic law" cropped up in my numerous conversations with Muslims in Lucknow. However, my aim in this paper is to illustrate the flexibility of the Shariʿah and the diversity of interpretations, inscribed in fiqh, that scholars derive from it. Muslim and non-Muslim scholars alike increasingly are recognizing the Shariʿah for its remarkable internal diversity and adaptability to innumerable local and temporal contexts, in contrast to simplistic portrayals of Islamic law as a static legal "code" or claims about the closed "gates of ijtihad."[4] This paper shows that the diversity of ethical concerns embedded within the Shariʿah is particularly evident in discourses on zakah.

The first section of the paper discusses what I term the "purity ethic" in Islamic charity. This ethic is concerned primarily with the obligation of Muslims to give, focusing attention on zakah-givers and how they and their wealth are "purified," with correspondingly less focus on the recipients of zakah. The second section turns to a short case study of a new Islamic charity and its turn-of-the-21st-century practices.

This organized Islamic charity and its supporters adhere to what I term a "developmentalist ethic" in Islamic charity. My data center around two of the moral concerns that comprise this newly emerging orientation: work ethic and public institutionalization. These concerns are defined as developmentalist because they focus attention on the recipients of charity, how it is spent, and how zakah-takers utilize alms to "develop" themselves and to advance the ummah in

India. How are we to understand these two divergent sets of moral concerns motivating Islamic charity practices?

The purity ethic is clearly rooted in Islamic scriptural injunctions for Muslims to purify their wealth, and regards zakah as "worship" (Urdu: *ʿibādāt*) for the donor. Critics could potentially accuse the organized charities of simply disregarding the spiritual teachings of Shariʿah about giving zakah modestly and in secret. Is the institutionalization of Islamic charity resulting in a reduced role for Shariʿah and for the spiritual teachings of the *ʿulamā*? On the other hand, newly organized Islamic charities are focusing attention on zakah as a financial transaction (*muʿāmalāt*) and on the socioeconomic impact it has on recipients of charity, and their moral concerns are also rooted in scriptural teachings of Islam. Charity organizations' supporters justify their existence in light of the waste and inefficiency they see in popular practices of zakah, which are falling short of its role as a system for redistributing the wealth that is the "right" of the poor.

This paper demonstrates that the accusations of critics against organized charities are quite mild and trivial, and that the seeming divergence between the purity ethic and the developmentalist ethic in Islamic charitable giving actually points to the internal diversity and responsiveness of the Shariʿah to historical contexts. Utilizing ethnographic data, I show that Muslims in Lucknow often imagine zakah to be a clear and straightforward obligation in Islamic "law," but that when this prescription is applied in practice a diversity of moral concerns become evident. The *ʿulamā* and organized charities I observed are embracing Shariʿah legal and ethical norms in a way that selectively introduces new practices into zakah rituals, while representing the new organized practices as age-old injunctions from the Prophet Muhammad. By employing an anthropological approach to "ethics in practice," this paper argues that such change in a normative ethical system like *fiqh al-zakāh* is, ironically, the result of efforts to properly understand that very ethical system and preserve it as a sacred tradition.

The Purity Ethic

Ritual Obligation

The purity ethic is comprised of three main concerns focused on the zakah-giver – the simple obligation to give, the purification of the donor, and secrecy.

The simple obligation to give zakah is seen as a straightforward obligation for which no rationale need be sought (although scholarly rationales exist), given that zakah is a practice of financial purification and a requirement for all Muslims. Zafar Ahmed[5] was the clerk of a firearms store on one of the main roads of Lucknow's Aminabad bazaar. I interviewed him during a systematic survey of donors:

> Chris: Which of these is the most important reason you give alms?[6]
> Zafar: It's Allah's order [*hukum*]. That's why! In place of these three reasons you are asking me, you only need one. "Nothing" is the reason! Just follow the order. Who needs a reason?

Zafar articulated a sentiment I heard numerous times: almsgiving is not complicated, and Islamic law regarding alms is clear and authoritative. On another day, outside Lucknow's oldest mosque after prayers, a worshipper who had been curious to find I was a researcher exclaimed "Hold on. You're writing a book on zakah? Why?! What's there to say about alms?! You just give 100 rupees here, 500 rupees there, and it's done (*bas*)! That's it!" In a third instance, a friend who was both a *madrasah* graduate (*ʿālim*) and the holder of a Ph.D. frankly told me, "Your [Ph.D.] topic [of zakah] is an excellent one... But it's one month of work; that's all [*bas*]... Read in a book what is the system of zakah in Islam. Just write that down." For these three informants and many others, the Islamic teachings on zakah are themselves quite clear. In their view, Muslim preachers and scholars may convolute the issues, and ordinary Muslims may misunderstand (deliberately or out of ignorance) what is otherwise a clear order (*hukum*) of Allah, but the obligation itself is indisputable.

Is zakah such a clear and straightforward practice in Islamic law? The diversity of practices and beliefs that I describe in this paper will belie such a notion. Among many Muslims in Lucknow, however, zakah is imagined to be a simple and obligatory act.[7] Scriptures articulate this duty in the verse "[Oh Muhammad!] Out of their wealth take alms [Arabic: *ṣadaqah*] in order to purify them" (Qur'an 9:103), and in another verse "Whatever profits you may gain, assign one fifth to Allah, the Prophet, his relatives, and also orphans, the poor, and needy travelers" (8:41). This latter verse is interpreted by Twelver Shiʿites as the duty to give as alms one-fifth of profits, whereas for Sunnites, "profits" here has meant only the spoils of war or treasure. For Sunnite Muslims, 2.5%, or one-fortieth, is the amount that Muslim scholars have determined as the fixed rate on money for Muslims of sufficient means to pay in alms, based on a hadith that reads "on silver coins one-fourth of one-tenth [is due]."[8] The variation in rates for alms depends on one's sect and on what type of property is owned (e.g., money, crops, livestock), but these variations are irrelevant alongside my larger point: The clear-cut obligation to give alms in Islam has scriptural origins which (unlike in the other Abrahamic faiths of Judaism or Christianity) specify details of the rate and recipients, giving rise to a normative consensus about the obligation (*farḍ*, Urdu *farz*) of almsgiving upon Muslims.

The repetitive insistence on the obligation of zakah is one aspect of what I term the purity ethic in Islamic charitable giving. This ethic is an orientation comprised of three main moral concerns that focus attention on the giver of zakah, as the one who is obligated to give. The second and third concerns, respectively, are the notion of zakah as "purification" and teachings about giving zakah in secret.

Purification

The Arabic term for almsgiving (zakah, Urdu: *zakāt*), a verbal noun, means, among other things, "to purify." The Qur'an, in fact, switches between the two meanings "purification" and "alms", twice utilizing the word zakah in the sense of "purification" (18:81, 19:13) while employing it thirty other times to mean "alms." In another verse (9:103), the Qur'an does not use zakah to mean "alms" but orders Prophet Muhammad to collect charity (*ṣadaqah*) in order to "purify" (*tuzakkīhim*) Muslims, indicating that the need to purify themselves by almsgiving is an obligation. In this sense, ritual almsgiving and ritual washing have been considered parallel acts of purification. For example, Imam Shāfiʿī wrote extensively on the resemblance of zakah and the ablution (*wuḍū'*) required before prayer.[9]

While zakah is also, of course, a transaction between two people, the purification referred to here exclusively affects the donor. What of the impact of zakah upon those Muslims who are recipients? The Qur'an (9:60) does offer specific guidance, listing eight categories that scholars of fiqh have taken to be exclusively eligible for receiving charity if it is to be counted as zakah.[10] This list of eight categories of recipients is quite broad, employing two nearly synonymous words for those in financial need, "the poor" (*al-fuqarā'*) and "the needy" (*al-masākīn*), and anticipating that even wealthy people stranded on the road (*ibn al-sabīl*) and those who once had wealth but fell into debt (*al-ghārimīn*) may be in dire straits. During ethnographic research in Lucknow, I found that most Muslims considered the list of potential zakah recipients broad and expansive. Needy people were ubiquitous, in their view, and aiding them was straightforward. What concerned them most was that zakah was an obligation in Islamic "law", which must be met, and that they must give the stipulated percentages with the right intentions.

The most famous scholar to head the madrasah of Nadwat ul-ʿUlama in Lucknow, Abu Hasan Ali Nadwi, wrote in an instructional text that zakah "cleanses and purifies the soul (*nafs*) as well as the wealth."[11] This point was emphasized to me repeatedly during my time researching discourses on zakah at this madrasah, Lucknow's largest Sunni seminary and one of India's most well-known. In a class taught by a mufti at the *madrasah*, he instructed me and other students:

> Although it has a financial dimension [*māli pehlū*] as well... since you are transacting with another person, almsgiving is basically worship [*asl main ʿibādat hai*]... [If a Muslim does not give zakah] along with his wealth his soul will also be unclean because it is filled with such ingratitude and is so forgetful of [Allah's] favor.

His lecture emphasized that the spiritual aspect of zakah as worship is what takes precedence in the minds of many Muslims, while the reality of zakah as a financial transaction was less significant from a standpoint of Islamic ethical and religious instruction offered in the *madrasah*.

The intensity of the focus of *ʿulamāʾ* and their fiqh scholarship upon zakah as a purification ritual for the donor is evidenced as well by the fact that when scriptural teachings do address the poor, they do so as donors. Though the poor are often in a position to receive zakah from wealthier Muslims, the Qur'an and hadith (as well as Urdu texts based upon them) rarely address the poor as recipients of charity or comment on how zakah should be utilized by them. A hadith quoted in the well-known instructional manual of India's missionary "preaching society" Tablighi Jama'at states:

> Even if a date is given away as *ṣadaqah* (charity) out of the lawfully earned property, with sincerity of intention, Allah Taʿala grants increase in the recompense for it, till it becomes as large as the Mount Uhad.

This hadith is quoted more than once in this Urdu instructional manual, *Fazāʾil-i Aʾmāl*, widely read by South Asian Muslims in India and worldwide since its publication in the 1930s.[12] Throughout the same manual, Muslims are addressed consistently as donors of zakah, never as receivers or even as managers of zakah distribution. The above hadith clearly indicates that even the poor are to imagine themselves as potential charitable donors to those in need, "even if [only] a date is given." Other hadith, also recorded in the manual of Tablighi Jama'at, reinforce this theme: even a "smile" is considered charity, even "half a date" is charity, and when a servant gives charity from his master's goods (because he has nothing of his own to give) he too receives spiritual merit despite not being the owner of the gift.[13]

Secrecy

Another popularly known theme in Islamic teachings on zakah is that alms are to be given modestly, ideally in secret. All *madrasah* graduates and most other Muslims in Lucknow paraphrased (or recited from memory) familiar verses in the Qur'an which teach that religious charity is best given secretly and is invalidated by public comment, "reminders of generosity," or other verbal injuries to recipients' dignity. One Qur'anic verse (2:264) reads, "Oh Believers, cancel not your charity by reminders of your generosity, or by injury." Another verse (2:271) warns almsgivers, "If you disclose [acts of] charity, even so it is well, but if ye conceal them, and make them reach those [really] in need, that is best for you: It will remove from you some of your [stains of] evil."[14] One hadith was universally popular among Lucknow Muslims: "Give from your right hand so the left will not know." I heard this hadith recited to me more than any other. One of my neighbors, Uncle Husain, for example, replied this way when I asked about Hindu charity (*dan*):

> What is there to tell? ...The purpose of that is just so they can get their names on a stone at the *mandir* (temple). That's it. It's not right. Whereas, zakah you give from the right hand so the left won't know. And, you shouldn't feel that you will get something in return.

The ethics of secrecy surrounding almsgiving in Islam, he and some Muslims told me, is one of the key criteria that distinguishes zakah from Hindu and other non-Islamic charity.[15]

When previous social ties already existed, such as that between neighbors or family, preserving secrecy became more difficult but remained a strong concern for the sake of modesty. The Qur'an encourages giving to relatives and close neighbors (e.g. 4:36), and nearly all donors accordingly prioritized these recipients. Modesty in the form of anonymity was, of course, impossible. Donors had a variety of creative responses. "My mother is very clever when she gives her zakah to our neighbors who she knows are needy," a young Muslim friend of mine in Lucknow told me in an interview in English. His family was relatively well-off but lived on a street in old city Lucknow that is dotted with make-shift shanty homes. "She bunches up the rupee notes, clenches her fist, and sometime during the visit just waves her hand over her friend's purse and drops them in. Sometimes the other woman doesn't even notice! Or, more often, she just doesn't say anything and ignores it."

The possibility of hiding one's identity as a donor was also an attractive option. The director of one of the charity organizations in which I volunteered told me:

> Donors often come to us and want to fund a family member's education. But they don't want the family to know. So they give us the money and we approach the family and tell them only that 'someone' has told us you may need help. They usually accept. This happens all the time. Perhaps ten to fifteen of our students [out of over 300] I can think of are funded like that.

Using an intermediary in this way, particularly for large zakah payments which might bring shame upon recipient family members, was a strategy I heard of occasionally, and a growing number of charity organizations in Lucknow facilitated this practice.

In short, the bulk of Hanafite jurisprudence that I encountered in *madrasah* teachings and in popular discourse reinforces what I call a "purity ethic" in zakah, exhorting Muslims to give zakah as an obligation that purifies their wealth without shaming the recipient with public recognition of their poverty or the donor's surplus wealth. This "repaying without displaying" view of zakah is one that seeks to mitigate the shame of the recipient. The purity ethic in practice, ultimately, accomplishes an erasure of the recipient in Muslims' moral imagination of the almsgiving transaction. The donor and his or her purification becomes the ethical subject and focus of these teachings.

Historical Contexts for the Purity Ethic

How did these particular teachings comprising the purity ethic come to be so important in the north Indian Muslim imaginary? One key factor, I suggest, was the scriptural revivalism that swept colonial India, resulting in new *madrasahs* founded at Deoband, at Lucknow (the Nadwa *madrasah* in which I researched and studied), and elsewhere in north India.[16] One aspect of this revival was an emphasis on scriptures as the authoritative roots of Islam. A second aspect of this revival was the effort to individualize and internalize Islam in order to preserve it in a time of societal upheaval. With the loss of Muslim political rulers as defenders of the faith, ordinary Muslims now filled that role.

These two aspects led to ideas about charitable giving that focused on pietistic reform for the Muslims who kept the obligation of zakah: the donors. The constant repetition of didactic moral instruction aimed at how to give zakah resulted in the three intertwined concerns that I have called the purity ethic. Comparatively less instruction was focused on how to receive zakah, who should receive it, and in what ways zakah is best utilized after it is given. The intensity of the focus of *ʿulamāʾ* and their fiqh scholarship upon zakah as a purification ritual for the donor is heightened by the fact that when scriptural teachings do address the poor, they do so as donors who may offer charity even if it is merely a smile or half a date. This is unsurprising, considering that the primary role of the *ʿulamāʾ* is to offer guidance for Muslims' spiritual well-being, while their material well-being had historically been the responsibility of rulers, local political elites, and kin.

The Developmentalist Ethic in Zakah

In the opening vignette, I described an Islamic charity organization's distribution event that occurred in public, complete with photography, and was eventually shared online. This and other Islamic charity organizations with which I volunteered in Lucknow performed and promoted many similar practices that spring from a developmentalist ethic. I characterize this developmentalist ethic as a set of moral concerns focused on the recipients of zakah (rather than the donors): who the recipients are, why they are in poverty or in need, what conditions contributed to their neediness, and how to utilize zakah efficiently and systematically to alleviate widespread poverty and, more broadly, support development.

Muslim givers of a more developmentalist mindset are focused on the life of the alms-gifts after they leave their hands, rather than (or in addition to) the purificatory act of giving itself. The focus of alms-giving rotates from the giver to the receiver. How will the charity be utilized by the recipient? Will the recipient work hard to invest it? Or will it make him or her lazy and dependent? Most importantly, will it lift the poor Muslim out of poverty? The developmentalist efforts of Muslim associations involves employing modern management practices such as fundraising pledges, recipient application forms, recipient eligibility criteria related to work ethic, bundling financial aid with sermons and "coaching" intended to discipline the poor as hard-working productive members of society, monitoring visits, and bureaucratic surveillance.

In this section, I highlight the moral concerns that are coming to define the work of new Islamic charity organizations in Lucknow, through a case study of one such organized charity, the Society for Divine Welfare. In contrast to the moral concerns of the purity ethic described in the previous section (obligation, purification, and secrecy), this section presents data on two concerns of this organization that exemplify the developmentalist ethic: (1) inculcating work ethic among the poor, and (2) the public nature of zakah-giving in institutional settings.

Work Ethic

The Society for Divine Welfare (Anjoman Falāḥ-e Darain; hereafter "The Society") is located in the heart of Lucknow's popular Aminabad Bazaar. The Society was founded in 1992 and is run by a Muslim preacher (Urdu: *maulānā*) who is a graduate of the *madrasah* at Deoband, Maulana Jahangir Qasmi. It is worth noting that all of the charity associations I found to be promoting the developmentalist ethic were founded since the 1990's. This association is notable, however, for being led by a Muslim preacher and for operating out of the tiny, back-alley mosque in which Maulana Jahangir leads prayers, while the others are run by businessmen. Nevertheless, the Society is heavily influenced by the concerns of businessmen and wealthy storekeepers who are the main donors and who form a large portion of the mosque-goers in Maulana Jahangir's neighborhood mosque. The following data is drawn specifically from one activity held about three or four times a year: a charity distribution event.

Maulana Jahangir, now in his fifties, grew up in a crowded Calcutta neighborhood and attended madrasah from an early age, achieving the honor of becoming a memorizer of the Qur'an by adolescence. He is not – nor has he ever been – a businessman, yet he presents the main mission of his charity as "business development". By this he means that his charity, while it collects zakah from local Muslims of means, does not simply distribute these as handouts. Instead, he spends the funds on eligible poor Muslims in ways that increase their potential for gainful employment or running their own business. The following hadith was an oft-repeated favorite of his, a metonym for his theological perspective on almsgiving:

> In a hadith, the Prophet said ... After faith and prayer, the next obligation is earning income in a halal way [*'īmān aur namāz ke bād, Ḥalāl kamānā farz hai*] ... So, the purpose of zakah is for the poor to stand up on their own. Do you see? ... Otherwise some of them go to Hell.

In this conversational interview with me, he elaborated at length on the variety of social ills that fester in the absence of a halal income: begging, dependency on others, lying, cheating, thievery to make ends meet, broken homes, and a cycle of poverty inherited by the next generation. Let us now zoom in the ethnographic lens to bring into focus two aspects of the Society's charity distribution event: the form zakah took as "instruments of employment" and moral sermonizing on "work ethic".

Each item to be distributed was an instrument of self-employment. Sewing machines, push carts for street selling, cycle rickshaws, and a milk-steamer for chai tea stalls were cluttering the room. Each was marked with the words "The Society for Divine Welfare" ("Anjoman Falāḥ-e Darain") hand-painted in cursive Urdu. The items were all hand-made or assembled in the Old City. The Society had acquired them after soliciting quotes from local businesses around the bazaar. Each item came with a warranty, negotiated with each seller by the Maulana, to provide lifetime repairs when beneficiaries presented their receipt from the Society which named them as the owner. The Maulana emphasized the warranty in his speech. Sturdily made, the solid iron body of the sewing machine and rough-hewn wood of the push carts declaimed their practicality, durability, and ease of repair.

All these elements combined – the Society's moniker, warranty, durability – conveyed the Maulana's ultimate intention that incentives for resale be mitigated as much as possible. His concern was real. Barter thrived in the Aminabad bazaar and even trash was traded daily for a handsome price. The speeches he made during distribution events covered other themes, but each one addressed the maulana's concern that beneficiaries see the charitable donations not only as a free gift but also as a means of self-employment. He articulated this in a lengthy appeal at the end of his speech:

> I'm on my knees asking you not to misuse these machines... not to sell them. If you're not using it, find another poor woman. Give it to your poor Muslim sister, she at least will make some money.... A few years back we spent 8-9,000 rupees on rickshaws for these regular mosque-goers (*namāzi*), for Hajjis. I won't say their names. They were poor. ... After a month of driving it, one guy sold his 8,000 rupee rickshaw for 2,100 rupees! After only a month! And mosque-goers! Hajjis! ... For the love of God, this is a loan (*amānat*) from Allah. ... If you sell it, what answer would you give to God? ... You're promising me that you won't sell it. And if you're lying, and you sell this, that means that you are betraying Allah. I won't be able to hold you accountable. You're taking up this loan [from Allah]. This [zakah] is your right. I won't be able to expect any favor (*ehsān*) from you. However, it's important to note the purpose (*maqsad*) with which this was given to you. Use it as it was intended.

With this warning of divine omniscience, the maulana concluded his appeal for the beneficiaries' commitment. The maulana was requesting the audience to adopt his perception of these donations as instruments of self-employment rather than see them for their inherent value in the barter economy of Lucknow's bazaar.

Maulana Jahangir also directly instructed the audience recipients to be hard-working in addition to prohibiting the resale of donations. To one man, for example, he wagged his finger while instructing, "This money that we're giving you, use it and work hard. Don't spend it on the wrong things." He instructed the women to save their money by avoiding tobacco-like stimulants and spending instead on education.

The emphasis on work ethic is clearly intentional and derives from scriptural teachings. One such teaching is the hadith on making a halal income cited above, with the logical corollary that zakah should lead unemployed Muslims to have such an income. Another set of relevant teachings emphasizes the need for Muslims to give zakah to the "correct" recipients, such as the eight categories specified in the Qur'an (9:60) which I discuss below. A third set of teachings that undergirds the work ethic consists of hadiths that forbid begging and dependency.[17]

Public Institutionalization

The public nature of zakah giving in organized charity associations is vividly displayed in the vignette that opened this paper, to which I now return briefly. The distribution event run by Maulana Jahangir entailed the public recognition of zakah recipients, reading their names, and photographing them (in fact, I once was asked to serve as photographer). A concern for recipients' accountability, which was shared by many supporters of the Society, led to practices that made the recipients (and their neediness) even more visible and put them under the observation of donors, the maulana, and Allah. Local Muslim businessmen and shopkeepers comprise nearly all of the Society's donors, and a few were present in the audience to witness the transfer of donations to the beneficiaries. This level of transparency was critical to the popularity of the Society.

A growing number of Muslim givers in Lucknow lack faith in the ability of charity associations to operate cleanly until they see it with their own eyes. The recipients were required to present themselves in front of the audience's gaze and to be photographed and sign for the amount of their recorded charitable donation. The needy beneficiaries publicly accepted the donors' largesse and consentingly posed for a photograph documenting the transaction. Such a practice socially defined the recipients as visible subjects with visible neediness. The ritual secrecy usually associated with Islamic almsgiving was in this instance overturned, replaced by these embodied performances that were intended to instill a sense of accountability.

Historical Contexts for the Developmentalist Ethic

Earlier I explained the moral concerns of the purity ethic as particularly salient during the colonial era, when reformist *ʿulamāʾ* turned their didactic focus toward ordinary Muslims in ways that individualized and internalized Islamic piety. At the turn of the 21st century, however, new groups of Muslims – organized Islamic charities – have made forays into the public discourse on zakah. *ʿUlamāʾ* are no longer the primary producers and circulators of authoritative Islamic teachings on zakah, as studies of Muslim societies around the world have noted. Dale Eickelman and James Piscatori refer to this process as the "fragmentation" of Islamic authority in an age of mass education.[18] New Islamic charities in which I volunteered in Lucknow were led by businessmen (four of the six charities profiled in my dissertation) or had businessmen as their primary donors (such as Maulana Jahangir's charity profiled in this paper). These organized charities and the Muslims working with them operate within a different set of moral concerns than the Deobandi *ʿulamāʾ* of the 19th century.

First, one primary concern of Muslims today is to systematize and institutionalize zakah, even if it means implementing methods of public distribution and accountability. A recent government report[19] has identified Muslims as rapidly becoming the most socioeconomically underdeveloped group in India. Many Muslims see this as a crisis – not only an economic crisis but a spiritual one as well. Muslim poverty is evidence that many are not paying their zakah and that zakah is not being distributed effectively. As the Muslim community in India gains the technological and organizational means to monitor and manage the utilization of zakah by recipients, some organized charities are beginning to do so.

A second concern originates with Islamic revivalist movements that motivated many Indian Muslims to return to the scriptures and to attempt to discern "correct" Islamic practices by separating authentic beliefs from inauthentic (or deviant) ones. This impulse to discern "correct" Islam extends to a search for the correct recipients of zakah. There is some indication in the Qur'an that certain categories of recipients are eligible (e.g., the needy, stranded travelers) while others outside these categories are not. Scholars traditionally hold that those Muslims below the threshold of sufficient means (*niṣāb*) are eligible for zakah. But the scholarly fiqh discourses about preferred recipients are not as well developed as are the discourses instructing the donors how to give and how to feel while giving. Very little fiqh, if any, has attended to the issue of what recipients are expected to do with zakah. Yet these issues are rapidly becoming more urgent for organized charities.

Debating the Developmentalist Ethic in the *Madrasah*

In describing this developmentalist ethic and two of its moral concerns, work ethic and public giving, this short case study has explored the ways that Muslim givers are focused on what happens to zakah after it is given – after the ritual requirement has been met. For those with developmentalist ideas, the original intent of alms-giving as the circulation of wealth to alleviate poverty is of primary concern. It is perhaps a useful oversimplification to view the developmentalist ethic as concerned with the material well-being of the recipients and the purity ethic as concerned with the spiritual well-being and modesty of the donor.

While there is universal agreement among Muslims over the zakah obligation itself, what do Islamic teachings say should be the end of giving zakah? Madrasah teachings and scholarly writings on fiqh can be read several ways on this issue. Islamic scholarship is at times remarkably specific on certain criteria for alms-recipients, without which the transaction is not eligible to be counted towards the obligatory annual tithe of zakah. For example, a donation to a destitute family utilized for food or clothing may be counted as zakah, but same donation if utilized to purchase the burial shroud (*kafan*) could not be counted as zakah, according to *Al-Hidaya*, a standard text taught in the Sunni *madrasahs* in north India, even though the shroud is an Islamic requirement.[20] It is also *ḥarām*, or prohibited, to give one's zakah to a known drunkard or someone who plans to spend it on a prohibited item such as alcohol or pork. Yet how does the donor know? The intention (*niyyah*) behind alms-giving, rather than how the zakah is ultimately spent or (mis)used, is also said to determine its efficacy in purifying the donor's wealth in traditional writings on Islamic almsgiving. According to the majority opinion in Hanafite fiqh, if the donor's intention is to give alms to a recipient who appears eligibly needy (according to the standard stipulations of who is "needy", which are quite broad, covering eight categories of "needy" in Qur'an 9:60) then regardless of what happens afterward the alms are considered valid zakah. This focus on donors' intentions restricts the determination of alms' efficacy to the period of time while it still remains in the donor's hands.

A minority opinion, however, which is just as valid and consistent with the beliefs of some Muslims in Old Lucknow (whether they are aware of the scholarly opinion itself or not), holds that if a donor finds that a portion of their zakah has been paid incorrectly then that amount must be paid a second time. This minority opinion is attributed to Abū Yūsuf, the famous student of Imam Abū Ḥanīfah.[21] This concern with zakah after it leaves the donor's hands is characteristic of the developmentalist ethic that motivated Muslims who expressed anxiety that their alms were not "correct" if not given to the right people for the right ends.

Islamic jurisprudence and scholarship taught in *madrasahs* in Lucknow does not mention a role for charity associations. Rather, alms are primarily the individual responsibility of the donor, or are to be collected by an Islamic government as in the time of the Prophet's caliphate. In the minds of some Muslims, Islamic charity associations are taking on responsibilities which are potentially not justifiable by Shariʿah. All students at Dārul 'Ulūm Nadwatul 'Ulama (Urdu, known as "Nadwa"), an urban *madrasah* in Lucknow, are familiar with contemporary Islamic reformist trends, but at least two students separately declaimed a more critical view of developmentalist charity organizations who collect and disburse zakah. One younger student explained that the village *madrasah* where he studied taught that Islamic charity associations that collected zakah were not justifiable, including the new Islamic charities with which I volunteered in Aminabad bazaar. Another older student was not opposed to alms-distribution associations, necessarily, but cautioned that many do not operate Islamically. Muslims must take care to only utilize associations run by *ʿulamā'*, graduates of a *madrasah*, he said. He recommended that in my dissertation I perform a survey and try to catch associations that do not distribute alms according to the eight categories of needy Muslims specified in the Qur'an: "My suggestion to you, is that you ask around within these organizations where you volunteer, 'Where are you spending this zakah money that you are receiving? Which category [of needy Muslim, as specified in the Qur'an] do you distribute to?'"

Maulana Sayyid Abul A'la Maududi (d. 1979), a Muslim born in British India and considered one of the world's most influential ideologues of political Islamism, is most well known for the party he founded, the Jama'at Islami, as well as his widely read Islamic scholarship.[22] Yet his theological writings on almsgiving are remarkable for their lack of attention paid to Islamic charity associations performing economic development. The organization he founded, Jama'at Islami, now manages millions of rupees in charitable donations in its chapters across South Asia. Most of his writings advocate for, or already assume, the establishment of an Islamic government in India. A collection of his significant Urdu writings on almsgiving, *Haqiqat-i Zakat* ("The Reality of Zakah"), however, ends with a long passage on what Muslims in India should do in the absence of a true Islamic state.[23] It discusses spending alms for one's needy kin and neighbors, but notes that there can be no centralized collection of alms without an Islamic state, so therefore "Muslims in India should think about what can be done." No explanation is given, nor is any mention even made of the sort of non-state civil society associations currently operating across India, which were less numerous but already present in his time. My teacher in Nadwa *madrasah* replied that there is not much in historical Islamic jurisprudence (which must meet the strict principles of Islamic legal argumentation, *uṣūl al-fiqh*) with which to justify Islamic charity associations. Despite this legal lacuna, he explained that Muslim scholars today tend to allow for Islamic charity organizations operating outside the jurisdiction of an Islamic state given the changed conditions of modern society.[24]

I asked my instructor – a mufti – about the permissibility of practices instituted at new Islamic charities that followed a more developmentalist ethic. I described their process of approving and rejecting certain poor Muslims for receiving alms, distributing in public and photographing them, and giving sermons that exhorted the poor to attain a better work ethic. Critics of new Islamic charities, I mentioned, had inveighed against the shaming practices of monitoring recipients as immodestly following up on charity after it is given.

On the issue of requiring applications to receive funds, and selecting hard-working recipients, the mufti stated that many people, especially professionals, have preferences for spending alms in areas of their expertise, such as education or health. Muslim givers may allocate their obligatory alms towards only those needy Muslims who have certain exam scores, or who have certain jobs, as long as those recipients are truly financially needy. However, he added emphatically, such donors must not direct all alms in this way. They are also under an obligation to withhold a portion for whatever people may approach them unsolicited and in need. If everyone applied conditions to all their obligatory zakah, it defeats the purpose of ensuring the free circulation and redistribution of wealth to all those in need. Thus, "There must be a balance (*tarāzū*)," he concluded, such that the poor overall receive their just due.

The mufti, however, did not go so far as to advocate that Islamic charity remain the sole province of religious leaders and *madrasahs*. His view stood in stark contrast to some students at his own *madrasah* (quoted above) who criticized new Islamic charities for taking alms funding away from *madrasahs* and for institutionalizing almsgiving outside the aegis of an Islamic state. Rather, he launched into an explanation that began with an Urdu proverb:

> Look, it's said that "If a man tries to do everything, he will end up getting nothing done."... How many people are there that need *madrasah* education in India? Tens of thousands! ... Some don't even know how to say their prayers. ... That should remain the main goal of *madrasahs* and Muslim scholars.

The equanimity of this mufti, and of most of the scholars I encountered while researching and studying in the madrasah, was evidence of their sound knowledge of sociological principles and plain common sense. The mufti propounded a model society characterized by a division of labor and channels of clear support and communication between religious specialists and experts in other fields. This complexity was in stark contrast to critics that I heard elsewhere in Lucknow, including the traditionalist Muslims who doubted the ability of modern-educated businessmen to manage religious alms in the correct manner, and the developmentalist Muslim givers who lambasted the madrasah system as outdated and as depriving Muslims of their place in the modern economy.

Conclusion

Popular conceptions view Shariʿah and the fiqh scholarship that derives from it as Islamic "law", a code that is singular and static. Just as the man I quoted above became indignant at my questioning, and responded that "It's Allah's order…Who needs a reason for giving zakah?" Muslims in Lucknow often regarded Shariʿah as a clear set of ethical-legal rules to discern and to follow, but not to question very deeply. Our translation of Shariʿah as "Islamic law" at times reinforces such a view. Even more precise translations, such as "the path" or "the way", still represent the Shariʿah as singular, a single normative order to be followed. A Muslim follows the Shariʿah to progress closer to Allah or to reach Heaven in the Hereafter, just as a person follows the path to get closer to the water-spring or to reach his or her home.

The *ʿulamā'* especially, as the scholarly preservers and interpreters of the intellectual tradition of Islam, have represented Islamic law as "unchanging" to bolster their authority, in colonial times and today.[25] "In a time of change, we did not change," wrote Qari Muhammad Tayyib, a director of Deoband and grandson of the founder, looking back on the achievements of his grandfather's scriptural revivalist movement in the colonial era.[26] The scholars who retreated to Deoband to found a *madrasah* in the late 1900s are an emblematic example. Barbara Metcalf and other scholars have shown that the very invention of tradition as "tradition" is very much a part of how people define the modernity in which we imagine that we live.[27] *ʿUlamā'*, however, in their representation of an unchanging tradition of interpretations of Shariʿah, are most often aware of the vast internal diversity of that tradition, as was the case with the mufti instructor who recognized that a sense of "balance" must guide Muslims as they navigate competing interpretations of Shariʿah and worldly concerns while giving zakah. Yet they still rely on constructions of the Islamic intellectual tradition as unchanging. Why does this not result in more vituperative attacks by *ʿulamā'* on the divergent developmentalist practices I described earlier, if only to maintain their authoritative connection to this construction of an unchanging normative system?

The entrance of new Islamic charity organizations into the public sphere in Lucknow, I argue, has largely served to bolster the authority of *ʿulamā'*, rather than threaten it. As I have described, the businessmen and community leaders who support these charity organizations are self-proclaimed revivers of zakah. Muslims of all types recognize the positive socioeconomic benefits these charities bring to Lucknow, providing welfare in a systematic way to the city's poor. Besides these material benefits for Muslims, most *ʿulamā'* also recognize the immense benefit to the spiritual health of the Muslim community that charity organizations bring. Some *ʿulamā'*, such as Maulana Jahangir, have even begun their own charities in the developmentalist model. Although organized Islamic charities are sacrificing some of the historically more prevalent concerns that comprised the purity ethic, they have brought Islamic teachings on zakah into the public eye in a way that madrasahs have been unable to do for the majority of Muslims. Operating as social welfare organizations, they partner at times with other charities run by Christians or Hindus. As Muslim organizations that are seen by all Indians as providing an indisputable public service, they appear in news articles and in government discussions in a more positive light than the madrasahs which focus largely on religious education. Thus, the net result is something that is also a shared goal of the *ʿulamā'*: a more significant role for the Shariʿah in the lives of Muslims, channeled through institutions that exhort them to maintain their zakah obligations.

Analyzing the power of the Shariʿah cannot be separated from an analysis of how its ethics are applied in practice. The power of Shariᶜah does not merely derive from politics, such as the backing of a state with a monopoly on the use of force, despite the étatization of Shariᶜah by Islamic states. Nor does the power of Shariᶜah ethics derive from its ability to be represented as a consistent, unitary, or static code. Its moral power derives from the extent to which the Muslim public at large embraces its ethical injunctions, even if they hold differing interpretations of those injunctions, as do the Muslims animated by the purity and developmentalist ethics. The anthropological approach of this paper suggests that an analysis of "ethics in practice" makes clear the internal diversity of beliefs and practices among actors that claim to follow the same ethical code. In such cases, the democratization of Shariᶜah occurs when new actors and organizations are empowered to act as revivers and preservers of Islamic ethical norms. As Robert Hefner wrote:

> The moral power of the sharia has always derived from the fact that its most gifted practitioners have never allowed it to be just an abstract dogma made consistent with its own premises, indifferent to the circumstances of the age. The sharia acquires ethical power when believers are able to draw its message deep into their everyday lives, so that it informs and resonates with their moral circumstances.[28]

This principle is something that the *ᶜulamā'* themselves, by and large, grasp intuitively or even consciously. It is no mistake that the case study for the developmentalist ethic that I presented is an organized Islamic charity run by a member of the *ᶜulamā'*. He and others are fast realizing the influential position of such an associational form, at a time when the influence and societal authority of traditional *madrasahs* is declining. Although the transformation is far from complete, and Islamic charity organizations are still a minor player in the Muslim public sphere in Lucknow, my data suggest that this will not long be the case.

The new developmentalist practices of Islamic charity organizations might be an inflammatory source of tension if *ᶜulamā'* believed their authority to be threatened by the changes such organizations are introducing into ritual practices of zakah giving that have been taught in *madrasahs* for centuries. Yet the *ʿulamāʾ* in Lucknow perceive this transformation of zakah giving not as a departure from the teachings of fiqh, but as a different choice of emphasis in interpreting the same scriptures. The example of such *ʿulamāʾ* in Lucknow highlights the importance of analyzing Islam as a "discursive tradition,"[29] tacking off of Alistair MacIntyre's notion of tradition as "an argument extended through time" that is defined more by the criteria of the debate than by the positions taken in it.

REFERENCES

Al-Marghinani, *Al-Hidayah: The Guidance*. Trans. by Imran Ahsan Khan Nyazee (Bristol: Amal Press, 2006).

Arjomand, Said Amir, 'Philanthropy, the Law, and Public Policy in the Islamic World before the Modern Era', in *Philanthropy in the World's Traditions.* (Ed.), W.F. Ilchman, et al. (Bloomington: Indiana University Press, 1998), pp.109–32.

Asad, Talal, 'The Idea of an Anthropology of Islam'. Occasional Papers Series. (Washington, D.C.: Center for Contemporary Arab Studies, Georgetown University, 1986).

Benthall, Jonathan, 'Financial Worship: The Qur'anic Injunction to Almsgiving', *Journal of the Royal Anthropological Institute* 5 (1999), pp.27–42.

Benthall, Jonathan, and Jerome Bellion-Jourdan, *The Charitable Crescent: Politics of Aid in the Muslim World* (London: I.B. Tauris, 2003).

Bornstein, Erica, 'The Impulse of Philanthropy', *Cultural Anthropology* 24 (2009), pp.622–651.

Deeb, Lara, *An Enchanted Modern: Gender and Public Piety in Shi'i Lebanon* (Princeton Studies in Muslim Politics. Princeton: Princeton University Press, 2006).

Eickelman, Dale F., and James Piscatori, *Muslim Politics* (Princeton: Princeton University Press, 1996).

Hallaq, Wael B., *Shari'a: Theory, Practice, Transformations* (Cambridge: Cambridge University Press, 2009).

Hefner, Robert W., *Shari'a Politics: Islamic Law and Society in the Modern World* (Bloomington: Indiana University Press, 2011).

Ibn Qudamah, Abu Muhammad ʿAbd Allah ibn Ahmad, *al-Mughnī*. (Ed.), Muhammad Rashid Rida, vol.2 (Egypt: Maṭbaʿat al-Manār, 1345/[1927]).

Kandhalvi, Zakariya, *Faza'il-e A'mal.* San Francisco: Islamic Bulletin. http://www.islamicbulletin.org.

Marsden, Magnus, *Living Islam: Muslim Religious Experience in Pakistan's North-West Frontier* (Cambridge: Cambridge University Press, 2005).

Maurer, Bill, *Mutual Life, Limited: Islamic Banking, Alternative Currencies, Lateral Reason* (Princeton: Princeton University Press, 2005).

McChesney, Robert D., *Waqf in Central Asia: Four Hundred Years in the History of a Muslim Shrine, 1480-1889* (Princeton: Princeton University Press, 1990).

Nadwi, Abul Hasan Ali, *The Economic Order of Islam* (Rae Bareli, UP: Dar-e Arafat).

Nasr, Seyyed Vali Reza, *Mawdudi and the Making of Islamic Revivalism* (New York: Oxford University Press, 1996).

Osella, Filippo, and Caroline Osella, 'Muslim Entrepreneurs in Public Life between India and the Gulf: Making Good and Doing Good', *Journal of the Royal Anthropological Institute* 15 (2009), pp.S202–S221.

Powell, Russell, 'Zakat: Drawing Insights for Legal Theory and Economic Policy from Islamic Jurisprudence', *University of Pittsburgh Tax Review* 7 (2009), pp.43–159.

Qaradawi, Yousef, *Fiqh al-Zakah* (Jeddah: Scientific Publishing Centre, King Abdulaziz University, 2000).

Sachar, Rajindar, *A Report on the Muslim Community of India: High Level Committee Report on Social, Economic, and Educational Status of the Muslim Community of India* (Delhi, 2006).

Singer, Amy, *Charity in Islamic Societies* (Cambridge: Cambridge University Press, 2008).

Taylor, Christopher B., 'Receipts and Other Forms of Islamic Charity: Accounting for Piety in Modern North India', *Modern Asian Studies* 52(1) (2018), pp.266–96.

Weber, Max, *Economy and Society: An Outline of Interpretive Sociology* (Berkeley: University of California Press, 1978).

Zaman, Muhammad Qasim, *The Ulama in Contemporary Islam: Custodians of Change* (Princeton: Princeton University Press, 2002).

NOTES

1. The saying is a hadith, or saying of the Prophet Muhammad, documented in *Ṣaḥīḥ al-Bukhārī*, Book 24, Number 504.
2. Pew Research Center, *The World's Muslims: Unity and Diversity* (Washington, D.C., 2012).
3. Max Weber, *Economy and Society: An Outline of Interpretive Sociology* (Berkeley: University of California Press, 1978).
4. See for example the influential article by Wael Hallaq, 'Was the Gate of Ijtihad Closed?' *International Journal of Middle East Studies* 16 (1984), pp.3–41. See also Robert Hefner, *Shari'a Politics: Islamic Law and Society in the Modern World* (Princeton: Princeton University Press, 2011).
5. All names from my research interviews are pseudonyms to protect the privacy of interviewees.

6. The survey question was worded (in Urdu): "We have discussed each of these reasons separately, but please tell me which of these three reasons is the MOST important reason you give alms: #1 Aid to the poor, #2 Avoiding punishment in the Afterlife, #3 To purify or protect my wealth from harm, or #4 some other reason." I selected these three reasons for the closed-ended survey questionnaire after months of preliminary open-ended interviews of donors regarding the most resonant motivations behind their almsgiving.
7. Anthropologist Jonathan Benthall similarly wrote, "Zakat's importance seems to be one principle on which almost all devout Muslims are united." See Jonathan Benthall, 'Financial Worship: The Qur'anic Injunction to Almsgiving', *Journal of the Royal Anthropological Institute* 5 (1999), p.35.
8. Quoted by Ibn Qudāmah in *al-Mughnī*. (Ed.), Muhammad Rashid Rida (Egypt: Maṭbaʿat al-Manār, 1345/[1927]), vol.2, p.596.
9. Wael B. Hallaq, *Shari'a: Theory, Practice, Transformations* (Cambridge: Cambridge University Press, 2009), p.231.
10. Verse 9:60 reads: "Alms are for the poor; and the needy, and those employed to administer the (funds); for those whose hearts have been (recently) reconciled; for those in bondage; and in debt; in the cause of Allah; and for the wayfarer" (Yusuf Ali translation).
11. Abul Hasan Ali Nadwi, *The Economic Order of Islam* (Rae Bareli, UP: Dar-e Arafat), p.41; cf. Qur'an 9:103.
12. Authored by Maulana Zakariya Kandhalvi (1898-1982), an influential scholar of the Tablighi Jama'at founded by his uncle, the *Faza'il-e A'mal* has been the key instructional text of that preaching society in their missionary activities across India and the world. The section on charity and zakah, titled Fazail-e Sadaqaat, is comprised of a simple numbered list of verses from the Qur'an and then hadiths, each with brief lines of interpretation. Zakariya Kandhalvi, *Faza'il-e A'mal* (San Francisco: Islamic Bulletin) http://www.islamicbulletin.org, pp.6 and 27.
13. Kandhalvi, *Faza'il-e A'mal*, pp.25, 67, and 95.
14. Yusuf Ali translation.
15. Hindus themselves, of course, do not view *dan* in this way, and anthropologist Erica Bornstein has detailed the religious teachings on "detachment" (*tyag*) when giving *dan* as part of efforts to escape from the cycle of death and re-birth in the material world. See Erica Bornstein, 'The Impulse of Philanthropy', *Cultural Anthropology* 24 (2009), p.3.
16. Elsewhere, I have discussed the historical rise of the purity ethic in the context of Indian Muslim scriptural revivalism. See Christopher B. Taylor, 'Receipts and Other Forms of Islamic Charity: Accounting for Piety in Modern North India', *Modern Asian Studies* 52(1) (2018), pp.266–96. While scriptural literacy has often been the factor in reformations that shape religious life by linking believers more closely to the scriptural roots of their faith, a look at zakah

receipts illustrates how financial literacy and accompanying desires for documentation also facilitated Indian Muslim revivalist organizing.

17. One such hadith is recorded by *al-Bukhārī*, Book 5, Number 2253, "The upper hand is better than the lower one, the upper being the one which bestows and the lower one which begs."
18. Dale F. Eickelman and James Piscatori, *Muslim Politics* (Princeton: Princeton University Press, 1996), p.131.
19. Rajindar Sachar, *A Report on the Muslim Community of India: High Level Committee Report on Social, Economic, and Educational Status of the Muslim Community of India* (Delhi, 2006).
20. The reasoning has to do with the fact that the true recipient is the deceased, and alms only may be counted as zakah when they are taken by living persons in need. See Al-Marghinani, *Al-Hidayah: The Guidance*, trans. by Dr. Imran Ahsan Khan Nyazee (Bristol: Amal Press, 2006).
21. Al-Marghinani, *Al-Hidayah*, p.291.
22. Seyyed Vali Reza Nasr, *Mawdudi and the Making of Islamic Revivalism* (New York: Oxford University Press, 1996).
23. Sayyid Abul A'la Maududi, *Haqiqat-i Zakat* (Karachi, n.d.), p.32.
24. For an overview of zakah in modern legal systems, see Russell Powell, 'Zakat: Drawing Insights for Legal Theory and Economic Policy from Islamic Jurisprudence', *University of Pittsburgh Tax Review* 7 (2009), pp.43–159.
25. In colonial India, these representations of Islamic law as unchanging were often in response to British accusations of arbitrariness. See Muhammad Qasim Zaman, *The Ulama in Contemporary Islam: Custodians of Change* (Princeton: Princeton University Press, 2012), p.25.
26. Cited in Barbara Metcalf, *Islamic Contestations: Essays on Muslims in India and Pakistan* (New Delhi: Oxford University Press, 2004), p.10. Metcalf goes on to comment, "My study of Deoband, in short, provided one of the many examples of how the very concept of 'traditional' becomes part of the self-definition of modernity. It also showed how what is often taken as tradition turns out to be a relatively recent product of the colonial past."
27. Barbara D. Metcalf, *Islamic Revival in British India: Deoband, 1860-1900* (Oxford: Oxford University Press, 1982). See also Lara Deeb, 'An Enchanted Modern: Gender and Public Piety in Shi'i Lebanon', *Princeton Studies in Muslim Politics* (Princeton: Princeton University Press, 2006).
28. Robert W. Hefner, *Shari'a Politics: Islamic Law and Society in the Modern World* (Bloomington: Indiana University Press, 2011), p.45.
29. Muhammad Qasim Zaman, T*he Ulama in Contemporary Islam: Custodians of Change* (Princeton: Princeton University Press, 2002). See also Talal Asad, 'The Idea of an Anthropology of Islam', Occasional Papers Series (Washington, D.C.: Center for Contemporary Arab Studies, Georgetown University, 1986), pp.381–406.

6

The Concept of *Riḍā* in the Qur'an: Popular Misunderstanding and the Westernization of Jews and Christians

Asaad Alsaleh

ABSTRACT: Due to its increasing popularity and a whole array of representations associated with it, verse 2:120 of the Qur'an's *Surah al-Baqarah* will be the center of this chapter. I render the verse in English as: "Never will the Jews or the Christians approve of you until you follow their religion. Say, 'Indeed, Allah's guidance is the guidance.' If you were to follow their liking after the knowledge you have received, you would have no protector from Allah or any helper." The chapter provides an exegetical study of the meanings and representations of *riḍā* (approval) in this verse, as contrasted with the "popular" understanding this verse has gained among many Muslims, particularly in the modern age of communication. I argue that both the verse and the concept of *riḍā* therein have been taken out of context and misunderstood as part of a reactionary discourse against the West. As seen in social media, online commentaries, and other virtual venues, many Muslims quote the verse to declare that there is an innate attitude of plotting or hatred on the part of an imagined monolithic Jewish-Christian West. Overwhelmingly popular, this misquoting has established a fixed meaning and a static understanding of a text that has its own context, reference, and interpretations. Misinterpretations of this verse have eclipsed and blurred an established opinion that the verse was directed to Prophet Muhammad within a specific historical context, and that its use as a timeless reference overlooks that context. The established, non-politicized understanding of verse 2:120 will be demonstrated through classical commentaries, which show that the verse indicates a certain religious position of some Jews and Christians who were not presented in an antagonistic state, and does not incite such a state against them.

Disapproval of the West

Anecdotal experiences sometimes motivate one to do research that eventually becomes indebted to those experiences. In an article I published in Arabic on my Facebook page (1 November, 2013) entitled "Islam in the World," I demonstrated that Islamic centers and mosques are flourishing in the United States. As someone who witnessed the advent of ISIS in his own homeland in eastern Syria,[1] I noticed that its military advancement was accompanied by rhetoric and ideologies that preach hatred, uninformed understanding of Islam, and confrontational religiosity. Alongside all the other things it damaged in the Arab world and beyond, it ushered in an increasing hostility against everything Western. ISIS insisted on, and perhaps was influenced by, the long-established dogma that the West presumably wants to destroy Islam. This dogma is held by many political Islamic movements, but has also become common among average Muslims in the Arab world. I wanted to point out in the article that fanatical discourses in the Middle East ignore the freedom of worship in the West and the presence of Muslims, with their culture and religious practices, in Western countries. I also argued that these discourses insist on depicting Western countries as "infidel" and "immoral" while idealizing the East and ignoring its prevailing problems that demonstrate non-Islamic principles, including resorting to terrorism and the extremist voices that feed it.

The readers' comments on my Facebook post were largely disapproving. I was not addressing my Arab audience (some highly educated and some with minimal education) to defend the West, as I do not believe that the East and West can exist as unique entities drawn geographically and historically to be separate from each other. I was writing with the intention to appreciate opportunities for coexistence. Though this piece can be criticized on different levels, one particular response stood out. I detected in the comments a serious problem with misquoting the Qur'an, particularly verse 2:120, which is often used as a "final world" that the West is innately bad and its inhabitants are the "Jews and Christians" mentioned in the verse. If the English poet Rudyard Kipling said in 1889 that the "East is East, and West is West, and never the twain shall meet,"[2] many still believe, in the East and the West, that religion is the reason why this meeting is impossible. As I found after examining an enormous number of citations of this verse, the historical and religious frames were mixed to form a lens by which some Facebook and Twitter commentators looked at the West, assuming a connection between the West and the people mentioned in the Qur'an. This one verse was widely used to justify attitudes against the West. Obviously, any Muslim might have many legitimate reasons to criticize the West, but one cannot see the West in the Qur'an in the way these critiques assume. These comments are hardly "personal" or expressing merely individual attitudes, but are part of a legacy of misunderstanding, misquoting, and misusing religious texts, as well as mixing the political with the religious.

Revisiting the Facebook comments on my afore-mentioned article will provide a clear picture of the attitudes shared by many Muslims about the West, Jews and Christians. I will give glimpses of these attitudes, and translate them, in the same order as they were received, before moving to the comments that took the Qur'an as a reference for their attitude, relying on verse 2:120, whose discussion lies at the core of the next section. One comment stated, "the Crusades against Islam have not stopped at all. The United State is responsible for Afghanistan, Palestine... Syria and Libya, as well as all divisions in the Arab world, which are facilitated by some Arabs. Why did they give Iraq to the Shiites? Why did Sudan become two states? All these are dimensions of a war on Islam." Another commentator, who might have read the above-mentioned comment, wrote, "We do not see it as a crusade. But, if you remember what Bush said when invading Iraq, they [Westerners] explicitly declared it to be so. Islam is all the same, but they are the ones who invented such terms as Islamists and fundamentalists." Another response was as follows: "Extremism is a concept made by the West and Arab regimes as a pretext to suppress the Islamic awakening." Referring to the events of 9/11, and obviously with a conspiracy theory attitude, one respondent wrote that "after the towers reached the end of their life span, the United States destroyed them but accused [for such an act] those whom they previously embraced, as their mission ended and they needed to be terminated. The United States occupied the Muslim countries that it considered no longer obedient to its will. It sought Iran's help by taking advantage of sect differences among Shiites and Sunnis, and declared a crusade war." One comment went like this: "The dirty face will remain dirty regardless of attempts to polish it. The United States shed the blood of Muslims and drank it to the full." Another person stated: "Somewhere in the Western mind, particularly in the United States, hostility exists against Islam. It sometimes shows openly and cannot be overlooked... A glaring example which cannot be ignored at all is [the question of] Palestine."

If we stop here for a moment, any cultural studies critic interested in Arab political culture might recognize that these attitudes are prevalent in the Arab world. They unveil political reactions largely fueled by the reality of skewed Western politics in the Middle East, particularly regarding the question of Palestine, which contributes to an increasing consensus among Arabs who did not like the suspicious foreign policy that defied their will.[3] The war in Iraq and Afghanistan, as mentioned in the introduction, has fueled yet more antagonism. According to a major poll commissioned by the Arab American Institute (AAI) and conducted in June 2004 by Zogby International, unfavorable impressions of the United States in five Arab countries had worsened substantially from 2002 – before the war against Iraq and Afghanistan. For example, 98% of the Egyptians surveyed expressed "a negative view of the US" showing a 22% increase from 2002.[4] This disaffection is based more on political grounds than religious reactions. Yet, religion could be used to give a push for certain political winds, causing confusion, negative reactions, and more politicization of religion; for example, President George W. Bush used the term "crusade" in response to the 9/11 terrorist attacks as an insensitive articulation of what his administration wanted to do against the culprits, marching toward a global and largely flawed war. Used by a Western leader, this term is nefarious and highly loaded with unpleasant history, and it backfired, as can be seen from the comments of some Arab citizens who fallaciously assumed that a president recklessly resorting to these inflammatory remarks spoke for all Western or American people. It is evident that this and similar attitudes against "all Western or American people" are reactionary and based on generalizations far from rational thinking – which is something a Western leader might also lack when talking about Islam or Muslims. Like Bush, then presidential candidate Donald Trump talked about Islam and Muslim immigrants in a CNN interview, saying, "I think Islam hates us."[5]

Quoting the Qur'an as a Political Reaction

Of the comments I received, several quoted the Qur'an to support their attitudes against the West. Verse 2:120 is highly quoted all over the Internet, and it is very common to find the following phrase taken from the verse: "Never will the Jews or the Christians approve of you until you follow their religion." This part, which I call the *riḍā* verse, is more commonly present and highly cited than the second part of 2:120: "Say, 'Indeed, Allah's guidance is the guidance.' If you were to follow their liking after the knowledge you have received, you would have no protector from Allah or any helper." After quoting the *riḍā* verse, one reader wrote "Shall we believe Allah or the United States?" This rhetorical question is repeated often and stands as an example of how this verse became so popular among Arab Muslims, giving them (they think) an already packaged discourse about the West. Even though most Western countries have adopted secularism, and neither have religious states (like the Jewish state in Israel) nor affiliate themselves with a single religion, the dominant view is that the West is composed of Jews and Christians. Thus, directing the verse to the West based on this political designation is misleading, even if justified by those who share this verse repeatedly out of context. Associating Christianity and Judaism with the West, and making them a target for an assumed Qur'anic reproach, often does not include those Jews and Christians who do not have the dominant power that the West has, including those who live in Arab countries.

The concept of Jewish-Christian disapproval dominates certain social media and online commentaries without sorting out the political from the religious. It implies that the West is an essentially coherent religious unit shaped by Christianity. Historian of religion Philip Jenkins points out that the future of Christianity is characterized by significant geographic changes, including the decline of Western Christianity, projecting that "in 2050, 72 percent of Christians will live in Africa, Asia, and Latin America."[6] Moreover, labeling the West as the locale of Christians and Jews ignores atheism in Western countries. Surveys show that some Western countries can hardly be labeled as religious, with 72 percent of Norwegians and 60 percent of Finns declaring no belief in a "personal God."[7] Thus, Christendom in the West is not as active in identifying the region as it is thought to be, nor do Christianity or Judaism have the dominant role in politics, as assumed by those who quote the Qur'an for the purpose of condemning the West. The *riḍā* verse is used in many contexts not only as a reference to support an argument against the West, but to be in itself a critique of the West. Oftentimes, mentioning the verse itself summarizes the position or opinion of the speaker. For example, when Samir Nassri, the French professional footballer, was left out the French World Cup team in 2014, his girlfriend from England made news headlines when she used Twitter to insult the French coach. The news reached the Arab world, and because Nassri has Algerian heritage, his story became the talk of the town in Algerian media. One commentator in the popular Algerian newspaper *Echorouk* used the *riḍā* verse to assume that the coach's dismissal was motivated by religious disapproval, claiming that what happened to Nassri was "the penalty for everyone who forgets his homeland."[8]

In February 2011, the Egyptian television presenter, Hafiz Mirazi, resigned from the Saudi-owned Satellite station, Alarabiya, after being denied the chance to talk about some of the consequences of the Arab Spring on Saudi Arabia. One reader of the news (named Salim) commented that conspiracy theory is a fact as clear as the light of the sun, as he put it, then also referred to the "Qur'an and its method" and quoted the verse.[9] Nassar al-Abd al-Jalil, a Kuwaiti journalist and once a Salafi nominee for the Kuwaiti Parliament, used the first words of the verse in a 2013 article directed to Turkish Prime Minister Recep Tayyip Erdogan entitled "Never will the Jews or the Christians approve of you... Mr. Erdogan." He claimed that Turkey and some Arab countries worked to please the West by adopting "false freedoms, a civil state (the separation of religion and state) and cancelation of Shariʿah." He concluded his argument by quoting the verse again, and the first commentator followed him by citing the verse to show sympathy for Hassan Nasrallah, the Secretary General of the Lebanese political and paramilitary party Hezbollah: "Never will the Jews or the Christians approve of you... Mr. Hassan Nasrallah."[10] Hundreds of other examples exist on social media in which this verse is used as a tool to express an essentialized view of the West, with Jews and Christians collectively and timelessly disapproving of Muslims and their religion to the point of unwavering hostility.

The *riḍā* verse is also often cited in a political context when an influential, well-known Western figure engages in political or cultural outreach to Arab countries. It is used as a way of refuting what the official says, or to raise suspicion about his or her actions. For example, in a lecture dated April 3, 2014, U.S. Undersecretary for Terrorism and Financial Intelligence David Cohen accused the Kuwaiti Islamic Affairs Minister Nayef al-Ajmi of supporting terrorism in Syria, stating that "Al-Ajmi has a history of promoting jihad in Syria. In fact, his image has been featured on fundraising posters for a prominent al-Nusra Front financier."[11] The Minister responded by calling the accusations groundless, but a Kuwaiti journalist had another way to refute Cohen. In an article defending al-Ajmi, the writer argued that the United States has no right to accuse these figures when it has a history of terrorism, then went on to state that Kuwaitis support the Syrian opposition and the efforts to topple the dictatorial rule of Bashar al-Assad. But he concluded his article by citing the *riḍā* verse, as if to say that the United States and its official would not be satisfied with what he assumed were actions done for the sake of Islam (at the hand of the Minister Nayef al-Ajmi). On the other hand, when U.S. Senator John McCain, who is a vocal supporter of the Syrian opposition against the regime of al-Assad, crossed the Syrian borders and met with local rebels in 2013, his picture appeared on a website that used the verse as the title of a report expressing suspicion of the senator's actions. Thus, the verse was cited against both Western opponents and supporters of the rebel groups in Syria.

Many other websites, including Facebook pages and Twitter accounts, link the *riḍā* verse with the news about the West. The Pope's visit to the United Arab Emirates and Jordan in May 2009 occasioned many comments on these websites criticizing the heads of state who received the Pope. Once again, the verse was used to undermine the value of relations with the West, and many citizens were playing the preposterous role of preaching to Arab rulers that their international outreach was against the Qur'an's teachings. On October 24, 2012, al-Qaeda leader Ayman al-Zawahiri released a video statement entitled "Cairo and Damascus are the two gates to Jerusalem,"[12] in which he warned his audience about the West "and the forces hostile to Islam." But al-Zawahiri's main targeted audience was then President Mohammad Morsi, whom he asked to "remember the words of Allah Almighty," and these words, according to al-Zawahiri, were the *riḍā* verse. Though his message was not called for, and only al-Qaeda followers take al-Zawahiri seriously, a similar discourse was used by others when commenting on the relationship between Morsi and the West, particularly the United States.[13]

Some conservative Muslim scholars also link Jews and Christians with the modern West, interpreting the verse to indicate an essential collective hostility between them and Muslims. They use this move without presenting established interpretations by Muslim exegetes. For example, Abdulaziz al-Turaifi, a Saudi scholar and a social media personality whose Facebook page has more than 127,000 likes, posted the following statement on his page on 8 October 2013: "If the West said: 'We are not enemies of Islam,' either they are lying, or we are not following the true Islam (Never will the Jews or the Christians approve of you until you follow their religion)."[14] This post was shared by 251 Facebook users, and it appeared on his Twitter page on February 11, 2014, with 3,902 retweets. Interestingly, on his page there were readers who opposed this understanding. "Our problem is that we always read the West from our narrow angle... we need only to think from a different angle," commented one reader. Another reader wrote: "there is a difference between hostility and lack of approval because your father might not approve of [something you do] but this does not mean he became your enemy." Nevertheless, if one searches for "Never will the Jews or the Christians approve of you until you follow their religion," the Twitter search engine shows what seem to be endless results. Another preacher, named Abdul Muhsin al-Ahmad, has a Twitter account with more than 1,156,000 followers, and appears in a YouTube video using this verse, which becomes the title of the video. In what seems to be a Friday sermon al-Ahmad says, "Take it as a rule: Everyone who is commended by the West, then know that they approve of him. And whomever they are satisfied with, he will not be on the right *millah* (religion) that Allah approved, otherwise (he reaches to a copy of the Qur'an and raises it in front of the audience) this Qur'an is fraud – Allah forbidding."[15] This preacher is so certain of his understanding of the verse that it could only be wrong if the Qur'an itself were a fraud. Such a reading calls to mind Khaled Abou El Fadl's thesis: "Since the Islamic text is mediated through human agents, it would make little sense to speak of an authoritarian text. Rather, it is the human agent who would transform the authority of the Islamic text into human authoritarianism... Fundamentally, authoritarianism is an act of abuse of authority."[16] Apparently, al-Turaifi and al-Ahmad believe that their attitude about the West is informed by the Qur'an, without critically thinking about it in another way, or allowing the possibility that their attitudes might in fact be imposed on the text, charging it with an unintended meaning, so that it is they who are informing the text and not vice versa.

Misinterpretations of the *riḍā* verse are extremely common among contemporary Muslim commentators. They use social media and other internet communications to propagate a message against the West either by circulating this verse as a comment on something related to the West, or simply by sharing explications of the verse by preachers or so-called religious figures. The examples that exist in Arabic media are overwhelmingly numerous. They come from both moderates and extremists. For example, the famous Muslim preacher Ahmad Deedat (1918-2005), whose interreligious debates made him a celebrity in many Muslim countries especially during the 1970s and 1980s, has used it in one of his videotaped lectures.[17] Known for debating Christian televangelists while demonstrating knowledge of both the Bible and the Qur'an, Deedat also stands for political causes affecting Muslims in his country of South Africa and beyond. His videotape, which is available on YouTube and social media, has the date 1987 and Arabic captions; its title is the *riḍā* verse itself.[18] In it, Deedat addresses an audience in the Maldives, reminding them of the Portuguese presence in the past and the Pope-ordained attempts to convert Muslims to Christianity. He also reminds them of their national hero, al-Azam who is credited for expelling the foreign colonizers. But since his speciality is to talk about the Qur'an, Deedat focuses more on the *riḍā* verse. After citing it, he immediately says: "And this is an eternal truth with us. Wherever we are, we find the same situation."[19] Deedat devotes a few minutes to explaining his point, mixing postcolonial narrative with Qur'an interpretations that do not seem to be informed by the context of the verse or by exegetical tradition.

On August 7, 2011, the official spokesman of the then so-called Islamic State[20] used the same verse to justify opposing and killing those who participated in the political system in Iraq. Addressing the Sunni Muslims in Iraq, the statement asks sarcastically: "Have you satisfied America and its allies or not? Are they pleased with the government, MPs, and parliament or not? The answer is definitely yes. Then have you what Allah said: "Never will the Jews or the Christians approve of you until you follow their religion."[21] This misquoting of the verse presents the text as having a definitive, final meaning, makes it political, and blurs the established opinion that it was directed to Prophet Muhammad in a specific historical context. Using this verse as a timeless reference misses that context.

If the verse is providing general reference, then the assumption is that all Christians and Jews have the same feeling towards their religion, which motivates them to have the same disapproval not only of Prophet Muhammad but of all Muslims everywhere and all the time. Logically, people cannot have the same feeling of disapproval. When this disapproval is associated with the faith of others, Muslims or non-Muslims, one cannot help but find exceptions; some do not care to disapprove and others do not feel that they should be targets of any religious disapproval. Therefore, the generalization of the verse is impossible to establish on logical grounds, the same grounds on which many classical exegetes built their interpretations. Whether in groups or as individuals, and throughout the ages, people of different faiths have varying degrees of commitment to their faith or their attitudes about those follow a different faith. Therefore, the assumption of a universal attitude by Jews and Christians does not seem to have a realistic or logical ground, even though it is commonly taken for granted in the Arabic online and print media.

Contextualizing *Riḍā*

But did the Qur'an actually provide the textual base for aggressive attitudes against Jews and Christians? Not in Qur'an 2:120, which is the verse most cited for directing such an attitude against the West. *Riḍā* in Arabic means satisfaction, approval, or to be totally pleased or contented with somebody or something. Classical Arabic lexical scholars often define it as the opposite of the word *sakhaṭ*, which means anger and describes the state of being displeased. In his authoritative Arabic dictionary, Ibn Manzur states that "approval [*riḍā*] and *sakhaṭ* are two adjectives [describing the state] of the heart."[22] He also explicates that when the Qur'an says "He will be in a pleasant life" (101:7) the adjective *rāḍiyah* – which literally means being satisfied – actually means *marḍiyah*, being the object of satisfaction, hence the fitting English translation "pleasant."

Riḍā is not easy to analyze either linguistically or psychologically. It is an emotion that has different dimensions. It can be expressed by silence, as in the hadith when ʿĀishah, the Prophet's wife, asked about the consent of women before their marriage, saying "O Allah's

Apostle! A virgin feels shy." The Prophet explained to her that "Her approval is (expressed by) her silence."[23] *Riḍā* in Islamic traditions can also be from Allah towards people, as in Qur'an 9:100, "Allah is well-pleased with them, and they are well-pleased with Him," which is explained in William Lane's *Arabic-English Lexicon* as "God is well pleased with their deeds and they are well pleased with the recompense that He has bestowed on them."[24] While *riḍā* is used in many hadiths with different connotations, the word and its variant derivatives are mentioned 30 times in the Qur'an.[25]

In verse 2:120, *riḍā* among Jews and Christians is conditional upon the Prophet's following their religion, but it does imply that they have *sakhaṭ* against the Prophet or that they are plotting against him or Muslims, which is what we saw Abdul Muhsin al-Ahmad emphatically (and wrongly) imply. In contrast, an established scholar like Yusuf al-Qaradawi, who can be polemical due to some of his political views, finds in this verse "praise for Jews and Christians" as it shows that they are committed in their religion.[26]

In Qur'an 2:120 the Jews and Christians are preceded with the Arabic definite article *al*, which in the Arabic science of rhetoric (*ʿilm al-balāghah*) is called *al al-ʿahdiyyah*.[27] Roughly translated as "the definite article of familiarity," it indicates a specific subject with which the listener is familiar, and about which he or she is previously informed. The Arabic rhetorician al-Qazwīnī (d. 739/1338) gives this illustrative example. The first speaker says: "A man from a tribe came to me." The second speaker replies (or asks later): "What did the man do?,"[28] where "the man" here does not refer to every man but a particular one familiar to the listener. The man becomes in this example not general, as in the sentence "The man did not exist without the woman," but specific, as in the sentence "The man who first landed on the moon is American." While Muslims can easily and rightly identify *al-nās* (the people) in Qur'an 114:1 as all people and all humankind, this word does not mean the same in Qur'an 3:173, as we will see. When commenting on Qur'an 9:30, "And the Jews say: ʿUzayr (Ezra) is the son of Allah," al-Qurṭubī (d. 671/1273) elaborates on this question of general versus specific. He maintains that "this statement is articulated in the general but it means the particular, as not all the Jews said so. This is similar to [Qur'an 3:173] 'Those to whom the people said,' when not all the people said so."[29] Qur'an 3:72 likewise describes what *some* Jews and Christians have done. Both Qur'an 2:120 and 3:72 follow up by asking the Prophet to say that the true guidance is the guidance of Allah, though with a slight change of word order. This connection establishes that Qur'an 2:120 is a particular reference to some Jews and Christians, not a general reference to all of them, made in the specific context of their historical interaction with Islam.

Though many Muslims associate *riḍā* in Qur'an 2:120 with the West, early works of *tafsīr* do not demonstrate a consensus on the meaning of the verse, or make such an association, which is highly politicized and hardly a well-informed opinion. There is no reference to this verse by Mujāhid ibn Jabr (d. 104/722), one of the earliest exegetes,[30] but his contemporary Muqātil ibn Sulaymān (d. 150/767) specifies that the Jews in this verse are from Madinah and the Christians are from Najrān.[31] Muqātil, who ironically is accused by latter Muslim scholars of heavily relying on Jews and Christians as informants in his book,[32] does not say much about this verse, except to mention that it was addressed to the Prophet. He maintains that the subject of the verb "say" in the verse is the Prophet, and he does not suggest that the entire Muslim community is the addressee. His reference to Christians from Najrān occurs in many places when interpreting Qur'anic verses about Jews and Christians. Gordon Nickel finds more than 80 verses at the beginning of *Sūrah Āl ʿImrān* that deal with "the Christological confessions of a delegation of Christians from the Arabian town of Najrān."[33] This contextualization in the *tafsīr* literature is missed by contemporary Muslim commentators. They cite the *riḍā* verse to claim that all Jews (not those in Madinah as stated by Muqātil), all Christians (not only those of Najrān), and all Muslims (not only their Prophet) are the subjects of this verse.

Another early exegete, ʿAbd al-Razzāq ibn Hammām al-Ṣanʿānī (d. 211/827), who records opinions about verses of the Qur'an mostly in a chain of narration, has nothing related to this verse. When commenting on Qur'an 3:72 ("And a group of the People of the Book has said [to each other], 'Believe in what was sent down unto those who believe [the Muslims] at the start of the day, and disbelieve at its end, so that they may abandon their religion'"), he paraphrases "Believe in what was sent down unto those who believe" as "*riḍā bi-dīnihim,*"[34] or "to be pleased with their religion." This means that he finds the act of belief equivalent to *riḍā*. Thus, "Never will the Jews or the Christians approve of you until you follow their religion" implies not a mere approval (secular and otherwise) but rather "*riḍā bi-l-dīn,*" to use al-Ṣanᶜānī's way of describing accepting a religion. On this interpretation, the negation of *riḍā* by Jews and Christians is a way of saying that they will not trade their religions for Islam. Qur'an 3:72 is clearly discussing only a "group of the People of the Book" that was involved in an on-again/off-again relationship with Islam.

In the exegetical literature, the *riḍā* verse continues to be about only the Prophet and the Jews and Christians of his time and in a specific geographical location: Jews in Madinah and Christians from Najrān. The language used by exegetes in explicating this message is almost always neutral. For example, the traditional Muᶜtazilite exegete al-Zamakhsharī (d. 538/1144) contributes his opinion that it is about the Prophet, without lumping Muslims into the scenario: it is "as if they said: We will not be satisfied with you, regardless of how much you insist, until you follow our religion. They said this to make him give up on their becoming Muslims. Thus Allah narrated their [intended] words."[35] For al-Zamakhsharī, these Jews and Christians wanted to deliver a message to the Prophet that their collective conversion to Islam was not attainable. Fakhr al-Dīn al-Rāzī (d. 606/1209), who also sees the entire verse as about the Prophet and the Jews and Christians of his time, agrees with al-Zamakhsharī's view but uses more aggressive language. According to al-Rāzī, Allah demonstrated in this verse "the intensity of their hostility to the Prophet and explained what necessitates giving up on their following [the Prophet]."[36] They both understand the text as delivering a message to the Prophet, though they differ in sensing the tone of this message.

It is only the second part of Qur'an 2:120 that had some exegetes include the ummah, or the entire Muslim community, as being addressed with the Prophet. Ibn Kathīr (d. 774/1373), whose *tafsīr* is widely read in the Muslim world, does this by contending that the *riḍā* verse is about the Prophet only, while the second part is extended to all Muslims. He begins his interpretation of the verse by quoting Muhammad ibn Jarīr al-Ṭabarī (d. 310/923): "The meaning of 'Never will the Jews or the Christians approve of you' is that Jews and the Christians will never approve of you, O Muhammad. Therefore, do not seek to achieve what pleases or suits them, and thrive to seek the approval of Allah by calling them to the truth that Allah sent you with."[37] But al-Ṭabarī, unlike Ibn Kathīr, does not include the ummah in the second part of Qur'an 2:120, and his interpretation is exclusively centered about the Prophet.

Ibn Kathīr is known to rely on *riwāyah*, or narration of former *tafsīr* opinions starting with the Sunnah (the sayings of the Prophet), then the Prophet's companions (*ṣaḥābah*), who are widely thought of as reliable due to their direct contact with and learning from the Prophet, and then by the *tābiʿīn*, who learned about the meanings of the Qur'an and the circumstances of its revelation from the *ṣaḥābah*. In the case of the second part of Qur'an 2:120, Ibn Kathīr quotes other later sources, or established opinions by scholars that came after these first generations and provided a respected legacy of *tafsīr*. Ibn Kathīr's decision to go back to al-Ṭabarī for the *riḍā* verse is meaningful because they both have the same methodology in compiling all the *tafsīr* narratives – with the latter also being known to have been "shaped by the theological discussion of his time, which then molded his approach to exegesis."[38] Though both preferred the documentation of narrated exegesis over personal opinions, neither al-Ṭabarī nor Ibn Kathīr could record an established interpretation of this verse rendered by the Prophet, his companions, or *tābiʿīn*. Therefore, they sought the alternative: providing a personal interpretation based on their knowledge of all related disciplines of Islam, and based on their linguistic, literary, and legal grounding. Both saw the *riḍā* verse as about the Prophet only, though they disagreed about the second part of the verse.

The lack of interpretation of Qur'an 2:120 from the Sunnah or the generations close to the Prophet indicates that whatever is said about it is the product of a human being approaching it – with no authoritative interpretation surrounding it. Either there was no opinion on the verse by the Prophet, the authoritative source for mediating meaning, or such an interpretation existed but fell into the cracks of documentation and memory. The lack of oral narrative or written documentation concerning this verse could also be because it was the business of the Prophet, not anybody else's, so to speak; but this is not how the traditional exegesis works, as meanings are instilled even by reconstructing the relationship between the Prophet and his community (Muslim and otherwise) and imagining the psychological, historical, and even didactical dimensions pertaining to that relationship and the text associated with it. In addition to what Ibn Kathīr quoted from al-Ṭabarī, we read in the latter's book a personal attempt to come up with an interpretation that provides a meaningful view of Jews and Christians and their lack of *riḍā* towards the Prophet. Al-Ṭabarī builds his exegesis on the following argument:

> Calling them [to Islam] is the [only] way for them to meet with you on grounds of love and religious values. Otherwise, you cannot satisfy them by following their religion because Judaism is against Christianity, and Christianity is against Judaism. They are not in accordance with each other, as it is impossible for one person to be Christian and Jewish at the same time. Jews and Christians do not agree to be well pleased with you, except if you become a Christian Jew, which you can never achieve, because you are a single person, and it is impossible to have two opposite religions in one (personal) condition. Since combining two religions at one time is impossible, it is also impossible to satisfy both of them. And since you cannot achieve this, you need to observe the guidance of Allah.[39]

This interpretation relies on logical argumentation. Al-Ṭabarī utilizes logic to determine how the meaning of approval can be negotiated, referring in the process to the context of the life and character of the Prophet Muhammad. Unlike Ibn Kathīr, al-Ṭabarī does not involve all Muslims. The gist of the verse, as al-Ṭabarī suggests, is that it is a message for the Prophet to focus on calling people to Islam, rather than on the psychological responses or intentions of the Jews and Christians, whose approval in the realm of faith is logically impossible to bring about. Thus neither Ibn Kathīr nor al-Ṭabarī (nor the exegetes who came before them) could find established evidence to state that such lack of *riḍā* is innately directed against Muslims in a timeless and essentialized manner.

As for al-Qurṭubī who focuses on the legal and linguistic aspects of the Qur'an, his methodology reveals a different dimension to Qur'an 2:120. Sometimes more detailed to the point of digression, as an English translator of his work points out, al-Qurṭubī tends to provide "a detailed explanation of the entire *fiqh* of the area concerned, including all the differing opinions of different *fuqahā'*, and the weight of their respective arguments."[40] Thus, he quotes Muslim jurists arguing whether or not the Jew can inherit from the Christian based on the word *millah*, which is mentioned in the verse in the singular. This legal debate provides an insight into how Jurists attempted to regulate community affairs, with its inter-faith diversity. There is no evidence, however, that this verse carries the textual potential to be about legal regulations. As for the *riḍā* verse, al-Qurṭubī maintains that it is about the Prophet's relationship with Jews and Christians, not about the latter's antagonism toward Muslims. Though his commentary on the *riḍā* verse includes only Muhammad and Jews and Christians, al-Qurṭubī sees in the second part of the verse ("if you were to follow their liking") a possibility of wider inclusion: "There are two aspects regarding the way this verse is directed. One is that it is addressed to the Messenger, because he is the one to whom the speech is directed. Second, it is directed to the Messenger but his entire ummah is meant by it. Accordingly, it is meant to discipline his ummah."[41] Al-Qurṭubī, who witnessed the fall of al-Andalus to Christian armies, caught the attention of Asma Afsaruddin, who said that his "enthusiasm for the view that fighting was a religiously prescribed, individual duty is at least partially explained by the circumstances of his own historical period."[42] His expansion of the scope of interpretation of this verse is also possibly motivated by the politics of his time, which saw the end of a long history of peaceful co-existence among Muslims, Christians, and Jews.

Yet neither al-Qurṭubī's method in commentary nor his own view on this particular verse supports the misreading that the negation of *riḍā* in this verse is meant to discourage coexistence based on an assumed universal antagonism of Jews and Christians toward Islam. Contributing his personal opinion, al-Qurṭubī explicates the verse as follows: "O Muhammad, when they [Jews and Christians] inquire about verses, it is not their purpose to believe. If you answer whatever questions they have, they will not like (approve of, be well pleased with) you. What satisfies them is both your renouncement of the religion you are following and accepting theirs."[43] As per his normal method, al-Qurṭubī reports what this verse provided for the *fuqahā'*, arguing that some of them understood from this and other verses that all disbelievers constitute equally the same non-Islamic religion. Still, al-Qurṭubī presents a neutral meaning of the verse, without claiming that there is something antagonistic about Jews and Christians because they refused Islam and adhered to their religion.

Is *Riḍā* a Universal and Timeless Reality?

Classical exegetes agree that the first part of the verse, about *riḍā* among Jews and Christians, is directed to the Prophet, and the occasion of revelation that they cite indicates that it is about only certain Jews and Christians. For example, Abū al-Ḥasan ʿAlī al-Wāḥidī (d. 468/1076), in his book about the occasions of revelation, states that it is about the Jews and Christians who were asking the Prophet for a truce. They were "enticing him that if he had a truce with them and gave them more time, they would follow him."[44] This opinion is taken verbatim by al-Baghawī (d. 516/1122), who is known for choosing sound narratives.[45] Another exegete, al-Khāzin (d. 725/1324), adopts the same opinion with almost the same wording. All three commentators also refer to the *qiblah* being the reason for the disapproval of the Jews and Christians. According to al-Wāḥidī, in a reference to Ibn ʿAbbās, "Jews in Madinah and Christians from Najrān hoped that the Prophet would direct his prayer to their *qiblah* [in Jerusalem], but when Allah directed the *qiblah* to the Kaʿbah [in Makkah], they found it difficult to bear and gave up hope that he would agree with them on their religion."[46] It is only the second part of Qur'an 2:120 ("If you were to follow their liking after the knowledge you have received, you would have no protector from Allah or any helper") that some latter exegetes, not the first generation ones, contended is a message to the Prophet and all Muslims. After citing this part, we see al-Baghawī, al-Khāzin,[47] Ibn Kathīr, and al-Qurṭubī mention that the Prophet is addressed but also the ummah.[48]

Why was the entire Muslim community assumed to be the addressee of the second part of Qur'an 2:120? The reason for this assumption in the exegetical tradition is the strong language of the text, which some exegetes thought could hardly be for the Prophet only. For example, al-Qurṭubī provides an explanation for including all Muslims in the second part of Qur'an 2:120 when he comments on the last part of Qur'an 2:145, which has the same message. Both parts come after mentioning the People of the Book, and both deliver a warning that starts with "If you were to follow their liking after the knowledge you have received," with Qur'an 2:120 continuing "you would have no protector from Allah or any helper," while Qur'an 2:145 continues "you would then be among the wrongdoers." For al-Qurṭubī, it is possible for someone to follow his liking (*hawā*), but the Prophet cannot possibly do this *li-ʿiṣmatihi*, because of his immunity from sin and his moral infallibility.[49] But al-Rāzī, who does not state that there is a reference to Muslims other than the Prophet, finds a logical argument to justify that even this part of the verse ("If you were to follow their liking after the knowledge you have received, you would have no protector from Allah or any helper") is for the Prophet only. He contends that "if Allah knows that someone does not do something [sinful], He can still warn him [about it]."[50] According to this scenario, as proposed by al-Rāzī, Allah is addressing the Prophet who is still the recipient of warning messages, even though he has immunity and is infallible.

The assumption that verse 2:120 is about lack of *riḍā* among all Jews and Christians towards all Muslims ignores the fact that while the Qur'an often addresses Muslims directly, in this verse it does not do so. The verb *tarḍā* (approve) in the verse refers to Jews and Christians, but is followed immediately with the prepositional unit *ʿanka*, "of you" – with the second person singular pronoun – *ka* (you) referring to Prophet Muhammad. The next verb appearing in the verse is *tattabiʿ* (follow), whose subject is also in the second person singular (you), which is also a reference to the Prophet, who is then addressed again with the same verb: "If you were to follow their liking." Another verb, *qul* (say) has a second person masculine singular subject, the Prophet, and the verb *jā'aka* (received) has the pronoun *ka* as a second person masculine singular object, referring again to the Prophet.

The linguistic references to Prophet Muhammad should be considered along with the textual context of this particular verse, which provides an illustration of the general statements given in the surrounding verses. Following a chronological context, and providing more context to verse 2:120, some commentators maintain that verse 2:118 ("Those who do not know say, 'Why does God not speak to us, nor a sign come to us?'") is about Christians, Jews, and polytheist Arabs,[51] and it shows their similar inclinations against Islam: "Their hearts resemble each other." Next, verse 2:119 shows the role of the Prophet to be revealing the truth, regardless of the reactions to it and no matter how stubborn his audience is: "Indeed, We have sent you, [O Muhammad], with the truth as a bearer of good tidings and a warner, and you will not be asked about the inhabitants of Hellfire." After these verses establish this place for the Prophet in the community, whose members are also the Christians and Jews, verse 2:120 describes a specific reaction to the Prophet by some of these community members, showing also that their questions are hardly sincere but merely a taunt.[52] If we take *millah* (creed) to mean Shariʿah or Islamic law, as al-Qurṭubī contends, then (some) Jews and Christians in this verse were reacting to a change in the community or the law of the society. This change, according to some commentators, is when the *qiblah* was no longer Jerusalem and the Kaʿbah was adopted instead.[53] Furthermore, if we take the entire *Sūrah al-Baqarah*, which was revealed in Madinah,[54] as a textually unified unit, then the other place where *riḍā* occurs merits consideration. This other occurrence is in Qur'an 2:144, regarding the new *qiblah* with which Allah promises His Prophet will be pleased (*tarḍāhā*). The connection that Muslim exegetes made in Qur'an 2:120 between Jews and Christians and their displeasure with the new *qiblah* is given some justification by the context of 2:144, and *riḍā* is shown to be associated with being pleased (or not) with the *qiblah's* position. Thus the lack of *riḍā* among Jews and Christians towards the Prophet in verse 2:120 is the semantic equivalent of the *riḍā* the Prophet has about the *qiblah* in verse 2:144.

In contrast, a modern interpreter such as Sayyid Qutb (1906–1966) offered a totally different context when dealing with this verse ideologically: "We see its truth throughout history and everywhere. It is the [Muslim] faith. This is the reality of the attack against the Muslim group [*jamāʿah*] by the Jews and Christians everywhere and at any time. It is the battle of faith... Global Zionism and crusadeism, as well as communism, are all participating in this battle."[55] This approach to the Qur'anic verse about *riḍā* is not adopted by Muhammad al-Tahir Ibn ʿAshur (1879–1973), Qutb's contemporary and a more established scholar in Qur'anic studies than Qutb. Ibn ʿAshur does not even make a case that the verse can be about the Prophet and all Muslims,[56] nor does Wahbah al-Zuhayli,[57] Rashid Rida, or Muhammad ʿAbduh.[58]

There are many verses in the Qur'an that specifically address the Prophet and give him guidance as he engages in his call to Islam with different communities. For example, in *Sūrah Āl ʿImrān*, following a verse that confirms that Islam is the only religion accepted by Allah, the Qur'an addresses the following directly to the Prophet:

> So if they argue with you, say, "I have submitted myself to Allah [in Islam], and [so have] those who follow me." And say to those who were given the Scripture and [to] the unlearned, "Have you submitted yourselves?" And if they submit [in Islam], they are rightly guided; but if they turn away—then upon you is only the [duty of] notification. And Allah is Seeing of [His] servants.[59]

This verse has the same style as the *riḍā* verse, and both give psychological assurance to the Prophet about the way his message is received, and that he is only responsible for calling people to submit to Allah, regardless of who and how many reject him.

Conclusion

In his regular appearances on a YouTube channel, the Egyptian exiled preacher Wagdy Ghoneim often calls the Egyptian government and army non-Muslims, after the takeover of the presidency in Egypt and the removal of President Mohammad Morsi on July 3, 2013. Ghoneim appears in an Aug 7, 2016 YouTube video in the form of an interview with a rather long title that states his rejection for those who expressed "their prayer for mercy on the *murtadd* [labeled as non-Muslim, excommunicated] Ahmed Zewail, Israeli collaborator, [which] is forbidden in Islam." In both the title and the content of the video Ahmed Zewail (1946–2016), who died five days earlier, becomes the target of Ghoneim's harsh condemnation. He alleges in an authoritative manner that Zewail helped Israel to develop its missile systems, and consequently Zewail is no longer a Muslim and no Muslim should even say "may Allah have mercy on him." This might seem unethical, if not unexpected, but the explosive rhetoric of Ghoneim hardly stops there. When Ghoneim was asked why the Nobel Peace Prize for 2015 was awarded to the Tunisian National Dialogue Quartet – which the likeminded Egyptian interviewer describes as secularist – instead of the Turkish President Recep Tayyip Erdogan, he has an explanation. Ghoneim cites Qur'an 2:120 and says, "Because Allah says in *Sūrah al-Mā'idah* [sic], 'Never [and he repeats the word "never" in Arabic twice and spells it for emphasis] will the Jews or the Christians approve of you until you follow their religion'.... Will your enemies honor you? Will your enemies, the enemies of your religion say that you are a good man?"[60] The video has 131,991 views (327 viewers marked it with "dislike"), and it shows how the Qur'an can be abused to serve extremist agendas, which can be directed against the West and even against Muslims themselves.

A careful and ethical (rather than politicized or polemical) analysis of verse 2:120 shows that it was Prophet Muhammad who was addressed by it, and that it was meant to give him assurance regarding the need for a continuous call to Islam, and that satisfying all Jews and Christians is impossible, as they have their convictions already set. After citing this verse, as well as Qur'an 5:51, Mahmoud Ayoub, whose scholarly enterprise focuses on dialogue among monotheistic religions, argues that verses like these "often referred to specific political problems between the Prophet and the Jews of Madinah or neighboring Christians. They should not, therefore, be used to negate the positive verses which are, in any case, more numerous and more emphatic in their insistence on mutual recognition and fair dialogue between Muslims and the people of the Book."[61] It is almost inconceivable, though, that those who cite this verse and use it as the only lens to look at Jews, Christians, and the West, would allow a balanced approach to the Qur'an and look into the "positive" dimensions in the relationship between Muslims and the People of the Book.

To understand the world and the complexities of their position in it, many people seek heavenly guidance through their divine texts. The situation becomes more complex when there is a misinformed reliance on specific religious texts with the assumption that they have fixed meanings that apply to all situations regardless of place, time, and context. Such is the case of the popular understanding and circulating of this Qur'an verse: "Never will the Jews or the Christians approve of you until you follow their religion. Say, 'Indeed, Allah's guidance is the guidance.' If you were to follow their liking after the knowledge you have received, you would have no protector from Allah or any helper."[62] Modern developments in communication and social networking technology have allowed many Arab Muslims to comment on political, cultural, and religious issues. One way for them to express themselves and their attitudes is by citing the Qur'an. When it comes to the complex relationship between the West and the Arab world, the aforementioned verse is commonly used to summarize an individual's position in rejecting different forms of historical and contemporary Western dominance. Such rejection is often bolstered by quoting the verse while wrongly implying that Jews and Christians are hostile to Islam innately, historically, and universally.

NOTES

1. The terrorist group used to be called Islamic State in Iraq, and became in April 2013 Islamic State of Iraq and Syria or ISIS. For more on ISIS, see Michael Weiss, and Hassan Hassan, *Isis: Inside the Army of Terror*, 2nd edn. (New York: Regan Arts, 2016).
2. Rudyard Kipling, *Poems and Ballads* (New York: H.M. Caldwell, 1899), p.11.
3. Andrew Hammond, *Popular Culture in the Arab World: Arts, Politics, and the Media* (Cairo: American University in Cairo Press, 2007), p.16.
4. Benjamin Duncan, 'Poll Reveals Arabs' True Feelings on US', Al Jazeera English, July 26, 2004, http://www.aljazeera.com/archive/2004/07/200841016355992889.html.
5. https://www.youtube.com/watch?v=C-ZjotfZY60
6. Philip Jenkins, *The Next Christendom: The Coming of Global Christianity* (Oxford: Oxford University Press, 2002), p. xi.
7. Michael Martin, *The Cambridge Companion to Atheism* (New York: Cambridge University Press, 2007), p.50.
8. http://sport.echoroukonline.com/articles/193048.html
9. 'Hafiz Al-Mirazi Fired from Alarabiya', http://www.factjo.com/pages/fullnews.aspx?id=24312.
10. http://kuwait.tt/articledetails.aspx?Id=281364#
11. http://www.treasury.gov/press-center/press-releases/Pages/jl2308.aspx
12. http://www.almadenahnews.com/article/print/181311-تنظيم-القاعدة-القاهرة-ودمشق-بوابتا-تحرير-فلسطين
13. https://khelafah.wordpress.com/2013/01/27/خبر-وتعليق-ولن-ترضى-عنك-اليهود-ولا-النص
14. https://www.facebook.com/A.Tarifi.1/posts/634016193296337?stream_ref=5
15. https://www.youtube.com/watch?v=hbtDZclnluw
16. Khaled Abou El Fadl, *And God Knows the Soldiers: The Authoritative and Authoritarian In Islamic Discourses* (Lanham, Md.: University Press of America, 2001), pp.33–34.
17. For more on the influence of Deedat, see Brian Larkin, 'Ahmed Deedat and the Form of Islamic Evangelism', *Social Text* 96 (2008), pp.101–21.
18. Using the verse as a title for a YouTube clip is very common. Searching the verse in YouTube will result in tens of videos, such as the one done by the exiled Egyptian preacher Wagdy Ghoneim, dated December 12, 2016: https://www.youtube.com/watch?v=wJKpNvkTjvI. Ghoneim uses the political situation in Egypt as a reason for his position against Jews, Christians, and some government members whom he calls non-Muslims.
19. See https://www.youtube.com/watch?v=8yk6nyn_wSk, where the video ends with an imposed recitation of Qur'an 2:120.
20. It became in April 2013 Islamic State of Iraq and Syria or ISIS.

21. See the entire statement at http://www.muslm.org/vb/showthread.php?447253.
22. Ibn Manzur, *Lisān al-ʿArab* (Beirut: Ṣādir, 2003), vol.6, p.168.
23. Ibn Qudamah, *al-Mughnī* (Cairo: Maktabat al-Qāhirah, 1968), vol.7, p.45.
24. Edward Lane, *Arabic-English Lexicon* (London: Williams & Norgate, 1863), p.1099.
25. For more on the context of each occurrence of *riḍā* and its variables in the Qur'an, as well as the different meanings of the word occurring in the Arabic language, see Muntaha Mahfouz Jallad, 'Satisfaction: Qur'anic Study,' M.A. thesis, Najah University (Nablus), 2010, at https://scholar.najah.edu/sites/default/files/all-thesis/satisfaction_Qur'anic_study.pdf.
26. https://www.youtube.com/watch?v=F3PHJL5sBmU
27. For the relationship between *'ilm al-balāghah* and exegesis, see Josef W. Meri, *Medieval Islamic Civilization: An Encyclopedia* (New York: Routledge, 2006), pp.679–80.
28. Jalāl al-Dīn Muḥammad ibn ʿAbd al-Raḥmān al-Qazwīnī, *al-Īḍāḥ fī ʿUlūm al-Balāghah.* (Ed.), Muhammad ʿAbd al-Munʿim Khafaji (Beirut: Dār al-Jīl, n.d), p.32.
29. *Tafsīr al-Qurṭubī* (Damascus: Dār al-Fikr, n.d.), vol.2, p.51.
30. See *Tafsīr al-Imām Mujāhid ibn Jabr.* (Ed.), Muhammad ʿAbd al-Salam Abu al-Nil (Madīnat Naṣr [Cairo]: Dār al-Fikr al-Islāmī al-Ḥadīthah, 1989).
31. *Tafsīr Muqātil ibn Sulaymān.* (Ed.), Ahmad Farid (Beirut: Dār al-Kutub, 2003), p.75.
32. For more on critiquing the reliability of *Muqātil*, see *Tafsīr Muqātil ibn Sulaymān.* (Ed.), ʿAbd Allah Mahmud Shihatah (Cairo: al-Hay'ah al-Miṣriyyah al-ʿĀmmah lil-Kitāb, 1983), vol.5, p.43.
33. Gordon Nickel, 'Conquest and Controversy: Intertwined Themes in the Islamic Interpretive Tradition', *Numen* 58 (2011), pp.234–35.
34. ʿAbd al-Razzāq al-Ṣanʿāni, *Tafsīr ʿAbd al-Razzāq.* (Ed.), Mahmud M. ʿAbduh (Beirut: Dār al-Kutub al-ʿIlmiyyah, 1999), p.397.
35. Mahmud ibn Umar Zamakhsharī, *al-Kashshāf ʿan Ḥaqā'iq Ghawāmiḍ al-Tanzīl wa-ʿUyūn al-Aqāwīl fī Wujūh al-Ta'wīl* (Riyadh: Obeikan, 1998), p.316.
36. Fakhr al-Dīn al-Rāzī, *al-Tafsīr al-Kabīr* (Beirut: Dār al-Kutub al-ʿIlmiyyah, 2004), p.30.
37. Ismāʿīl ibn ʿUmar Ibn Kathīr, *Tafsīr al-Qur'ān al-ʿAẓīm* (Riyadh: Dār Ṭaybah, 2002), p.402.
38. Herbert Berg, *The Development of Exegesis in Early Islam: The Authenticity of Muslim Literature from the Formative Period* (Richmond: Curzon, 2000), p.127.
39. *Tafsīr al-Ṭabarī.* (Ed.), Mahmud Shakir (Cairo: Dār al-Maʿārif, n.d.), vol.2, pp.562–63.

40. Aisha A. Bewley, *Tafsir al-Qurtubi: Classical Commentary of the Holy Qur'an* (London: Dar al-Taqwa, 2003), pp. xv–xvi.
41. *Tafsīr al-Qurṭubī* (Damascus: Dār al-Fikr, n.d.), vol.2, p.91.
42. See Asma Afsaruddin, *Striving in the Path of God: Jihad and Martyrdom In Islamic Thought* (New York: Oxford University Press, 2013), p.71.
43. *Tafsīr al-Qurṭubī*, vol.2, p.90.
44. Abu al-Hasan ʿAli al-Wahidi, *Asbāb al-Nuzūl*. (Ed.), Kamal Basyuni Zaghlul (Beirut: Dār al-Kutub al-ʿIlmiyyah, 2006), p.43.
45. J. Robson, 'al-Baghawī', in *Encyclopaedia of Islam*, 2nd edn., http://dx.doi.org/10.1163/1573-3912_islam_SIM_1024, accessed May 15, 2017.
46. Al-Wāḥidī, *Asbāb al-Nuzūl*, p.43.
47. ʿAli ibn Muhammad al-Khazin, *Lubāb al-Ta'wīl fī Maʿānī al-Tanzīl* (Beirut: Dār al-Kutub al-ʿIlmiyyah, 2004), p.75.
48. Muhammad Rashid Rida (d. 1935) records the opinion of Muhammad ʿAbduh (d. 1905) that this part of the verse and the warning in it are also for the ummah, but when ʿAbduh discussed the first part of *riḍā* in the verse he contextualized with the Jews and Christians of the time, whose conversion to Islam was perhaps expected by the Prophet, and this verse announced to him that they would not embrace Islam. See *Tafsīr al-Manār* (Cairo: Dār al-Manār, 1947), p.445.
49. See *Tafsīr al-Qurṭubī*, p.151.
50. Al-Rāzī, *al-Tafsīr al-Kabīr*, p.30.
51. Al-Khazin, *Lubāb al-Ta'wīl fī Maʿānī al-Tanzīl*, p.74.
52. See Seyyed Hossein Nasr, *The Study Quran: A New Translation with Notes and Commentary* (New York: HarperOne, 2015), p.56.
53. Nasr, *The Study Quran*, p.56.
54. Al-Wāḥidī, *Asbāb al-Nuzūl*, p.24.
55. Sayyid Qutb, *Fī Ẓilāl al-Qur'ān* (Cairo: Dār al-Shurūq, 2003), vol.1, p.208.
56. Muhammad al-Tahir Ibn Ashur, *al-Taḥrīr wa al-Tanwīr* (Tunis: Dār al-Tūnisiyyah lil-Nashr, 1984), pp.692–97.
57. Wahbah al-Zuhayli, *al-Tafsīr al-Munīr* (Damascus: Dār al-Fikr, 2007), vol.1, pp.318–21.
58. Rida, *Tafsīr Al-Manār*, p.445.
59. Qur'an 3:20.
60. https://www.youtube.com/watch?v=UM-0569Jlgw
61. Mahmoud Ayoub and Irfan A. Omar, *A Muslim View of Christianity: Essays in Dialogue* (New York: Orbis Books, 2007), p.208.
62. Qur'an 2:120.

7

Social Justice and Islamic Legal/Ethical Order: The Madinah Constitution as a Case Study from the Prophetic Period

Katrin Jomaa

ABSTRACT: This paper analyses a case study from the prophetic period revealing how social justice is perceived from an Islamic perspective and how it is implemented in a legal setting. Prophet Muhammad established the first ummah in Madinah 622 CE through a constitution that organized the relations between Muslims, Jews and their allies. By analyzing the 47 decrees of this constitution, this paper explores a modern concern: how to organize differences in a pluralistic society legally and politically? Liberalism tolerates religious difference as long as it is confined to private practice, while one secular law dominates legal and public dealings. John Rawls proposes interaction based on the "veil of ignorance" in the political realm, where people interact publicly by stressing commonalities and ignoring/hiding private differences to avoid conflict. While the theory has been generally endorsed in the West, critiques attribute to its practice the absence of a sense of community, a lack of social cohesion, and injustices against minorities. One striking observation of the Madinah charter is its incorporation of religious and ethnic diversity in public through the constitution and through legal pluralism. Yet in matters that affect mutual dealings between the diverse communities, as well as common defense, the law becomes common. The layout of the constitution shows a buildup of multiple layers of rights and duties attributed to the respective communities. The ummah expanded from the Muslim community (along with its ethnic diversity) to incorporating the diverse Jewish community then enlarged to include allies or individuals, hence the addressee at the end of the charter became *ahl al-ṣaḥīfah* ("the people of the constitution"). What is consistent across the Madinah charter is the way the public legal document mirrored the private differences, not only by acknowledging them but also by organizing its law around these differences. This paper reveals a new perspective on social justice where differences are not hidden in private, yet their public manifestation does not jeopardize social harmony. The charter puts into practice the Qur'anic ethical understanding of diversity as enriching humans' knowledge about their differences rather than dealing with them behind a "veil of ignorance".

This paper analyses a case study from the prophetic period revealing how social justice is perceived from an Islamic perspective and how it is implemented in a legal setting. The paper explores a question quite relevant to the modern period: how does the modern state deal with different religious communities from a social and political perspective? The liberal secular model tolerates religious difference as long as it is confined to private practice, while one secular law dominates legal and public dealings. One criticism of this model revolves around the concept of identity and the constant need for people to demonstrate a public identity different from their private one for acceptance and assimilation. John Rawls, the leading theorist of modern Liberalism, proposes public dealings performed behind a "veil of ignorance" where people interact publicly by stressing commonalities and ignoring or hiding private differences to avoid conflict. While the theory has been generally endorsed in the West, critiques attribute to its practice the absence of a sense of community, a lack of social cohesion, and injustices against disenfranchised communities.

Islamic ideology, based on the Qur'an and Prophetic practice, sheds a different light on this matter. Prophet Muhammad organized a multi-religious community upon his immigration to Madinah in 622. A copy of the constitution which united Muslims and Jews in that nascent civic ummah was preserved in the Prophetic *sīrah*. This paper analyzes that constitution (comprising 47 decrees), along with the Qur'anic verses that descended in that period addressing the regulation of social, public and political relations between the different religious communities. This paper is part of a larger project exploring the concept of the ummah in the Qur'an (through the lens of four exegetical sources from the 9th century and the modern period) and the *sīrah*.

Community versus Ummah

The first two decrees of the Madinah Constitution (MC)[1] define the members of the Madinah ummah. The MC begins by referencing itself as a book upon which the ummah is to be established. Its decrees clarify the goal of the ummah, the covenants established, and their common leader and land.[2] The first decree, "This is a book / written agreement / accord (*kitāb*) from Muhammad the Prophet (the Messenger of God) between the believers and Muslims of Quraysh and the people of Yathrib and those who follow them, join them and strive along with them," starts with identifying the different members belonging to that one ummah. Hence the term is an active term which reflects a source of identification rather than an established identity. This diverse ummah directly reflects the element of choice associated with the concept and also shows that the term ummah does not depict a closed society. Rather it is an open community for whoever wishes to join and abide by its goals and covenant. Religion (*dīn*) is not the common element among the members of the ummah, which is further clarified in decree 25: "The Jews of Banī ʿAwf, together with the believers constitute an ummah[3] (constitute an ummah from the believers),[4] the Jews having their religion/law (*dīn*) and the Muslims having their religion/law (*dīn*)..."

The Jews and believers form a common ummah, despite each possessing their own religion (*dīn*). Denny argues that the Jews were an ummah "alongside" the Muslims, and that the term ummah represents a closed community defined by common religion.[5] Denny supports his claim by proposing a theory of rupture: establishing a new community in Madinah necessitated a prior break with the old ways of Christians, Jews and pagans; hence there was a continuous rupture with earlier traditions to establish the new order.[6]

Denny's interpretation can be challenged for several reasons. First, it is worth noting that the terms Jews and Muslims, not Jewish ummah and Muslim ummah, are used to refer to religious differences: "The Jews having their religion/law (*dīn*) and the Muslims having their religion/law (*dīn*)." However, ummah is the term used for describing both communities under one banner. Such inclusive phrasing is seen in decree 25, "The Jews of Banī ᶜAwf, together with the believers constitute an ummah," and in the beginning of the constitution through use of the term *ummah wāḥidah. Ummah wāḥidah* is a Qur'anic term used to reflect unity before God; hence the goal of this ummah in Madinah was to unite the different groups. This strongly suggests that the term ummah does not refer to a group of people following a specific sharīᶜah or *dīn*, rather it has broader implications as has been already shown. The Jews and the believers form an ummah united by the common four attributes mentioned earlier, which will be discussed in the ensuing decrees in greater detail.

Second, the inclusion of Jews and their law in the ummah and in the constitution reflects a desire to communicate with earlier traditions rather than forming a closed community breaking with them. On the other hand, the Prophet is described as the *ummī* prophet, foretold in earlier scriptures,[7] whose message confirms those earlier scriptures, and who acts as a guardian and witness to those earlier communities.[8] Thus, the Qur'anic message represents a continuation with earlier divine traditions, and Prophet Muhammad, whose Qur'anic model is prophet Abraham, functions as the father who embraces and unites all of them. The structure of the ummah reflects an ideological background in which not only are different religious groups respected, but also the different groups' religious laws.

Arjomand considers that the constitutional recognition of the Jewish religion represents the foundation of religious pluralism in Islam.[9] Islamic religious pluralism reflects the inclusive Qur'anic ideology which recognizes earlier communities as legitimately possessing the divine right to follow and implement their prescribed sharīʿah, as was discussed in Qur'an 5:48, "To each among you, we have prescribed a law and a clear way...." Common ethical values, which form the essence of any divine revelation as expressed by the Qur'anic concept of *taṣdīq* (later revelation confirms previous ones), make possible the introduction of a common law to organize a pluralistic society, which nevertheless is based on divine scripture. This is what happened in Madinah.

Fred Donner thinks that the first ummah established in the early period of Islam was "confessionally open"[10] and had an ecumenical character as it enjoined the worship of God and the observance of God's law whether it be the Torah, the Gospel or the Qur'an. This early ummah, inclusive by nature, cut across the boundaries of confessional communities. Donner calls the first ummah the Believers' movement. Donner also argues that the inclusion of Jews in the early ummah of Madinah makes one skeptical of accounts reported in traditional sources about the Prophet's conflict with specific Jewish tribes. He thinks that these stories could have been greatly exaggerated or even fabricated by later Muslim tradition to depict Muhammad as a strong character.[11] In response to scholars who regard Prophet Muhammad's preaching as anti-Jewish, Donner says: "in view of the inclusion of some Jews in the Believers' movement, we must conclude that the clashes with other Jews or groups of Jews were the result of particular attitudes or political actions on their part, such as refusal to accept Muhammad's leadership or Prophecy. They cannot be taken as evidence of a general hostility to Judaism in the Believers' movement, any more than the punishment of certain of Muhammad's persecutors from Quraysh should lead us to conclude that he was anti-Quraysh."[12]

If the Prophet had not been sent to a universal ummah, and if the Qur'anic ideology had been exclusive, it would have been impossible to establish that united ummah in Madinah given its significant ethnic, religious and cultural diversity. Politically, Muhammad Mahdi Shams al-Din thinks that decree 25 reflects a political community that unites two communities following two different creeds. Its public order is based on Islamic values and led by Prophet Muhammad. Shams ad-Din calls it a "diverse contractual society" which maintains diversity while simultaneously establishing unity.[13] The statement "the Jews together with the believers constitute an ummah" conveys that, while both the Jews and the believers are distinct communities having their own religion and law, neither group forms a separate political community on its own. In addition, decrees 33-35 acknowledge and confirm Jewish alliances that already existed before the arrival of Muslims in Madinah.

Decrees 2 and 25 are the only decrees in which the term ummah is mentioned. The remaining decrees of the charter discuss the ideas and governing relations between the members of the ummah. It describes the ummah's rights and obligations, thereby clarifying how its members will be judged and how to organize their life together. The first decrees (3–24) address the believers (*al-mu'minūn*). Decrees 25–36 specifically address the Jews (*al-yahūd*) and the remaining decrees (37–47) address the people of the document (*ahl al-ṣaḥifah*). There is one decree that addresses polytheists (20 B). The term Muslims is mentioned only three times, twice to differentiate them from Jews (25 & 37) and once in the beginning of the document.

Serjeant translates *mu'min* as someone who is secure or granted security (*amān*), a definition related to the linguistic root *ʾ-m-n*. Then he argues that the Jews formed a separate ummah parallel to the believers, and he therefore endorses the reading "*yahūd Banī ʿAwf ummatun maʿa al-mu'minīn*" ("The Jews of Banī ʿAwf are an ummah with the believers").[14] Denny does not agree with this translation because the constitution addresses all parties involved equally; it would be unlikely that only one party would be granted security and not others. He favors the translation "believers" instead of "those granted security."[15]

Rubin also translates *mu'minūn* as believers and endorses the second reading, "*yahūd Banī ʿAwf ummatun mina al-mu'minīn*" ("the Jews form an ummah of [a part of] the believers"). He supports his argument by noting that the preposition min typically follows ummah in the Qur'an, e.g. *ummatan min al-nās, umam min al-jinn wa al-ins*, etc. He adds that this reading better explains the use of the term *ummah wāḥidah* in the beginning of the document (second decree), diction that implies uniting all the different parties under one ummah. Thus Jews are regarded as monotheistic believers distinguished from other monotheistic believers (e.g., Muslims who follow Prophet Muhammad). Rubin thinks that being recognized as believers in the MC granted them the privilege to practice their own *dīn*.[16] Arjomand combined the latter interpretations and translated *mu'minūn* as "faithful covenanters," referring to those who enjoy the security and protection of God through the covenant of Madinah, and he regards the MC as "the Covenant of Unity."[17]

Rubin's reading seems problematic for the constitution because there are decrees that clearly distinguish between Jews and believers (24, 38, 45). Decrees 24 and 38 use the preposition with (*ma*ʿ), stating that "Jews along with the believers shall bear (their own) war expenses during war." In addition, the first decrees (3–24) address the believers, while the decrees addressing the Jews (25–36) address them specifically as Jews. It appears that the terms believers and Muslims are used interchangeably in the context of the constitution, while we do not see that happen with the Jews. The reason may be attributed to the Qur'an's definition of believers: "The Messenger believes in what has been revealed to him from his Lord, and (so do) the believers (*al-mu'minūn*); they all believe in Allah and His angels and His books and His messengers; 'We make no distinction (they say) between one and another of His messengers.' And they say: 'We hear, and we obey: (We seek) Thy forgiveness, our Lord, and to Thee is the end of all journeys'" (2:285). The verse specifies that believers should not differentiate between God's messengers. In other Qur'anic verses, not distinguishing between any of God's prophets is directly correlated with submitting (acting as a Muslim).[18] Since the Jews do not recognize the prophecy of Jesus and Muhammad, they are distinguished from the believers who believed in all the prophets equally.

Fred Donner defines Muslim as "essentially, a committed monotheist, and Islam means committed monotheism in the sense of submitting oneself to God's will."[19] Therefore, the term Muslim encompassed Monotheists in general, including Christians and Jews. With time, the term Muslim starts to refer to 'new monotheists' who follow Qur'anic law.[20] Elsewhere I too have discussed the meaning of the term Muslim in the Qur'an, through the character of Prophet Abraham and earlier prophets who were referred to as Muslims. 'Muslim' in the Qur'an does not merely describe followers of Prophet Muhammad, but those who have accepted the divine message in its totality and submitted in sincere devotion to God's will, which "entails taking action accordingly."[21] Donner's argument that Muslim in essence refers to a submitting monotheist is plausible, but that the term Muslim became confessionally exclusive with time can be challenged. The term Muslim is 'cumulative' and requires a new action with the coming of a new prophet as the Qur'anic verses cited in the previous paragraph show. This is due to the fact that the coming of a new prophet signals the annulment of the previous law and the endorsing of the new law. Insisting on following the previous law and rejecting the new one in essence defies the core meaning of submission, and hence forfeits the significance of the term Muslim. Muslim is not a static or dogmatic term that requires a belief fixed in time; rather it has a dynamic and cumulative characteristic that acquires a new flavor with the coming of a new prophet. The person who embodies that dynamic trait (Muslim) is required to act based on the arising circumstances of God's revelation. The latter happened frequently during the Prophet's time. For example, Muslims had to reorient themselves to a new *qiblah* (direction of prayer) when the descending revelation required it.

Therefore, the first reading of decree 25 that the Jews form an ummah with the believers (*yahūd Banī ʿAwf ummatun maʿa al-mu'minīn*) seems more feasible in the context of this constitution from a Qur'anic perspective. From a political perspective, the constitution's main goal is uniting the different groups and establishing peace in Madinah. Saying that the Jews are an ummah of believers has no political or unitary connotations, but saying that they form an ummah with the believers implies socio-political unity.

Moreover, changing the addressee in an expanding sequence also supports the element of addition. The constitution starts with the basic unit of the ummah represented by the believers, and then expands the ummah to include Jews, though they are distinguished as following their own religion. Moreover, the ummah expands to include the respective communities' allies (*mawālī*) and protected persons (*jār*), privileging the latter identified members as well. Finally, the constitution begins to address its entire people (*Ahl al-Ṣaḥifah*). This cumulative addition, represented in changing the addressee terminology, shows that the *ummah wāḥidah*, in essence, is open to include whoever wills to be a member of it. It is not a closed society as Orientalists claim, and it does not merely represent a political confederation.[22]

The religious constituent in the MC is not equivalent to exclusive religious law (*dīn* or sharīʿah) applied to followers of a specific prophet and a divine book. This is confirmed in decree 25, in which each group is instructed to follow its own religious law. Rather, the religious foundation of the MC is reflected in the Qur'anic ideology behind its establishment. Belief represents the essence of its foundation. Believers form the founding unit or the building block for the embracing *ummah wāḥidah*. This is reflected in the terminology used in the MC. The word believers (*mu'minūn*) or its singular form (*mu'min*) is mentioned 32 times in the MC, while the word Muslims is mentioned only 3 times. The word Jews (*yahūd*) is mentioned 21 times. I think there is a significant point to be made here. Why is the word believers emphasized instead of Muslims? I would argue that this is not only meant to strengthen the relationships between Muslims and Jews and others by stressing commonalities, but also to emphasize another crucial point for everyone, Muslims included: belonging to the ummah requires choice and responsibility, not cultural, religious or ethnic affiliation. This critical point is related to the core concept of the ummah. Religion can be reduced to a set of rituals and practices, thereby losing its vigor. In order not to succumb to the problem of transforming belief into a passive affiliation (a problem emphasized in Qur'an 49:14–15)[23] the word believers was underscored.

Decrees Addressing the Believers

Decrees 3–23 address the believers and clarify their duties and rights in the MC. Decrees 5–11 repeat the wording of decree 4 while changing the name of the tribe being addressed:

> 4- The Banī ʿAwf are in charge of the management of their affairs, they shall continue to pay the costs of their bloodshed among themselves as has been the custom and each group shall ransom its war prisoner according to *maʿrūf* and equity (justice) among the believers.

Watt says that this organization shows that everything in the ummah is interpreted in terms of the kinship group.[24] Denny refutes Watt's claim and argues that the ummah is only arranged along kinship lines because the kinship system was the only means to describe and differentiate between the elements of the Arabian society.[25] Denny's argument is more feasible because by looking at the structure of the latter decrees, one will notice that each decree starts by addressing the specific name of a tribe and ends with common rules binding all believers, not just a specific tribe.

The second half of the decrees 3–11 are the same, "according to *maʿrūf* and equity among the believers" (*bi-l-maʿrūf wa al-qisṭ bayna al-mu'minīn*). Therefore, while using the tribe as a unit for organizing the pluralistic structure of the ummah, the MC did not judge each tribe by its own tribal rules, rather by the common rules binding all of them equally before the constitution. That is why each decree ends with the same binding statement, which identifies new regulations based on *maʿrūf* and justice between the believers.

Maʿrūf is a Qur'anic concept describing the action of the best ummah to be raised for mankind, an ummah that commands righteousness and deters wrongness while believing in God. The Qur'anic verses[26] mentioning this term relate *maʿrūf* to belief in God, similar to the decrees (according to *maʿrūf* and equity among the believers). *Maʿrūf*[27] is translated as "customary" by some scholars who argue that the Madinan ummah did not offer anything new to the Arabian society and was rather just maintaining Arab tradition.[28] This idea is refutable because the meaning of "*maʿrūf* and equity" is clarified in the remaining decrees that address the believers (12–23), where some decrees clearly contradict established Arabian customs preceding the coming of Prophet Muhammad. For example, decree 13 altered the pre-Islamic Arabian understanding of crime from a tribal responsibility to an individual one.

Decree 13 states: "All God conscious believers shall be against the person who intends to commit an aggressive and unjust act among them, or who aims to infringe one's rights or to cause turmoil among believers. And even if this person is the offspring of one of them, they shall all raise their hands against him." In this case, kinship and tribal rules are forfeited for the sake of establishing peace and equity among the believers, regardless of tribal affiliations. However, the custom of pre-Islamic Arabia associates the guilt of offence with the whole tribe, not the individual criminal, as explained by Serjeant:

> To expiate the guilt of offence, the guilty *tribe* must execute one of its own members, not necessarily the actual murderer, or else the other tribes will unite and attack it, remaining at war until they have exacted proper atonement in the way of killings adequate to the heinous crime of violating the sanctity of the sacred enclave.[29]

Arranging the Madinan ummah along tribal lines did not mean a loss of individual responsibility at the expense of the tribe. This idea is implied in Arjomand's analysis where he claims that "the ummah was organized as a community of clans, not individuals."[30] Arjomand's argument is problematic because there is an amalgam of rights and responsibilities associated with both the tribe as a community unit within the ummah and the individuals as affiliated ummah members. This idea is discussed by Fadlallah[31] in his interpretation and explanation of the concept of *ummah wasaṭ*, which offers a middle position in community organization and does not overstress the rights of the community at the expense of the individual or vice versa.

Shams al-Din also addresses this point by saying that the decrees that refer to the different tribes and their functions reveal a considerable internal independence of each tribe in managing its internal affairs. However, this privacy and independence is restricted for the sake of the idea of one ummah in which different communities merge into one society. Thus, the tribes were not destroyed as a social unit, but were kept and even used to strengthen the spirit of internal collaboration between the different parties.[32] The pluralistic structure did not threaten the unity of the ummah. This unity will be confirmed through studying the subsequent decrees (12–24), specifically decrees 12, 15, 17, 19, 22 and 23. In decrees 15 and 17 the word *wāḥidah* appears again, emphasizing the one common ummah for all:

> Decree 12: The believers shall not leave a *mufraḥ*[33] (one under financial burden) among them without giving him what is (established by) custom for ransom or blood-wit.
> 12 B- No believer shall oppose the *mawlā* (client/ally) of another believer. (According to another reading: No believer may enter into an agreement with the *mawlā* of another believer, so as to harm the latter.)

Decree 12 with its subsection reflects the mutual duties of believers. It may also reflect the concept of brotherhood (*mu'ākhāh*) established by Prophet Muhammad between the natives of Madinah and the recent immigrants. The institution of brotherhood was a critical step toward the final realization of the ummah. It facilitated reconciliation between the believers and increased their cohesion. The tribe and kinship were no longer the bonding link, and faith became the everlasting bond, as shown in Qur'anic verses referring to brotherhood in religion (*ikhwānukum fī al-dīn*).[34] The institution of *mu'ākhāh* was part of the development process from the tribe to the ummah.[35]

Individual versus Collective Responsibility

Decree 13, discussed earlier, urges collective responsibility as well as stressing individual accountability to hold the offender responsible for his or her offensive act. This idea of shared responsibility among the members of the ummah was introduced in the Makkan verses[36] urging believers to carry out continuous reform (*iṣlāḥ*). Then the Madinan verses[37] practically elaborated on the idea by stressing the need for interaction, discussion, and mutual advice among different people of the ummah since all members share the same destiny. The Madinan verses culminated with the notion of the best ummah, the successful one, whose belief will urge it to invite people to the good by enjoining righteousness and deterring wrongness (*ya'murūna bi-l-maʿrūf wa-yanhawna ʿan al-munkar*). The notion of being best instills in the ummah a culture of social and political obligations that are not dependent on a central power for implementation. This active ummah and its dynamic culture are inspired by a Qur'anic ideology that considers belief deficient if it does not blossom into right action and virtue in society.

Decrees 13 and 37[38] represent a practical realization of the Qur'anic concepts discussed thus far. An active ummah by default puts limitations on the central power. Again we may witness here a middle position best suited to realize politically the *ummah wasaṭ*, where central power and ummah assume different responsibilities without either negating the other. Shams al-Din considers the ummah in this case to be equivalent to the political community. The ummah is responsible for maintaining its integrity and deterring evil and injustice irrespective of tribal or even kinship affiliations.[39]

> Decree 14: No believer shall kill another believer for the sake of an infidel or shall assist an infidel at the expense of a believer.

This emphasizes collaboration of the believers to protect and defend each other as a united ummah against any external threat. This condition reflects the common goal for establishing the ummah and Constitution of Madinah: establishing security and peace between the different tribes and members in Madinah after a long period of strife and war. Similarly, the persecuted believers who emigrated from Makkah to Madinah with the Prophet were mainly concerned with practicing their religion in a secure environment without fearing loss of life.

> Decree 15: The security (*dhimmah*) of Allah (for life and property) is the same for everyone; this protection (acknowledged by the least important of the believers) applies to them all. And the believers, some are allies of others who are apart from the rest of the people.

This decree confirms the goal introduced in decree 14 by

representing the concept of security as a covenant with God. The covenant represents one of the constitutive principles in the ummah.[40] In *Lisān al-ʿArab, dhimmah* means covenant, security, assurance, inviolability and right (*al-ʿahd wa al-amān wa al-ḍamān wa al-ḥurmah wa al-ḥaqq*).[41] This decree reflects the Qur'anic verses (16:92–93)[42] that emphasize the critical importance of upholding covenants 'equally' between weak and strong *umam*. The Qur'an supports its argument using metaphorical imagery comparing the established covenants to the threads forming a piece of yarn: the loss of one thread will lead to the destruction of the whole piece. Similarly, decree 15 states that protection by God is bestowed equally upon the lowliest of believers (in terms of prestige and material status) as on the most privileged. God does not discriminate based on societal status; rather, all are equal before Him. In one respect, associating security with a covenantal status and religious inviolability maintains security for the Madinan ummah. Arjomand considers that the indivisible protection of God over the community and its members strengthened the covenantal solidarity by providing it a new dimension.[43]

Majority versus Minorities or Elite versus Marginalized

In another aspect, this decree again opposes established tribal values that consider the privileged more 'worthy' of protection in comparison to the marginalized. Shams al-Din translates the second part of the decree as "the believers are guardians of each other apart from the rest of the people." The decree reflects the equality of all people, irrespective of the statuses created by human societies. All members have the same rights including the right of giving protection to others, which was a right of only the most privileged in pre-Islamic Arabia but became the right of the least privileged as well in Madinah. All believers should acknowledge that right, honor it and endorse it because the security of God is the same for all believers. Shams al-Din concludes that the guardianship of believers (*wilāyah*) towards each other shows the responsibility of the ummah towards itself politically and reinforces the concept of *shūrā* practiced among the believers.[44]

Thus while keeping the basic structural unit of the society, the tribe, the MC introduced new modes of interaction based on Qur'anic ethics, which fosters a novel understanding of *ummah wāḥidah*. This unifying socio-political structure does not differentiate between its members based on kinship (decree 13), privileged status (decree 15) or religious difference (decrees 16 and 25–35). Rather, the *ummah wāḥidah* establishes its unifying order based on common principles of unbiased justice and equity.

Decree 16: "Among Jews, those who join (follow) us shall receive our assistance and equal treatment; they shall not be oppressed, nor shall we give assistance to their enemies" – is a clause of decree 15 whereby Jews who choose to join the ummah are also granted the indivisible protection of God under the common covenantal security of the MC. Hence the members or tribes of the MC should equally support them and not befriend their enemies; this implies that the enemies of the Jews become the enemies of the believers.[45] Shams al-Din says that equality extends to all parties involved in the socio-political contract. It is not only equality to believers of different status in society, but also to those of different religious background. The Jews here are granted support and equal treatment as long as they support the Muslims living with them in Madinah, and do not betray them or give assistance to their enemies.

> Decree 17: Peace is one among believers. No believer, in a war fought in the path of God, may agree to a peace accord by excluding other believers. This peace shall only be made among them (believers) according to the principles of equity and justice/fair dealing between them.

Shams al-Din thinks that decree 17 is a continuation of decree 15. This decree deals with peace treaties as a means to end war. It shows that being at peace or at war is a decision that cannot be taken by individuals. It is rather a collective decision of the whole ummah that results from *shūrā* and must "accord to the principles of equity and justice/fair dealing between them." Decree 15 talks about individuals. Any individual can give protection to another individual, such as a polytheist, and the rest of the ummah should accept this protection. Decree 15 is related to personal cases and it is not a political obligation of the whole ummah. However, in decree 17, war making or peace making decisions cannot be taken by separate individuals, rather by the whole ummah.[46] This decree reflects the goal behind establishing the ummah of Madinah, which is indivisible peace and security to all. While decrees 12–16 organized individual, internal relationships between Madinah members, decrees 17–22 will organize their dealings with each other as one coherent group fighting external enemies.

> 18- Each raiding party which raids along with us – one shall succeed another.
> 19- Believers shall execute retribution on behalf of one another with respect to their bloodshed in the path of God.
> 20- Surely, God conscious believers follow the best and straightest path.
> 20-B No polytheist [affiliated with the community] may protect the life and property of a person affiliated with Quraysh nor can intervene with a believer in this matter.

Decrees 17–20 establish an internal cohesion between the members of the ummah in cases of war against them, and ends stating that this represents better guidance than that which was followed in pre-Islamic Arabia. The statement "*ʿala aḥsan hudan*" (following the best path/guidance) in decree 20 reflects the Qur'anic promise of bringing better guidance than that of the forefathers: "*Qul a-wa-law ji'tukum bi-ahdā mimma wajadtum ʿalayhi ābā'akum?*" (43:24). The terms *hudan* and *ahdā* have the same root and imply the same meaning. Decree 20B shows that there are polytheists who are recognized as affiliate members of the ummah but this is the only decree that mentions a polytheist and his obligation towards the ummah of Madinah. I think that polytheists were not recognized as an organized community in Madinah like the Jews or the believers, which explains why they do not show up in the remaining decrees of the MC. This decree may reflect a protected person or client of any member or community of the Madinan ummah who happens to be a polytheist.

Since the context of decrees 17–22 is related to war situations, it is conceivable that Quraysh and its affiliated members will be addressed in the MC. Quraysh represents the main enemy of Prophet Muhammad and his followers, not only for its persecution of the believers and its expelling them from Makkah, but also because of its ideology. The word *mushrik* (polytheist), which represents the creed of Quraysh, opposes the word *mu'min* (believer) representing belief in one God. *Mushrik* means associating partners with God, implying following different directions or having different leaders. This usually leads to conflict and disunity, ultimately resulting in war and strife. On the other hand, the root of the word *mu'min* is *amn* (security), which comes as a direct result of belief in God and is due to the unifying power such belief instills in followers.

The socio-political conditions of strife and war in the pre-Islamic tribal society reflect the state of *shirk* (polytheism) endorsed by the pagan society. That state is contrasted with the peaceful state of the believers and the covenanted members of the one ummah, a state resulting from a unity inspired by belief in one common God and enacted through a treaty based on Qur'anic universal ethics. The Qur'anic inference of 'monotheistic belief versus *shirk*' and its socio-political consequences will be addressed in detail in decree 39. Decree 20B shows that polytheist confederates are part of the ummah through abiding by the decrees of the confederation; hence they cannot support their fellow polytheists of Quraysh or interfere with a believer in this matter. This decree shows again that religion does not form one of the constitutive principles of the ummah; rather, it is the covenant that relates and unites the members of the ummah.

Public Norm & Individual Choice

21- If it is proven with certainty that one person has killed a believer (unjustly without a reason that necessitates killing), then it is his own responsibility unless the guardian of the victim grant him a pardon; and all believers shall be against him. And it is not permissible for the believers to fight for him.

22- It is not lawful for any believer approving the contents of this sheet (document) and believing in God and the Day of Judgment, to support or shelter an aggressor; whoever supports or shelters him shall receive the curse and wrath of God on the Day of Judgment, when financial compensation or sacrifice shall no longer be accepted.

23- In whatever thing you are at variance, its reference back (*maradd*) is to Allah and to Muhammad.

Decree 21 shows the individual's responsibility for a crime, rather than the individual's tribe or people. Simultaneously, it stresses the importance of the collective responsibility of the ummah in maintaining this norm (instead of tribal norms) and ensuring implementation: "all believers shall be against him." Decree 22 is a direct result of establishing one ummah because it again revokes the tribal order for the sake of the unified ummah. It emphasizes maintaining the public order in society instead of chaos and mischief. It also highlights the responsibility of the ummah to implement law as the ummah has guardianship over itself (*wilāyat al-ummah ʿala nafsihā*).47

Thus, both decrees link individual responsibility to the collective's, so that individuals cannot fulfill their obligations without the community's committing to establish a norm in society. At the same time, a community cannot maintain its norms and order without the contribution of each constituent member. Therefore, the success of the ummah is a direct result of fulfilling both obligations, the individual and the collective. It is the direct interaction between the two that creates a healthy balance in society and ensures the maintenance of order with the least need for intervention from a central power. Then it becomes possible genuinely to account for the rule of the people and understand the meaning of "the ummah's guardianship over itself" endorsed by Shams al-Din.

The collective obligation of the members of the ummah to fight an aggressor among them and hold him the only one responsible for his crime is emphasized only in the decrees addressing the believers. It is worth noting that this collective attitude is not present in the decrees addressing the Jews. The believers could not have implemented that constitutional norm if they were not educated accordingly, especially as it directly opposes established tribal norms. Hence we find the link in decree 22 between implementing decree 21 and believing in God and the Day of Judgment and fearing His wrath. This direct relationship reflects the Qur'anic education of the believers for a period of thirteen years before they emigrated to Madinah to establish the ummah.

The Madinan verses addressing the collective commitment of the members of the ummah towards each other in enjoining right conduct and fighting aggression are directly implemented in decrees 21 and 22. These constitutional decrees represent a cultivation of the new Islamic values and norms taught by the Prophet in the pre-Hijrah period. Thus, there was a process of socialization before institutionalization. It is obvious from the Madinah constitution that the concept of socialization of norms is rendered seriously for the ummah's establishment and continuation. That is why there is a stress on the collective obligation of the believers in this transitional period. The Jews as a collective body are addressed differently (as will be discussed later) because the Jews of Madinah were not socialized in Islamic values like the Muslim immigrants.

Decree 22 invokes the concept of choice before requiring loyalty to the covenant between the affiliated members by saying "any believer approving the contents of this document." This statement shows that the MC came about through the agreement and consensus of its members, and explicitly states that they have willingly chosen to be part of the covenanted ummah. Consequently, they are obliged to assume the responsibility associated with their choice by upholding their covenant with each other. Strengthening their covenant is realized by equating their covenant with each other to taking a covenant with God. Hence, decree 22 associates revoking the covenant with provoking God's wrath and punishment.

Decree 23 comes directly after the decree requiring constitutional loyalty, which reflects that the judicial authority of Prophet Muhammad is also part of the covenant chosen and enacted by the covenanted members of the ummah. Thus, abiding by Prophet Muhammad's leadership in settling disputes is another form of upholding the agreed upon covenant. Prophet Muhammad's leadership is not above the constitution and therefore, it does not make sense to consider his authority a real theocracy as Denny claims.[48]

Decrees Addressing the Jews

Decree 24 – "Jews along with the believers shall bear (their own) war expenses as long as they are fighting" – is repeated in decrees 37 and 38. Shams al-Din regards this decree to be representative of a "political community." The responsibility of defending Madinah is a shared responsibility for all its residents because the beneficiary of the independence and safety is the whole political community.[49] Arjomand thinks that obligating the Jews to pay the war levy is the Prophet's condition in return for their protection by the law and assuring them religious tolerance.[50] I do not think that the war levy was imposed on the Jews, as Arjomand argues, because the same condition applies for the believers. It appears to be a shared duty of both communities in the ummah rather than a tax imposed on one community in return for granting equal rights.

In addition, the decree specifies that the Jews will pay the war levy "as long as they are fighting with the believers." This last condition implies that they do not have to pay the war levy if they are involved in fighting for communal defense. Decree 45, for example, distinguishes between a war for common defense, which is the duty of all affiliated members of the ummah, and a war for religious reasons, which would be carried out by one group without involving the other members of the ummah.

> 45- If they (the Jews) are invited (by the Muslims) to make and adopt a peace agreement, they shall make that agreement and adopt it; and if they (the Jews) suggest the same thing (to the Muslims), they shall have the same rights from the Muslims; except in cases of war over religious issues.
> 45-B) Each group is responsible for the area belonging to it (with regards to defense and other needs).

Therefore, if the Jews are not fighting alongside the believers in a war carried out for religious reasons, they do not have to pay the war levy since the decree explicitly states "as long as they are fighting." In conclusion, the decree is not an imposition by the Prophet; rather it is assuring that every group is equally and 'fairly' responsible for upholding its duties towards the one ummah.

> 25- The Jews of Banī ʿAwf, together with the believers, constitute an ummah, the Jews having their religion/law (*dīn*) and the Muslims having their religion/law (*dīn*). This includes both their *mawlā* and themselves personally. But whoever performs an unjust action or commits a crime shall harm solely himself and the people of his house.
> 26- The Jews of Banū al-Najjār shall have the same (rights) as the Jews of Banī ʿAwf.

Decree 25, as discussed earlier in detail, represents the pluralistic socio-political foundation of the ummah. The following decrees (26–35) basically mention each tribe by name to guarantee all of them the same rights as the tribe of Banī ʿAwf mentioned in decree 25. What is worth noting here is that the same tribes mentioned earlier as believers are mentioned again in decrees (25–30), but in this case represent Jews. There are six tribes (Banū ʿAwf, Banū al-Najjār, Banū al-Ḥārith, Banū Sāʿida, Banū Jashm and Banū al-Aws) mentioned both in decrees 4–8 and 11 as representing the believers, and in decrees 25–30 as representing the Jewish members of the tribes.

Therefore, the tribe is no longer the main source of affiliation and the ummah cannot be interpreted in terms of kinship as Watt argued, or in conformance with Arab tradition as Serjeant claimed.[51] Both arguments are problematic because the tribe was divided into two communities, or affiliated members, recognized by their religion and law (*dīn*) before their tribal affiliation. There would be no point in mentioning the believers of each tribe and then identifying their Jewish members, uniting them to form an ummah, if they were from the same tribe in the first place. What we witness in the MC is totally new – a dismantling of the Arabian society and tradition, replaced with a new form of affiliation according to new laws and a new social order. The tribe was kept as a 'secondary' source of affiliation because it was the only means to distinguish the elements of the society, as Denny rightly argued.[52] The ummah in the MC represents the primary form of affiliation for its members as shown in decrees 1–2 and 25. Religious and tribal affiliations are secondary. Thus, the ummah cannot be represented as a tribe or as a real theocracy, although it does include tribe as a form of social organization and religion as a personal right of affiliation.

Decrees that govern interactions of the members of both communities seem to be based on the religious law of each community. For example, we have already shown that the governing ideology of the decrees addressing the believers is the Qur'an, as referenced in decrees 13, 15, 17, 21 and 22. The decrees that address Muslims are identifiable from the use of specific expressions such as "according to the principles of justice and equity among the believers," or "God-conscious believers," or "*ḥalāl*." These decrees invoke in the believers a sense of collective responsibility by enjoining right conduct in society and forbidding wrongness, both directives being based on a belief in God and the Day of Judgment. We do not see similar decrees aimed at fostering communal action in the decrees addressing the Jews. This could be due to the difference between the teachings of Islamic and Jewish law. We notice that decree 25 explicitly states that the Jews have their own religion/law, which implies that the Jews are free in organizing their internal affairs based on Jewish law. However, there needed to be a way to insure stability in the ummah as a whole and prevent aggression between its different members.

Since Islamic values are specified as non-binding on the Jews, a different approach is used to preserve order and justice. For example, in decrees 25 and 31 "whoever performs an unjust action or commits a crime shall harm solely himself and the people of his house." If a Muslim commits an act of injustice, all Muslims are against the offender based on the Qur'anic teaching of enjoining goodness and deterring wrongness; for a Jewish offender the social pressure is exerted by the people of his house. In Jewish law, the Torah states "And he that kills any man shall surely be put to death…Breach for breach, eye for eye, tooth for tooth: as he has caused a blemish in a man, so shall it be done to him again" (Leviticus 24:17–20). The Jewish law allows for personal retaliation for a wound or harm, but there is no equivalent for the social pressure exerted by the community fostered in Islamic law.

Therefore, citing "the people of his house" as responsible for sharing blame[53] is a means to foster positive community relations among the Jews, hindering unjust acts and maintaining peace and justice. In addition, decree 36 B – "It shall not be forbidden to take revenge of a wound. Surely if a person happens to kill another, both he and his family shall be responsible as a consequence, except if he kills one who acts wrongfully (*ẓalama*). God is with those who best obey this document" – clearly reflects Jewish law by allowing personal retaliation for a wound. This decree initially appears to contradict decree 21 that addresses the believers stating that "if a person kills a believer (unjustly), then it is his own responsibility unless the guardian of the victim grants him pardon; and all believers shall be against him…." The question raised here is: why can the killer of a believer be granted pardon from the believer's guardian, but for one who wounds a Jew, retaliation should be enacted? Al-Ṭabarī says that retribution for a murdered or wounded person was obligatory on Banī Isrā'īl, i.e., there was no *diyah* (blood wit) as compensation for murder or wound in Jewish law. However, God relieved the community of Muhammad by allowing them the option of paying blood money in cases of murder and injury if the family of the victim agreed to it.[54] Therefore, the difference between the decrees addressing the believers and those addressing the Jews in the case of murder and injury can be explained by referring to the difference between Islamic and Jewish law.

> 37- In the case of war Jews bear their expenses and the Muslims theirs. Surely they shall cooperate among themselves, in opposing those who wage war against the people designated on this sheet (document). There shall be good counsel and advice between them. Observation of one's undertakings eliminates treachery/breaking of treaties.
> 37.B- No one may commit a crime against his ally; surely the oppressed shall receive help.
> 38- Jews along with Muslims shall bear the expenses of wars fought together.

Starting with decree 37, the addressee changes into *Ahl al-Ṣaḥīfah* (the people of the constitution) to reinforce the feeling of socio-political unity. The decree implies external as well as internal threats because it invokes collaboration between both the Jewish and Muslim communities to stand together against anyone fighting the people of the constitution. The decree also declares that both communities should interact with each other in good counsel and mutual advice, which implies deterring any internal threat from among them that could cause chaos and mischief between the two communities.

Decree 37 ends with a general unifying statement that defends the oppressed's rights, irrespective of his/her affiliation. At the same time it stresses the individual responsibility of an aggressor, stating that a human being cannot be accused of a sin committed by his ally. Despite the fact that allies have the same rights as the members of the community, responsibility for an act of aggression by an ally would not be shared by other members as well (following the same logic of rights). Instead, the aggressor must carry sole responsibility for his or her crime and justice will prevail in favor of the oppressed.

Decree 38 is the same as decree 24. Shams al-Din considers it to be a copying mistake by those who transmitted the constitution.[55] This assumption could be challenged. First, there is a possibility that we have two separate documents, one specifically addressing the Muslims and the other addressing the Jews. Second, despite the seeming repetition, decree 37 describes general threats (which include internal ones, and that is why there is the specific mention of allies), while decree 38 specifies external threats. Decree 38 is directly followed by specifying the sanctity of the land, which means that war cannot be conducted inside Yathrib (the previous name of Madinah). Thus, decree 38 specifically addresses cases of war against external threats, which should be conducted outside the borders of Madinah. It is not redundant; rather it is clearly emphasizing the specific duties and obligations. I think that decrees 38 and 39 could be joined together as one verdict.

Decrees Addressing *Ahl al-Ṣaḥīfah* (the People of the Constitution): Sacred Land (*Ḥaram*)

39-On behalf of the people designated by this document (constitution), the Yathrib (*jawf*) constitutes a protected territory.

Decree 39 defines the borders of the land that contain the people addressed by the constitution. The concept of the ummah, in this case, embraced the concept of the land within it. The land is considered sacred (*ḥaram*), which means that no wars are to be conducted within its borders. However, I think that the idea of a "sacred land" for the ummah has a deeper significance than what was stated. In traditional Arabia the concept of *ḥaram* or *ḥawṭah* signified a secure location established by a holy person or family in agreement with diverse neighboring tribes. The agreement allows different tribes to safely come together in this location and conduct business or resolve disagreements, etc., while all the affected parties pledge to preserve its sanctity and neutrality. Murder is one of the biggest offenses within the *ḥaram*.[56] Thus, the central point is securing a safe common area for the competing tribes. While there is a great emphasis on safety or security, there is also a need to provide a common, legitimate ground by which differences can be settled and negotiated. That is why a "holy" person or family establishes the *ḥaram*, because trust and legitimacy play a critical role in preserving the sanctity of the place and upholding the trust of the diverse tribes.

In the Qur'anic context, the *ḥaram* represents the center of peace and safety and is directly related to belief. The symbolism of peace and safety that is associated with the territorial piece of land is a direct result of believing in one God (in contrast to polytheism). In the Qur'an[57] the word *ḥaram* is defined by contrasting it with a state of fear, anxiety and disorder. The Qur'an invokes the spiritual dimension of the word *ḥaram* by highlighting the contrast between safety, associated with belief, and fear, associated with giving power to other entities besides God (polytheism).

The relationship between the security of the land and the belief in one God is traced back historically to the prayer of Prophet Abraham,[58] which implies that spiritual belief and peace will result in the betterment of the ummah's physical life by bringing sustenance in abundance; hence the word *balad* is used, which refers to a physical piece of land or country. Thus, there is a direct relationship between belief in God and receiving His sustenance and security, while those who reject belief are drawn to fear and anxiety (Qur'an 29:67) and hell as a final abode (Qur'an 2:126).

In another Qur'anic verse, Abraham's prayer is accepted and

again the theme of security and asylum is stressed in the context of the Kaᶜbah (first house on earth erected for the worship of God): "And (remember) when We made the House (the Kaᶜbah at Makkah) a place of resort for mankind and a place of safety. And take then the place whereon Abraham once stood as your place of prayer" (2:125).

The Kaᶜbah is described in another verse as *al-Bayt al-Ḥarām*, the sacred house, whereby the connotation of the word *ḥaram* is more clarified: "Allah made the Kaᶜbah, the Sacred House (*al-Bayt al-Ḥarām*), *qiyāman* for the people, and so too the sacred months, the offerings and the sacrificial animals with garlands; that you may know that God is aware of all that is in the heavens and all that is on earth, and that God has full knowledge of everything" (5:97). The word *qiyāman* has been translated differently by exegetes because it has no counterpart in the English language. However, the interpretation of this word is critical for exploring the word *ḥaram. Qiyām* is translated by al-Qurṭubī as both 1) maintaining a livelihood by establishing Shariᶜah (law), and 2) a basis and support.[59] Al-Ṭabarī said that the *qiyām* or *qiwām* of a thing is the means by which it is rectified. For example, the great king is the *qiwām* of his people because, through him, people's affairs are managed, their enemies are pushed away, and oppressors are withheld from those potentially oppressed.[60] The king's rules could be equivalent to Shariᶜah later. We can combine the meanings as "establishing founding principles that support and maintain a peaceful and righteous livelihood." The sanctity of the Kaᶜbah (*ḥarām*) is a derivative of its symbolic function in maintaining a peaceful livelihood for the people through establishing an ethical base governing their interaction with each other (*qiyām*). The same argument goes for the sacred months and rituals.

I think it is significant that in the constitution the word "*jawf*" is used to describe the inside of Madinah in decree 39: "the Yathrib *jawf* constitutes a *ḥaram*." *Jawf* is defined in *Lisān al-ᶜArab* as the interior or core of something. The *jawf* of a human being is his or her interior, and mainly refers to the abdomen. The *jawf* of a land is the portion of the land that is most stable (*mā ittasaᶜa wa-ṭma'anna faṣāra ka al-jawf*) and covers an area broader and deeper than a single valley. *Jawf* also describes the center.[61] I think that the word *jawf* is used in the constitution not just to describe a physical area of land, but also to convey a metaphorical significance.

The *jawf* of Madinah is described as sacred to stress again the connotation of sacredness of the core or essence, the center of the ummah of Madinah. The basis of unity for this new community is not territory, as Rubin claims,[62] and is not merely a political confederation, as previously discussed; it is a unity based on making the sacred represent its essence and core. This sacredness is manifest physically in the land where no bloodshed or oppression is allowed. It is also manifest in the just rules governing people's interaction with each other resulting in peace, as well as in its leadership.

The idea of the sacred being the center and its critical importance in preventing or dealing with conflict is shown in decrees 23 and 42. Decree 42 addresses all the people of the constitution: "whatsoever aggression/misdemeanor or quarrel that occurs between the people designated on this sheet, which is feared to cause dissension, will be referred to Allah and his messenger Muhammad." In both decrees, the centrality of God and his Messenger as the arbiter for resolving conflict enforces the connection between peace and the sacred. It also shows the interconnection between the different decrees in the constitution and the consistency in its formation.

> 40- The protected person is like (one's) self, he shall not be oppressed nor shall he commit any crime.
> 41- A woman shall not be accorded protection except by permission of her people.

Decrees 40 and 41 extended the protection enjoyed by the Madinah members to one's neighbors based on the custom of *ijāra* (making one a neighbor). However, the MC requires conditions in return for protection, first that a protected person should not commit a crime and second, that women should have the permission of their family beforehand.

Decree 39, which specifies borders, is directly followed by clarifying the neighboring borders in decrees 40 and 41. Defining who belongs to the ummah is not achieved by alienating the other, which is considered the same as the self. The latter represents a critical difference between the concept of the ummah and that of the nation state, which establishes itself by demeaning or alienating the different other. "The process of othering is a facet of the collective identity building that is related to a specific territory and refers to the building of the figure of the foreigner, the neighbor, the Other."[63] Bordering territories to create a nation state is obsessed with state sovereignty as well as security from external aggression. Randy Widdis defines the borderland as "a physical, ideological, and geographical construct, a region of intersection that is sensitive to internal and external forces that both integrate and differentiate communities and eras on both sides of the boundary line."[64] The ummah is not invested in creating boundaries, or ideological with respect to differentiating its members from outside members who represent a threat. In contrast, diversity is part of the internal structure of the ummah, resulting in accepting diversity from outside its borders as well. That is why the neighbor is framed as a friend deserving protection rather than as an enemy suspect of aggression. The physical boundary of the ummah is used as a symbol of peace and the sacred to unify members of the ummah and restrain them from aggression against each other. Aggression is not regarded differently outside or inside the borders; it is one and the same – no double standards! Aggression against any human being, whether a member of the ummah or not, is equally despised in the eyes of God. The ummah is open to whoever would like to abide by its ethics, hence its borders are porous and welcoming ideologically and physically. As shown in this paper, the concept of the ummah kept expanding by including more diverse members. In early Islamic history, the boundaries were expanded so that more nations, ethnicities and religious groups became part of the ummah. In this process of expansion, boundaries that separate people from each other were destroyed. In the early caliphate system, the ummah is sovereign, and not the state (or political power), contrary to the modern nation state.

The next decree confirms that the ummah is invested with

evading aggression among its members more than outside aggression.

> 42- Whatsoever aggression/misdemeanor or quarrel that occurs between the people designated on this sheet, which is feared may cause dissension, will be referred to Allah and his messenger Muhammad. Allah is (surety) for the truest and most righteous observance of what is in this document.

This decree reaffirms decrees 23 and 36 that assign judiciary authority to Prophet Muhammad; however the addressee in this decree is not only the believers or the Jews, but rather the united ummah of the constitution (*Ahl al-Ṣaḥīfah*). This decree reflects the Qur'anic verse 5:48[65] which assigns the governance of the ummah to its book and judgment to the one knowledgeable of its book. The book (*kitāb*) precedes the function of the judge and legitimizes the judge in the latter part of the verse. Hence the decree started by addressing the people of the constitution before assigning the Prophet the role of judge and ended with emphasizing that the people should follow its rules to ensure God's surety. Emphasizing God before the Prophet is critical because it makes the law objective, not subjective and biased to serve the elite or the privileged. In the same regard, if the law is objective in regards to aggression in general, there should be no difference between aggressive acts inside or outside the borders.

> 43- Neither Quraysh nor those assisting them shall receive protection.
> 44- There shall be cooperation among them (Muslims and Jews) against those who invade Yathrib.
> 45- If they (the Jews) are invited (by the Muslims) to make and adopt a peace agreement, they shall make that agreement and adopt it; and if they (the Jews) suggest the same thing (to the Muslims), they shall have the same rights from the Muslims; except in cases of war over religious issues.
> 45-B) Each group is responsible for the area belonging to it (with regards to defense and other needs.)

Decrees 43–45 address the defense of Madinah by calling for mutual participation of its members in war and peace, and singles out a common enemy. Quraysh represents the main opponent of

Muslims as it drove the Prophet and his followers out of their hometown, besides its persecution of Muslims. It is important to note that this is a specific case in which part of the ummah had an existing conflict with a tribe, rather than defining outsiders in general as a potential threat. Nevertheless, Quraysh did not represent a threat to the people of Madinah until Prophet Muhammad and his followers entered the city. In order to solve this problem, the Prophet adopted two strategies. First, it was expected that Quraysh would attack the Muslims in their new land (Madinah), so the Prophet cited Quraysh as an enemy to the general defense of Madinah, a space that is declared sacred (*ḥaram*) for all its inhabitants. Second, to ensure equality for all affiliated members of the MC, the Prophet obligated both communities, Muslims and Jews, to respect and support each other in peacemaking and in war.

Therefore, the Jews were not obligated to consider Quraysh as an enemy for the sake of the Muslim members in Madinah without expecting reciprocal support from the Muslims. However, decree 45 singles out religious war as a potential point of contention, which is understandable because the two communities have different religious affiliations. Serjeant interprets this decree as a deterrent from one of the parties entering into a peace agreement to preserve their own interests at the expense of the others.[66] In both cases, the decrees ensure the rights of both communities while maintaining unity by constantly reminding them of their common goals. Decree 45 B is a continuation of decree 45 as it makes each community responsible for defending the area within its domain.

Decree 47 represents a summary of the major points iterated in the whole constitution:

> 47- This book (*kitāb*) shall not protect the perpetrator of an unjust act or crime from punishment. Whoever goes out shall have security and whoever remains in Madinah shall also have security; except one who commits an unjust act or a crime. Allah protects the person who observes undertakings and keeps free of dishonorable acts and offences, and Muhammad the messenger of Allah, Allah bless and honor him.

Conclusion

The Madinah constitution describes an inclusive ummah receptive to any human being who is willing to be affiliated with its inclusive values. Many scholars and exegetes interpreted this global ummah, described in the Qur'an as '*ummah wāḥidah*', to be an ummah of a common humanity defined by a common innate nature (*fiṭrah*). That inclusive ummah does not eliminate religious, cultural or political diversity but acknowledges them as respected choices with merited consequences.

The constitution, with its principles and values, represents the foundation that unites the diverse communities of the ummah into one shared body, *ummah wāḥidah*. The decrees reflect different kinds of pluralism. Religious pluralism is manifested by inclusion of Muslims and Jews within the ummah, each community following its own religion and law. Cultural pluralism appears through the mentioning of each tribe by its own name, thereby reinforcing the connection between the private and public spheres. Political pluralism is evident from the way the constitution details reciprocal rights and obligations for its diverse communities.

Different decrees urge the members of the ummah to actively oppose an aggressor among them, even if a member of their kin. Thereby it portrays an active ummah assuming the responsibility of maintaining and implementing justice between its members and not confining the responsibility to the central power. In addition, mutual advice and consultation are urged between the various communities. The latter concepts are critical as societal public norms are used to enforce individual responsibilities, a concept alien to the structure of a modern state where laws are enforced by coercive central power, as the modern society represents a summation of alienated individuals rather than fellow members of one society.

Another noticeable feature of the Madinah constitution is its incorporation of religious and ethnic diversity in public through the constitution as a law document and through legal pluralism. Yet in matters that affect the mutual dealings between the religious communities and ethnic groups, as well as defense of the common territory, the law becomes common. The layout of the constitution shows a buildup of multiple layers of rights and duties attributed to the respective communities. What is consistent across the Madinah charter is the way the legal public document mirrors the private differences, not only by acknowledging them but also by organizing its law around these differences.

The ummah expanded from the Muslim community (along with its ethnic diversity) to incorporate the diverse Jewish community, then enlarged to include allies or individuals, hence the addressee at the end of the charter became *Ahl al-Ṣaḥīfah* (the people of the constitution). Associated with the latter term, a new concept is introduced, *ḥaram* (sacred land). This term implies peace, security and trust, which represent desired goals for the flourishing of the ummah. Contrary to the nation state, the bordering is not created to alienate the neighboring other and protect its members from outside aggression. Rather, the Ḥaram represents a symbol of peace for the ummah members which is aimed at constant expansion by welcoming more members to the ummah, thereby destroying boundaries that separate people from each other.

This paper shows a new perspective about social justice where differences are not hidden in private, yet their public manifestation does not jeopardize social harmony. The MC also addresses the individual citizen as a complete human being, rather than a number among many. This is evident in the ways the MC balanced between the elite and the marginalized as well as between the individual and the community. The charter puts in practice the Qur'anic ethical understanding of diversity as enriching humans' knowledge about their differences rather than dealing with them behind a "veil of ignorance."

REFERENCES

Arjomand, Said Amir, 'The Constitution of Medina: A Sociolegal Interpretation of Muhammad's Acts of Foundation of the Ummah', *International Journal of Middle East Studies* 41 (2009), pp.555–75.

Denny, Frederick, 'Community and Salvation: The Meaning of the Ummah in the Qur'ān'. Ph.D. dissertation, University of Chicago, 1974.

Denny, Frederick, 'The Meaning of Ummah in the Quran', *History of Religions* 15(1) (August, 1975), pp.39–42.

Denny, Frederick, 'Ummah in the Constitution of Medina', *Journal of Near Eastern Studies* 36(1) (January 1977), pp.39–47.

Donner, Fred M., *Muhammad and the Believers: At the Origins of Islam* (Cambridge: The Belknap Press of Harvard University Press, 2010).

Fadlallah, Muhammad Husayn, *Min waḥy al-Qur'ān* (Beirut: Dār al-Malāk, 1998).

Giannakis, Elias, 'The Concept of Ummah', *Graeco-Arabica* 2 (1983) pp.103–4.

Guillaume, A., *The Life of Muhammad: A Translation of Isḥāq's Sīrat Rasūl Allāh* with Introduction and Notes. (Oxford: Oxford University Press, 1955; reprinted Karachi, 1967).

Hamidullah, Muhammad, *Majmūʿat al-Wathā'iq al-Siyāsiyyah* (Cairo: Lajnat al-Ta'līf wa al-Tarjamah wa al-Nashr, 1941).

Ibn Hisham, Abu Muhammad ʿAbd al-Malik, *al-Sīrah al-Nabawiyyah.* (Ed.), Suhayl Zakkār (Beirut: Dār al-Fikr, 1992).

Ibn Kathīr, Abū al-Fidā' al-Ḥāfiẓ, *al-Bidāyah wa al-Nihāyah* (Beirut: Maktabat al-Maʿārif, 1966.).

Ibn Manzur, *Lisān al-ʿArab* (Beirut: Dār Iḥyā' al-Turāth al-ʿArabī, 1993).

Ibn Sallam, Abu ʿUbayd, *Kitāb al-Amwāl.* (Ed.), M. Khalil Haras (Cairo: Maktabat al-Kullīyāt al-Azhariyyah, 1968).

Jomaa, Katrin, 'A Conceptual Analysis of Umma in the Quran and Sunna and the Aristotelian Polis'. Ph.D. dissertation, Indiana University, 2012.

Lecker, Michael, *The "Constitution of Medina": Muhammad's First Legal Document* (Princeton, NJ: The Darwin Press, 2004).

Meier, Daniel, 'Bordering the Middle East', *Geopolitics* 23 (2018), pp.495–504.

Pickthall, Muhammad, *The Glorious Quran: Text and Explanatory Translation* (New York: Mostazafan Foundation of New York, 1984.).

al-Qurṭubī, Abū Abd Allāh Muḥammad ibn Aḥmad al-Anṣārī, *al-Jāmiʿ li-Aḥkām al-Qur'ān* (Beirut: Dār Iḥyā' al-Turāth al-ʿArabī, 1985).

Rubin, Uri, '"The Constitution of Medina": Some Notes', *Studia Islamica* 62 (1985), pp.5–23.

Serjeant, R.B., 'The Sunnah Jami'ah, Pacts with the Yathrib Jews and the Tahrim of Yathrib: Analysis and Translation of the documents comprised in the so-called

"Constitution of Medina"', *Bulletin of the School of Oriental and African Studies* 41(1) (1978), pp.1–42.

Serjeant, R.B., 'The Constitution of Medina', *The Islamic Quarterly* 8 (1964), pp.3–16.

Serjeant, R.B., 'Haram and Hawtah, the Sacred Enclave in Arabia', in *Mélanges Taha Hussein*. (Ed.), Abdurrahman Badawi (Cairo: Dār al-Maᶜārif, 1962), pp.41–58.

Shams al-Din, Muhammad Mahdi, *Fī al-Ijtimāᶜ al-Siyāsī al-Islāmī* (Beirut: al-Mu'asassah al-Jāmiᶜiyyah lil-Dirāsāt wa al-Nashr, 1992).

al-Ṭabarī, Abū Jaᶜfar Muḥammad ibn Jarīr, *Jāmiᶜ al-Bayān* (Beirut: Dār al-Fikr, 1995).

al-Ṭabaṭabā'ī, Muḥammad Ḥusayn, *al-Mīzān fī Tafsīr al-Qur'ān* (Beirut: Mu'asassat al-Aᶜlamī lil-Maṭbūᶜāt, 1983).

al-Wāqidī, Muḥammad ibn ᶜUmar, *Kitāb al-Maghāzī*. (Ed.), Marsden Jones (London: Oxford University Press, 1966).

Watt, W. Montgomery, *Muhammad at Medina* (Oxford: Clarendon Press, 1956).

Yusuf Ali, Abdullah, *The Meanings of the Illustrious Qur'ān: English Translation with Introduction* (New Delhi: Kitab Bhavan, 2000).

APPENDIX A

THE MADINAH CONSTITUTION[67]

1) This is a book (*kitāb*) from Muhammad the Prophet (the Messenger of God) between the believers and Muslims of Quraysh and the people of Yathrib and those who follow them, join them and strive along with them.

١- هذا كتاب من محمد النبي (رسول الله) بين المؤمنين والمسلمين من قريش و(أهل) يثرب ومن تبعهم فلحق بهم وجاهد معهم.

2) They are one ummah (*ummah wāḥidah*) apart from the people.

٢- أنهم أمة واحدة من دون الناس.

3) The *muhājirūn* (migrants) of Quraysh are in charge of the management of their affairs, they shall defray the cost of bloodshed among themselves and shall join in ransoming their war prisoners according to *maʿrūf* and equity (justice) among the believers.

٣- المهاجرون من قريش على ربعتهم يتعاقلون بينهم وهم يفدون عانيهم بالمعروف والقسط بين المؤمنين.

4) The Banū* ʿAwf are in charge of the management of their affairs, they shall continue to pay the costs of their bloodshed among themselves as has been the custom and each group shall ransom its war prisoner according to *maʿrūf* aand equity (justice) among the believers.

٤- وبنو عوف على ربعتهم يتعاقلون معاقلهم ألاولى، وكل طائفة تفدي عانيها بالمعروف والقسط بين المؤمنين.

5) The Banū al-Ḥārith (...)

٥- وبنو الحارث (بن الخزرج) على ربعتهم يتعاقلون معاقلهم ألاولى، وكل طائفة تفدي عانيها بالمعروف والقسط بين المؤمنين.

6) The Banū Sāʿida (...)

٦- وبنو ساعدة على ربعتهم يتعاقلون معاقلهم ألاولى، وكل طائفة تفدي عانيها بالمعروف والقسط بين المؤمنين.

7) The Banū Jashm (...)

٧- وبنو جشم على ربعتهم يتعاقلون معاقلهم ألاولى، وكل طائفة تفدي عانيها بالمعروف والقسط بين المؤمنين.

8) The Banū al-Najjār (...)

٨- وبنو النجار على ربعتهم يتعاقلون معاقلهم ألاولى، وكل طائفة تفدي عانيها بالمعروف والقسط بين المؤمنين.

9) The Banū ʿAmr bin ʿAwf (...)

٩- وبنو عمرو بن عوف على ربعتهم يتعاقلون معاقلهم ألاولى، وكل طائفة تفدي عانيها بالمعروف والقسط بين المؤمنين.

10) The Banū al-Nabīt (...)

١٠- وبنو النبيت على ربعتهم يتعاقلون معاقلهم ألاولى، وكل طائفة تفدي عانيها بالمعروف والقسط بين المؤمنين.

11) The Banū al-Aws (...)

١١- وبنو ألاوس على ربعتهم يتعاقلون معاقلهم ألاولى، وكل طائفة تفدي عانيها بالمعروف والقسط بين المؤمنين.

12) The believers shall not leave a *mufraḥ*[68] (one under financial burden) among them without giving him what is (established by) custom for ransom or blood-wit.

١٢- وأن المؤمنين لا يتركون مفرحًا بينهم أن يعطوه بالمعروف في فداء أو عقل.

12B) No believer shall oppose the *mawlā* (client/ally) of another believer. (According to another reading: No believer may enter into an agreement with the *mawlā* of another believer, so as to harm the latter.)

١٢ب- وأن لا يخالف مؤمن مولى مؤمن دونه.

13) All God conscious believers shall be against the person who intends to commit an aggressive and unjust act among them, or who aims to infringe one's rights or to cause turmoil among believers. And even if this person is the offspring of one of them, they shall all raise their hands against him.

١٣- وأن المؤمنين المتقين (أيديهم) على (كل) من بغى منهم، أو ابتغى دسيعة ظلم، أو اثمًا، أو عدوانًا، أو فسادًا بين المؤمنين، وأن أيديهم عليه جميعًا، ولو كان ولد أحدهم.

14) No believer shall kill another believer for the sake of an infidel or shall assist an infidel at the expense of a believer.

١٤- ولا يقتل مؤمن مؤمنًا في كافر، ولا ينصر كافرًا على مؤمن.

15) The security (*dhimmah*) of Allah (for life and property) is one; (a protection acknowledged by the least important of the believers) applies to them all. And the believers, some are allies of others apart from the rest of the people.

١٥- وأن ذمة الله واحدة يجير عليهم أدناهم، وأن المؤمنين بعضهم موالي بعض دون الناس.

16) Among Jews, those who join (follow) us shall receive our assistance and equal treatment; they shall not be oppressed, nor shall we give assistance to their enemies.

١٦- وأنه من تبعنا من يهود فإن له النصر وألاسوة غير مظلومين ولا متناصر عليهم.

17) Peace is one among believers. No believer, in a war fought in the path of God, may agree to a peace accord by excluding other believers. This peace shall only be made among them (believers) according to the principles of equity and justice/fair dealing between them.

١٧- وأن سلم المؤمنين واحدة، لا يسالم مؤمن دون مؤمن في قتال في سبيل الله، إلا على سواء وعدل بينهم.

18) Each raiding party which raids along with us — one shall succeed another.

١٨- وأن كل غازية غزت معنا يعقب بعضها بعضًا.

19) Believers shall execute retribution on behalf of one another with respect to their blood shed in the path of God.

١٩- وأن المؤمنين يبئ بعضهم عن بعض بما نال دماءهم في سبيل الله.

20) Surely, God-conscious believers follow the best and straightest path.

٢٠- وأن المؤمنين المتقين على أحسن هدى وأقومه.

20B) No polytheist [affiliated with the community] may protect the life and property of a person affiliated with Quraysh nor can intervene with a believer in this matter.

٢٠ب- وأنه لا يجير مشرك مالاً لقريش ولا نفسًا، ولا يحول دونه على مؤمن.

21) If it is proven with certainty that one person has killed a believer (unjustly without a reason that necessitates killing), then it is his own responsibility unless the guardian of the victim grant him a pardon; and all believers shall be against him. And it is not permissible for the believers to fight for him.

٢١- وأنه من اعتبط مؤمنًا قتلاً عن بينة فإنه قود به، إلا أن يرضى ولي المقتول (بالعقل)، وأن المؤمنين عليه كافة وانه لا يحل لهم الاقتتال عليه.

22) It is not lawful for any believer approving the contents of this sheet (document) and believing in God and the Day of Judgment, to support or shelter an aggressor; whoever supports or shelters him shall receive the curse and wrath of God on the Day of Judgment, when financial compensation or sacrifice shall no longer be accepted.

٢٢- وأنه لا يحل لمؤمن أقرّ بما في هذه الصحيفة، وآمن بالله واليوم الآخر أن ينصر محدثًا أو يؤويه، وأن من نصره، أو آواه، فإن عليه لعنة الله وغضبه يوم القيامة، ولا يؤخذ منه صرف ولا عدل.

23) In whatever thing you are at variance, its reference back (*maradd*) is to Allah and to Muhammad.

٢٣- وأنكم مهما اختلفتم فيه من شيء، فإن مردّه إلى الله وإلى محمد.

Decrees Addressing the Jews

24) Jews along with the believers shall bear (their own) war expenses as long as they are fighting.

٢٤- وأن اليهود ينفقون مع المؤمنين ما داموا محاربين.

25) The Jews of Banī ʿAwf, together with the believers constitute an ummah; the Jews having their religion/law *(dīn)* and the Muslims having their religion/law (*dīn*). This includes both their *mawlā* and themselves personally. But whoever performs an unjust action or commits a crime shall harm solely himself and the people of his house.

٢٥- وأن يهود بني عوف أمة مع المؤمنين، لليهود دينهم وللمسلمين دينهم، مواليهم وأنفسهم إلا من ظلم وأثم، فإنه لا يوتغ إلا نفسه وأهل بيته.

26) The Jews of Banī al-Najjār shall have the same (rights) as the Jews of Banī ʿAwf.

٢٦- وأن ليهود بني النجار مثل ما ليهود بني عوف.

27) The Jews of Banī al-Ḥārith shall have the same (rights) as the Jews of Banī ʿAwf.

٢٧- وأن ليهود بني الحارث مثل ما ليهود بني عوف.

28) The Jews of Banī Sāʿida shall have the same (rights) as the Jews of Banī ʿAwf.

٢٨- وأن ليهود بني ساعدة مثل ما ليهود بني عوف.

29) The Jews of Banī Jashm shall have the same (rights) as the Jews of Banī ʿAwf.

٢٩- وأن ليهود بني جشم مثل ما ليهود بني عوف.

30) The Jews of Banī al-Aws shall have the same (rights) as the Jews of Banī ʿAwf.

٣٠- وأن ليهود بني ألاوس مثل ما ليهود بني عوف.

31) The Jews of Banī Thaʿlabah shall have the same (rights) as the Jews of Banī ʿAwf. But whoever performs an unjust action or commits a crime shall harm solely himself and the people of his house.

٣١- وأن ليهود بني ثعلبة مثل ما ليهود بني عوف، إلا من ظلم وأثم، فإنه لا يوتغ إلا نفسه وأهل بيته.

32) The Jafnah (family) is a branch of the Thaʿlabah [tribe] and because of this they shall be considered as the Thaʿlabah.

٣٢- وأن جفنة بطن من ثعلبة كأنفسهم.

33) The Banū al-Shuṭaybah shall have the same rights as the Jews of Banī* ʿAwf. Observation of one's undertakings eliminates treachery/breaking of treaties.

٣٣- وأن لبني الشطيبة مثل ما ليهود بني عوف، وأن البر دون الإثم.

34) The clients/allies of Thaʿlabah shall be considered as Thaʿlabah themselves.

٣٤- وأن موالي ثعلبة كأنفسهم.

35) Those associated with Jews (by alliance and bonds of mutual protection) shall be considered as Jews themselves.

٣٥- وأن بطانة يهود كأنفسهم.

36) Among them (Jews) none may go (on a military campaign with the Muslims) without the permission of Muhammad.

٣٦- وأنه لا يخرج منهم أحد إلا بإذن محمد.

36B) It shall not be forbidden to take revenge of a wound. Surely if a person happens to kill another, both he and his family shall be responsible as a consequence, except if he kills one who acts wrongfully (*ẓalama*). God is with those who best obey this document.

٣٦ب- وأنه لا ينحجز على ثار جرح، وأنه من فتك فبنفسه وأهل بيته إلا من ظلم وأن الله على أبر هذا.

37) In case of war Jews bear their expenses and the Muslims theirs. Surely they shall cooperate among themselves, in opposing those who wage war against the people designated on this sheet (document). There shall be good counsel and advice between them. Observation of one's undertakings eliminates treachery/breaking of treaties.

٣٧- وأن على اليهود نفقتهم، وعلى المسلمين نفقتهم، وأن بينهم النصر على من حارب أهل هذه الصحيفة، وأن بينهم النصح والنصيحة والبر دون الإثم.

37B) No one may commit a crime against his ally; surely the oppressed shall receive help.

٣٧ب- وأنه لا يأثم امرؤ بحليفه، وأن النصر للمظلوم.

38) Jews along with Muslims shall bear the expenses of wars fought together.

٣٨- وأن اليهود ينفقون مع المؤمنين ما داموا محاربين.

Decrees Addressing *Ahl al-Ṣaḥīfah* (the People of the Constitution)

39) On behalf of the people designated by this document (constitution), the Yathrib (*jawf*) constitutes a protected territory.

٣٩- وأن يثرب حرام جوفها لأهل هذه الصحيفة.

40) The protected person is like (one's) self, he shall not be oppressed nor shall he commit any crime.

٤٠- وأن الجار كالنفس غير مضارّ ولا آثم.

41) A woman shall not be accorded protection except by permission of her people.

٤١- وأنه لا تجار حرمة إلا بإذن أهلها.

42) Whatsoever aggression/misdemeanor or quarrel that occurs between the people designated on this sheet, which is feared may cause dissension, will be referred to Allah and his Messenger Muhammad. Allah is (surety) for the truest and most righteous observance of what is in this document.

٤٢- وأنه لا ما كان بين أهل هذه الصحيفة من حدث، أو اشتجار يخاف فساده، فإن مردّه إلى الله وإلى محمد رسول الله (صلى الله عليه وسلّم)، وأن الله على أتقى ما في هذه الصحيفة وأبرّه.

43) Neither Quraysh nor those assisting them shall receive protection.

٤٣- وأنه لا تجار قريش ولا من نصرها.

44) There shall be cooperation among them (Muslims and Jews) against those who invade Yathrib.

٤٤- وأن بينهم النصر من دهم يثرب.

45) If they (the Jews) are invited (by the Muslims) to make and adopt a peace agreement, they shall make that agreement and adopt it; and if they (the Jews) suggest the same thing (to the Muslims), they shall have the same rights from the Muslims; except in cases of war over religious issues.

٤٥- وإذا دعوا إلى صلح يصالحونه ويلبسونه فإنهم يصالحونه ويلبسونه، وأنهم إذا دعوا إلى مثل ذلك، فإنه لهم على المؤمنين إلا من حارب في الدين.

45B) Each group is responsible for the area belonging to it (with regards to defense and other needs.)

٤٥ب- على كل أناس حصتهم من جانبهم الذي قبلهم.

46) The Jews of al-Aws, their *mawlā* and themselves, shall have the same rights agreed upon on this sheet (document), with sincere/complete observation from the people designated on this sheet. Observation of one's undertakings eliminates treachery/breaking of treaties. He who commits a breach (of this treaty) commits it against himself alone. God is with those who best and truly observe the rules described on this sheet.

٤٦- وأن يهود ألاوس مواليهم وأنفسهم على مثل ما لاهل هذه الصحيفة مع البر المحض من أهل هذه الصحيفة، وأن البر دون إلاثم لا يكسب كاسب إلا على نفسه، وأن الله على أصدق ما في هذه الصحيفة وأبره.

47) This book (*kitāb*) shall not protect the perpetrator of an unjust act or crime from punishment. Whoever goes out shall have security and whoever remains in Madinah shall also have security; except one who commits an unjust act or a crime. Allah protects the person who observes undertakings and keeps free of dishonorable acts and offences, and Muhammad the Messenger of Allah, Allah bless and honor him.

٤٧- وأنه لا يحول هذا الكتاب دون ظالم أو آثم، وأنه من خرج أمن ومن قعد أمن بالمدينة، إلا من ظلم وأثم، وأن الله جار لمن برّ واتقى، ومحمد رسول الله (صلى الله عليه وسلم).

NOTES

1. The full text and a translation may be found in Appendix A.
2. On the constituent features of the term ummah in the Qur'an, see Katrin Jomaa, 'A Conceptual Analysis of Umma in the Quran and Sunna and the Aristotelian Polis' (Ph.D. dissertation, Indiana University, 2012).
3. A reading is argued by Michael Lecker where he replaced umma by *amina* (secure) based on an Indian edition which was remarked by later editors to be inaccurate. However, Lecker still supported the reading (*amina*). Lecker's argument seems problematic for a simple grammatical reason, because if *amina* (in a verb or a noun form) was used, it has to be conjugated in the plural form to match the noun (the Jews). The reading argued by Lecker is in singular form, which is grammatically impossible. In Michael Lecker, *The "Constitution of Medina" Muhammad's First Legal Document* (Princeton, NJ: The Darwin Press, 2004), 139.
4. A different reading in Abū ʿUbayd Ibn Sallām, *Kitāb al-Amwāl.* (Ed.), M. Khalil Haras (Cairo: Maktabat al-Kullīyāt al-Azhariyyah, 1968), p.147. Also Ibn Kathīr, *al-Bidāyah wa al-Nihāyah* (Cairo: Maktabat al-Maʿārif, 1932), vol.1, p.43.
5. Frederick Denny, 'Community and Salvation: The Meaning of the Umma in the Qur'ān' (Ph.D. dissertation, University of Chicago, 1974), p.214.
6. Ibid., p.246.
7. For a detailed analysis about the relationship between the *ummī* Prophet and the ummah, see Jomaa, 'A Conceptual Analysis of Umma', pp.57–64.
8. Ibid., pp.137–39.
9. Said Amir Arjomand, 'The Constitution of Medina', *International Journal of Middle East Studies* 41 (2009), p.560.
10. Fred M. Donner, *Muhammad and the Believers: At the Origins of Islam* (Cambridge: The Belknap Press of Harvard University Press, 2010), p.69.
11. Ibid., pp.69–75.
12. Ibid., p.74.
13. Muhammad Mahdi Shams al-Din, *Fī al-Ijtimāʿ al-Siyāsī al-Islāmī* (Beirut: al-Mu'asassah al-Jāmiʿiyyah lil-Dirāsāt wa al-Nashr, 1992), pp.293–95.
14. R.B. Serjeant, 'The Sunnah Jami'ah, Pacts with the Yathrib Jews and the Tahrim of Yathrib: Analysis and Translation of the Documents Comprised in the So-Called "Constitution of Medina"', *Bulletin of the School of Oriental and African Studies* 41(1) (1978), pp.12–14.
15. Frederick Denny, 'Ummah in the Constitution of Medina', *Journal of Near Eastern Studies* 36(1) (January 1977), p.43.
16. Uri Rubin, '"The Constitution of Medina": Some Notes', *Studia Islamica* 62 (1985), pp.13–16.
17. Said Amir Arjomand, 'The Constitution of Medina', pp.562–64.

18. The same phrase occurs elsewhere in the Qur'an. "Say, [O believers], 'We have believed in Allah and what has been revealed to us and what has been revealed to Abraham and Ishmael and Isaac and Jacob and the Descendants and what was given to Moses and Jesus and what was given to the prophets from their Lord. We make no distinction between any of them, and we are Muslims [in submission] to Him'" (2:136). "Say, 'We have believed in Allah and in what was revealed to us and what was revealed to Abraham, Ishmael, Isaac, Jacob, and the Descendants, and in what was given to Moses and Jesus and to the prophets from their Lord. We make no distinction between any of them, and we are Muslims [submitting] to Him'" (3:84).
19. Donner, *Muhammad and the Believers*, pp.71–72.
20. Ibid., p.72.
21. Jomaa, 'A Conceptual Analysis of Umma', pp.90–100.
22. Rubin, '"The Constitution of Medina"', p.12. Rubin presents a survey of different scholars, such as Wellhausen, Wensinck, Watt, Serjeant, and Gil, reducing the ummah of Madinah to a mere political confederation.
23. "The desert Arabs (Bedouins) say, 'We believe (*āmannā*).' Say (to them, O Muhammad), 'You did not believe; but rather say, "we have surrendered" (*aslamnā*), for faith has not yet entered your hearts. Yet if you obey Allah and His Messenger, He will not belittle any of your deeds: for Allah is Forgiving, Most Merciful.' Indeed the believers are only those who have believed in Allah and his messenger and have never since doubted, and have striven with their wealth and their selves in the way of Allah, such are the truthful ones" (49:14–15). The verses address the problem of following a religion superficially by confessing adherence to it or merely endorsing its public manifestation. Belief, on the other hand, necessitates taking action by "striving with the wealth and the self." The same idea is stipulated in the first decree of the constitution, which describes the members covenanted to establish the ummah as "... those who follow them, join them and strive along with them." Thus, it is evident that establishing an ummah requires a choice and an ongoing responsibility to adhere to that choice.
24. W. Montgomery Watt, *Muhammad at Medina* (Oxford: Clarendon Press, 1956), p.242.
25. Denny, 'Community and Salvation', p.216.
26. "Let there be from among you (*minkum*) an ummah inviting to the good (*khayr*) and enjoining righteousness and deterring wrongness (*ya'murūna bi al-maʿrūf wa yanhawna ʿan al-munkar*) and those are the successful" (3:104). "You are (*kuntum*) the best (*khayr*) ummah ever raised up for mankind for you enjoin righteousness and deter wrongness and believe in God, and if the people of the book were to believe it would have been better for them, among them are believers but most of them are transgressors" (3:110). For a discussion of these verses see Jomaa, 'A Conceptual Analysis of Umma', pp.127–34.

27. Translated as "customary" by R.B. Serjeant and Arjomand, "uprightness" by Denny, and "proper" by Bulac.
28. R.B. Serjeant, 'Haram and Hawtah, the Sacred Enclave in Arabia', in *Mélanges Taha Hussein.* (Ed.), Abdurrahman Badawi (Cairo: Dār al-Maᶜārif, 1962), pp.41–58.
29. Ibid., p.47. Emphasis added.
30. Arjomand, 'The Constitution of Medina', p.565.
31. Jomaa, 'A Conceptual Analysis of Umma', pp.116–117.
32. Shams al-Din, *Fī al-Ijtimāᶜ al-Siyāsī al-Islāmī*, p.293.
33. In another reading *mufraj* (one turned Muslim among a people to whom he does not belong).
34. Qur'an 9:11. Also Qur'an 49:10: "The believers are but brethren, therefore make peace between your brethren and be careful of (your duty to) Allah that you may have His mercy."
35. Elias Giannakis, 'The Concept of Ummah', *Graeco-Arabica* 2 (1983), pp.103–4.
36. Jomaa, 'A Conceptual Analysis of Umma', pp.75–80.
37. Ibid., 127–34.
38. "Decree 37- In the case of war Jews bear their expenses and the Muslims theirs. Surely they shall cooperate among themselves, in opposing those who wage war against the people designated on this sheet (document). There shall be good counsel and advice between them. Observation of one's undertakings eliminates treachery/breaking of treaties. 37.B- No one may commit a crime against his ally; surely the oppressed shall receive help."
39. Shams al-Din, *Fī al-Ijtimāᶜ al-Siyāsī al-Islāmī*, p.295.
40. Jomaa, 'A Conceptual Analysis of Umma', pp.49–57.
41. Ibn Manzur, *Lisān al-ᶜArab* (Beirut: Dār Iḥyā' al-Turāth al-ᶜArabī, 1993), vol.5, pp.59–60.
42. See Jomaa, 'A Conceptual Analysis of Umma', pp.54–57.
43. Arjomand, 'The Constitution of Medina', p.566.
44. Shams al-Din, *Fī al-Ijtimāᶜ al-Siyāsī al-Islāmī*, pp.296–97.
45. Serjeant reports an incident mentioned in Ibn Isḥāq/Ibn Hishām: "In a quarrel, Abu Bakr struck Finḥāṣ the Jew, adding that but for the pact (ᶜ*ahd*) between them, he would have cut off his head. Finḥāṣ went for redress to Muhammad as head of the *Muhājirūn* and Muhammad rebuked Abu Bakr." Serjeant, 'The Sunnah Jami'ah', p.22. Cf. A. Guillaume, *The Life of Muhammad* (Oxford: Oxford University Press, 1955; reprinted Karachi, 1967), p.263.
46. Shams al-Din, *Fī al-Ijtimāᶜ al-Siyāsī al-Islāmī*, pp.297–298.
47. Shams al-Din, *Fī al-Ijtimāᶜ al-Siyāsī al-Islāmī*, p.300.
48. Denny claims that "Medina developed into a real theocracy" in Denny, 'Ummah in the Constitution of Medina', p.47.
49. Shams al-Din, *Fī al-Ijtimāᶜ al-Siyāsī al-Islāmī*, p.301.
50. Arjomand, 'The Constitution of Medina', p.567.

51. Serjeant, 'Haram and Hawtah', p.48.
52. Denny, 'Ummah in the Constitution of Medina', p.45.
53. Serjeant, 'The Sunnah Jami'ah', p.31.
54. Ibid.
55. Shams al-Din, *Fī al-Ijtimāᶜ al-Siyāsī al-Islāmī*, p.305.
56. Serjeant, 'Haram and Hawtah', pp.45–47.
57. "Do they not see that We have set up a secure sanctuary (*ḥaram āmin*), while people are ravaged all around them? Will they, then, [continue] to believe in falsehood and deny God's blessings?" (29:67).
58. "And, lo, Abraham prayed: 'O my Sustainer! Make this a land secure (*baladan āminan*), and grant its people fruitful sustenance – such of them who believe in God and the Last Day.' [God] answered: 'and whoever shall deny the truth, I will let him enjoy himself for a short while – but in the end I shall drive him to suffering through fire: and how vile a journey's end'" (Qur'an 2:126).
59. Al-Qurṭubī, *al-Jāmiᶜ li-Aḥkām al-Qur'ān* (Beirut: Dār Iḥyā' al-Turāth al-ᶜArabī, 1985), vol.6, p.325.
60. Al-Ṭabarī, *Jāmiᶜ al-Bayān* (Beirut: Dār al-Fikr, 1995), vol.5, p.104.
61. Ibn Manzur, *Lisān al-ᶜArab*, vol.2, pp.421–23.
62. Rubin, '"The Constitution of Medina"', p.10.
63. Daniel Meier, 'Bordering the Middle East', *Geopolitics* 23 (2018), p.500.
64. Quoted in Ibid., p.501.
65. "And to you We revealed *al-kitāb* in truth, confirming the Scripture that came before it and a guardian (*muhaymin*) over it (old Scriptures). So judge between them by what Allah has revealed, and follow not their vain desires, diverging away from the truth that has come to you. To each among you, We have prescribed a law and a clear way (*shirᶜatan wa minhājan*). If Allah willed, He would have made you one ummah, but that (He) may test you in what He has given you; so strive as in a race in all virtues. The return of you (all) is to Allah; then He will inform you about that in which you used to differ." This verse is discussed in Jomaa, 'A Conceptual Analysis of Umma', pp.137–39.
66. Serjeant, 'The Sunnah Jami'ah', p.38.
67. Muhammad Hamidullah, *Majmūᶜat al-Wathā'iq al-Siyāsiyyah* (Cairo: Lajnat al-Ta'līf wa al-Tarjamah wa al-Nashr, 1941), pp.1–7.
68. In another reading *mufraj* (one turned Muslim among a people to whom he does not belong).

Contributors

In alphabetical order

Kamal Abu-Shamsieh
PhD Candidate in Practical Theology at the Graduate Theological Union and Chaplain with Stanford Healthcare

Asaad Alsaleh
Associate Professor of Arabic Literature and Cultural Studies in the Department of Near Eastern Languages and Cultures at Indiana University

Samy Ayoub
Assistant Professor of Islamic Law at the University of Texas at Austin and the University of Texas School of Law

Katrin Jomaa
Assistant Professor of Islam and Middle Eastern Politics in the Departments of Political Science and Philosophy at the University of Rhode Island

Hamid Mavani
Associate Professor of Islamic Studies at Bayan Claremont Islamic Graduate School / Claremont School of Theology

Christopher B. Taylor
Post-doctoral fellow at the Ali Vural Ak Center for Global Islamic Studies and instructor in the Department of Sociology & Anthropology at George Mason University

David R. Vishanoff
Associate Professor of Islamic thought at the University of Oklahoma